LOOK

Jim O'Brien

BASKETBALL MEMOIR

ONCE AGAIN

Jim Eakins of Virginia Squires positions himself for rebound battle with Artis Gilmore of Kentucky Colonels.

Malcolm W. Emmons/Street and Smith's Archives

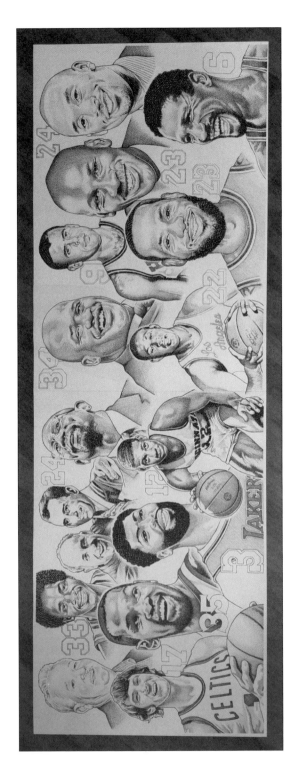

AUTHOR'S DREAM TEAM – From left to right, John Havlicek, Kevin Durant, David Thompson, Red Auerbach, Bob Cousy, Anthony Davis, Oscar Robertson, Spencer Haywood, Elgin Baylor, Shaquille O'Neal, Bob Pettit, LeBron James, Michael Jordan, Bill Russell and Kobe Bryant. Pictured on cover of prequel were Larry Bird, Magic Johnson, Wilt Chamberlain, Connie Hawkins, Jerry West, Pete Maravich and Julius Erving.

Artwork by Bob Weaver

Bob Netolicky's response to NBA pledge:

In August, 2020, the NBA Board of Governors
announced it was pledging $300 million to an
Economic Empowerment of Black Community.
Here is response offered by Bob Netolicky, best
known for his play for the Indiana Pacers and a
strong advocate for ABA pension:

*"What about the ABA players (85% black) who
pioneered today's game? We were promised
the same pension rights as NBA players in the
merger agreement. This is ludicrous! They could
at least gives us a small pension like the
pre-1965 NBA players received that just happen
to be 95% white. It would cost them 1% of this
so-called economic empowerment pledge.
SHAME ON YOU, NBA!*

Books By Jim O'Brien

COMPLETE HANDBOOK OF PRO BASKETBALL 1970–71
COMPLETE HANDBOOK OF PRO BASKETBALL 1971–72
COMPLETE HANDBOOK OF PRO BASKETBALL 1972–73
ABA ALL-STARS
PITTSBURGH: THE STORY OF THE CITY OF CHAMPIONS
HAIL TO PITT: A SPORTS HISTORY OF
THE UNIVERSITY OF PITTSBURGH
DOING IT RIGHT
WHATEVER IT TAKES
MAZ AND THE '60 BUCS
REMEMBER ROBERTO
PENGUIN PROFILES
DARE TO DREAM
KEEP THE FAITH
WE HAD 'EM ALL THE WAY
HOMETOWN HEROES
GLORY YEARS
THE CHIEF
STEELERS FOREVER
ALWAYS A STEELER
WITH LOVE AND PRIDE
LAMBERT
FANTASY CAMP
STEELER STUFF
PITTSBURGH PROUD
IMMACULATE REFLECTIONS
A WINNING WAY
GOLDEN ARMS
FROM A TO Z
LOOKING UP
FRANCO, ROCKY & FRIENDS
LOOKING UP ONCE AGAIN

To order copies of these titles directly from the publisher, send $29.95 for hardcover edition. Please send additional $4 to cover shipping and handling charges per book. Copies will be signed by author at your request. Discounts available for large orders. Contact publisher regarding availability and prices of all books in Pittsburgh Proud series, or to request an order form. 412-221-3580.

Dedication

Photos by Jim O'Brien

This book is dedicated to all those who served on the frontlines during the coronavirus pandemic, the doctors and nurses and EMS warriors, those who stayed at work to make sure we had all the essentials in our lives, the policemen and firemen who distinguished themselves in a positive manner, and the volunteers who made sure everyone had something to eat.

Copyright © 2020 by Jim O'Brien

All rights reserved

Published by James P. O'Brien — Publishing
P.O. Box 12580
Pittsburgh PA 15241
E-mail: jimmyo64@gmail.com
Website: www.jimobriensportsauthor.com

First printing, September 2020
Printed by R.R. Donnelley of Pittsburgh Printing
Typography by Cold-Comp
ISBN 978-1-886348-17-2

Cover artwork by Bob Weaver

Graphic design:
Cathy Pawlowski
Project assistance:
Denise Maiden
Kathleen O'Brien
Susannah Zirwas

Acknowledgments

My buddy Alex Pociask and my Good Guy friend Dallas Frey were both a big help in driving me on two different basketball odysseys. Alex made all the arrangements for us to travel to visit with some legendary basketball coaches and players in Indiana and Kentucky, and Frey accompanied me on a trip in the summer of 2018 to Indianapolis for the ABA's 50th anniversary reunion celebration. My wife Kathie accompanied me on a three-day visit to Louisville for the 2018 Kentucky Derby Week and the 50th anniversary of the Kentucky Colonels. My friend Bill Neal of Champions, Inc., a basketball maven in Pittsburgh and the founder of the Connie Hawkins Summer Basketball League, invited me to the 50th anniversary gathering of the Pittsburgh Pipers.

I have been fortunate to have met and interviewed and learned from so many outstanding individuals, most of whom have been associated with and excelled

Jim O'Brien

George Thompson of Pittsburgh Condors and Dallas Frey enjoyed ABA reunion in 2018 in Indianapolis.

in the world of sports. I am grateful for those who were generous with their time and thoughts, stories and insights.

Frey was the best fact checker of the staff of proof-readers I employed to proof-read this book, and am grateful for his efforts as well as those of Tom McGuire, Roberta Sarraf, Pat Santelli, Jack Sega, George Morris and Marvin Zelkowitz.

I am also grateful to Peter Vecsey, a retired sports columnist for *The New York Post* and *New York Daily News* for endorsing my nomination for the Curt Gowdy writers' wing of the Basketball Hall of Fame, and to Terry Lyons and Bryan McIntyre, retired NBA executives, for their Hall of Fame nomination.

Significant financial support has been offered through the years by the following: Atria's Restaurant & Tavern, Don Carlucci of Carlucci Construction of Cheswick, Pa., Eat'n Park Restaurants, James S. Hamilton of Federated Securities, Inc., Frank B. Fuhrer Wholesale Company, Hoddy Hanna of Hanna Real Estate Services, Thomas B. Grealish of Henderson Brothers, Andy Russell, Jack Mascaro of Mascaro Construction, Joseph A. Massaro Jr. of the Massaro Company, Dave Jancisin and Derek Jancisin of Merrill Lynch, Robert J. Taylor of Taylor & Hladio Law Offices, Jim Frantz of TEDCO Inc., Bob Randall of TRACO, Inc., Kenneth Codeluppi of Wall-Firma, Inc., Jack McGinley Jr. of Eckert Seamans Law Firm.

Others who have worked with me: Don DeBlasio of DeBlasio's Restaurant, Ralph Cindrich, Gregory L. Manesiotis, Robert F. McClurg, Dennis Meteny, Rebecca O'Brien, Andy Ondrey, Jim Roddey, Len Stidle, Barbara Stull, Judy Brown, Erica McElhone, Audrey Steiner, Laurie and Paul McGinnis, Scott Zecker.

I want to thank the following individuals for their loyal support: Tony Accamando, Suzy and Jim

Broadhurst, Ray Conaway, Judge Jeffrey A. Deller, Dick Goetz, Nancy and Pat McDonnell, Arthur J. Rooney Jr., Patrick J. Santelli, Dick Swanson of Swanson Group, Ltd., Joe Landolina, David O'Connor and John D. O'Connor & Son Funeral Home, Bill Priatko. My books are printed by RR Donnelley, with assistance from Jake Zoller, Bob Goodrick, Zachery Milano and Trudy Simpson.

I owe a debt of gratitude to Cathy Pawlowski and Denise Maiden of Cold-Comp Typographers and to artist Bob Weaver who make my books so beautiful.

My basic support team is my wife of 53 years, Kathleen, and our daughters, Sarah and Rebecca, and our grandchildren, Margaret, Susannah, Jeffrey and Madeline. They make it all worthwhile.

Jim O'Brien

Alex Pociask poses at Muhammad Ali Museum in Louisville.

Contents

"A must read for Steelers history buffs."
—**Pittsburgh Post-Gazette**

Preface
Some special men named George

Writing this book was my cure for the coronavirus. If we had to stay at home during the global pandemic, I was going to get something accomplished. I would write another book, the 30th in my Pittsburgh Proud sports series.

To write a book you have to sit down at your writing desk and stay the course. I found myself getting up earlier and earlier each morning, sometimes as early as 4 and 5 a.m., as I was eager to write. Writing had become easier for me, I was surprised to learn at age 77, and while my short-term memory wasn't nearly as reliable as it once was, my long-term memory was vivid and some say remarkable.

It was a blessing to be able to write this book, to have a purpose each day to do something. My wife Kathie and I both had health challenges during this time and overcoming them made us want to achieve even more. We are both avid readers, and I continued my education by reading lots of history books. At Pitt, they said to write well you had to read well.

Beyond the restrictions to combat the coronavirus, our world got even more challenging after a man named George Floyd died in Minneapolis after an overzealous policeman pressed his knee to the neck of Floyd for nearly nine minutes until he could no longer breathe. This ugly incident created world-wide turmoil and protest and violence in the streets of cities across our county and other parts of the world. George Floyd became a martyr for the "Black Lives Matter" movement. George Floyd, a husky 6–5 man, had played high school basketball and football, and basketball for two years at a junior college in Florida. He'd had many run-ins with the law in his life.

I was writing about some remarkable men named George, all rags-to-riches stories, the kind that were called "Horatio Alger stories" in my youth. Horatio Alger was a Harvard-educated author of popular books for young adults in the 19th Century. They were stories of the American dream, about impoverished boys who rose from challenging circumstances to become successful through hard work, determination, courage and honesty. My subjects were George Gervin, George McGinnis, George Thompson and George Tinsley. They all offer inspiring stories for all young people. They are all African-Americans.

I had their phone numbers and it was easy to contact them because they all had to stay at home, too, and had time to talk. I met and talked to George Tinsley for the first time at the 50th year reunions in 2018 of the ABA and then the Kentucky Colonels.

His is a remarkable story. I called him one day in June 2020 when I meant to call George McGinnis. The phone number was next to a notation that simply read "George." I called George Thompson twice when I meant to call George McGinnis. But I picked up a few gems that misguided way.

It gave me an opportunity to offer my condolence to George Tinsley about the death of his daughter, Penni, age 44, a beautiful and talented young woman who suffered greatly from a degenerative disease called multiple system atrophy.

This had happened after I had last talked to Tinsley. It had to be so difficult to deal with by George, his wife Seretha and their son, George II. Yet George Tinsley was talking in his signature upbeat manner.

"I'm positive we'll come out of all of this stronger than ever," he said. "Penni isn't suffering anymore. She's walking with The Lord, and I hope to join her someday and be with her again."

I thought it was remarkable that George Tinsley was still preaching a positive message. He had often said "the customer is always right and you have to give them an experience that they will want to come back to your restaurant."

He went on to tell me that he also had to shut down 20 restaurants that he owned because of the coronavirus. He was just starting to re-open some at airports. "But there are few travelers these days, so the traffic has been light so far."

George Tinsley has had a successful career as a businessman, helped in a considerable way by his wife Seretha. They met during their student days at Male High School in Louisville, and were among the few African-American students at Kentucky Wesleyan, a Methodist college in Owensboro, Kentucky.

He was a star basketball player and student leader, and she was a cheerleader, and both were involved in many student activities such as student council. They were the first African-American students to be admitted to the school's prestigious honor society.

Their story reminds me of another ambitious couple, Joy Maxberry and Dwayne Woodruff. The Woodruffs met as students at the University of Louisville, and Joy pushed Dwayne to be a more dedicated student when he was at risk to flunk out of school.

He went on to become an outstanding football player for the Cardinals and the Pittsburgh Steelers, an attorney and judge in Allegheny County Family Court. They have a model family. Their three children are all achievers.

I did some more research on George Tinsley and learned some details that I didn't have in my notebook the first time around. They enrich his story and that of his wife and family.

His holding company has many restaurants and food and drink outlets, such as Starbucks, Don Shula Steak House, TGI Fridays, at airports in Miami, Tampa and Louisville. He got his start in the restaurant business as a training manager for Kentucky Fried Chicken, and he still favors the sort of white or cream-colored suits that Col. Harland Sanders wore when he founded and became the ambassador for the chain of fried chicken franchises.

His wife Seretha had front office positions as a general manager, even a vice-president, of radio stations in Atlanta and Jacksonville. Then, in 1984, they combined their talents to take the leap into restaurant operations.

I already knew that George grew up under difficult circumstances in the Louisville inner-city community called Smoketown, the same section of the city that produced Cassius Clay, later to be known as Muhammad Ali.

But I learned some more details that flesh out his story. He was abandoned by his mother as an infant, just six months old, turned over to a widow named Willie Tinsley who looked after other children in a single room with a small kitchen. She had one leg—the other had been amputated—and required a crutch to get around. She managed to get by on $65 a month Social Security.

She died when George was 13 and her son Clarence took George into his home. That didn't work out as well. But George got a basketball scholarship to Kentucky Wesleyan and made the most of the opportunity. He belongs to many business associations and he and Seretha have served in Chamber of Commerce leadership roles.

George does a lot of motivational speaking, simply telling his own story the same way former Notre

Dame and Steelers star Rocky Bleier has been telling his story all these years. "We are all selling hope," as Bleier puts it.

"I've tried to let people know you can really achieve and have success by being positive," says George Tinsley. "I love people and I love to be involved."

Then, too, on another occasion, George Tinsley has said, "Don't be a prisoner of your own mind. If I can do it, you can, too."

This book is full of stories of men who lifted themselves to great heights, many escaping the ghettos of their childhood, to succeed in sports and, more importantly, in life.

Some remain challenged, as senior citizens after the bright lights of basketball arenas no longer shine on them. I enjoyed reconnecting with them, getting to know them better, getting their stories beyond the basketball courts.

They all started, as I did, shooting baskets in their backyard or in the front of their home, and we all found a way to make it in the world of sports.

One of my longtime friends, a retired neurological physician named Dr. Marvin Zelkowitz, who read these stories in advance of publication, sent me an e-mail "You lend dignity to these men you write about. People need to know about them."

When I was a student at the University of Pittsburgh, I befriended Dr. H.C. "Doc" Carlson, the director of the student health service. He removed a wart from my finger on one visit.

Doc Carlson counseled me about a lot of things, and I listened because he had been an All-America football player at Pitt, a basketball coach of a national championship team at Pitt, and he and one of his players, Charlie Hyatt of Uniontown, were honored in the charter class of the Basketball Hall of Fame.

Doc Carlson was big on charts and he drew one over a message he wrote above his signature in a book he gave me that had been written by Grantland Rice. It was called *The Tumult and the Shouting* (1954). Doc's hand-written message had an arrow pointing upward and an arrow pointing downward. With the upward arrow he wrote, "Positive like Grantland Rice." The downward arrow said, "Negative like the muckraker Westbrook Pegler." And he added, "Which direction will you follow?"

I think Doc Carlson would like this book. I hope you do, too. I loved Doc Carlson but I must tell you that the wart came back.

Artwork by Marty Wolfson

From Hail to Pitt

Pitt Hall of Fame basketball coach Doc Carlson

As good as it gets—
Kobe's Farewell Game

He was more noble than handsome, his head and face and body so chiseled. He was a bronze statue before anyone considered creating one in his honor. Women were attracted to him. He was a chick magnet. Other women scorned him because of what they considered bad behavior, being unfaithful to his beautiful wife. You either loved him or hated him. "Nobody loves Goliath," Wilt Chamberlain used to say of his life as a seven-footer.

But Kobe Bryant demanded your attention. He was so good at the game of basketball, if not perfect off the court, and he demanded the best of everybody, especially his teammates, and, like Michael Jordan, didn't hesitate to call them out if he found them lacking in dedication and desire. Basketball great Bill Sharman told me no one on the Lakers worked harder than Kobe Bryant.

There wasn't any delay in inducting Kobe into the Basketball Hall of Fame, and that was appropriate, even if a year early of five-year minimum requirement after retirement. Roberto Clemente of the Pittsburgh Pirates was inducted into the Baseball Hall of Fame shortly after his death. Clemente was coming to the rescue of earthquake victims in Nicaragua when the airplane in which he was traveling dropped into the waters outside of his native Puerto Rico, and he perished and disappeared in the crash.

How similar their fate. Bryant was traveling with his younger daughter Gianna, to a basketball game she was to play in, when his private helicopter pilot lost his way, or so it is thought, in dense cloud cover and crashed into a hillside, gone like so many of America's favorite singing stars. Seven others were killed in the crash. This happened on January 26, 2020.

Kobe Bryant scored 60 points in leading Lakers to comeback victory over Utah Jazz in his last NBA outing on April 13, 2016. He and his daughter Gianna were killed in a helicopter crash on January 26, 2020 in San Fernando Valley.

After I wrote this, I learned that Bryant was to be inducted into the Basketball Hall of Fame Class for 2020. He was not really eligible until 2021, but it was appropriate and fitting to include him in a Class that has Tim Duncan, Kevin Garnett and Tamika Catchings.

* * *

Bryant was born into basketball. His father, Joe "Jelly Bean" Bryant, was one of Philadelphia's rich basketball progeny. His father Joe played in the NBA and in Europe, where Kobe was a constant presence at his dad's side, and learned to play basketball and speak foreign languages. He was always one of the most well-spoken and gifted athletes on the planet.

Walt Sczerzbiak, who grew up on Pittsburgh's South Side and became a basketball star with a Spanish team in Europe, told me that Joe Bryant told him about his son and his development. "He's going to be a beast," said Jelly Bean. "You have to see him to believe how good he is already."

College wasn't for Kobe. He was prepared to play pro ball when he was in high school. He had a 20-year career with the Los Angeles Lakers—his favorite team as a kid—and he couldn't have asked for a better script. Except for the ending.

I talked to Joe Bryant once when he played in the NBA. He was a member of the Philadelphia 76ers for four seasons, and the 1976–77 version made it to the NBA finals before bowing to the Portland Trail Blazers in the championship series. His teammates included Julius "Dr. J" Erving, George McGinnis and Doug Collins. All good guys. In the first game of the 1979–80 season, Joe, then playing for the San Diego Clippers, scored on a slam dunk over Kareem Abdul-Jabbar of the Lakers. Lloyd Free scored 46 points for the Clippers in that game, but the Lakers prevailed on a final sky hook by Jabbar.

I have never met or spoken to Kobe Bryant. Never shook his hand or took a picture of him. I never saw him play in person. Only on television.

I have visited Staples Center and touched the statues honoring Jerry West and Magic Johnson, and Lakers' long-time broadcaster Chick Hearn. They have since been joined by statues of Shaquille O'Neal and Elgin Baylor.

"We've got this young guy who was full of himself," said Jerry West at the unveiling of Shaq's statue. "One of these days he's going to be here real soon." West had no idea how prophetic his words would be in the case of Kobe Bryant.

I did interview Shaq when he was with the Orlando Magic with Penny Hardaway. The team's president, Pat Williams, was a long-time fellow author and friend of mine. "There is magic in team work," Williams wrote to me when signing his book of the same name.

In Pittsburgh, we have Clemente and Willie Stargell and Honus Wagner and Bill Mazeroski statues outside PNC Park. Steelers' owner Arthur J. Rooney has an inviting statue outside Heinz Field, near where he grew up over his dad's saloon on the North Side. It invites you to sit down on a bench with The Chief. And talk to him. I've done that on several occasions. I always enjoyed talking to him, and like his admiring son Art Jr., still do. "What would The Chief do?" Art Jr. tells me he often asks himself when faced with a decision.

O'Neal thought that James Worthy and Wilt Chamberlain would be honored before him. Why is Wilt not there? There was no greater Laker, unless it was West, for his longer service in so many capacities. I still think Chamberlain is the greatest pro basketball player in history. There is a statue of Chamberlain outside the Wells Fargo Center in his hometown of Philadelphia.

All this history and Kobe's tragic ending all raced through my mind on a Saturday afternoon, April 4, 2020, as I sat in my family room alone and watched "Kobe's Farewell" on television. It wasn't one of the many salutes offered to him after his sudden demise, but rather a re-run of his final game with the Lakers.

Back on April 13, 2016, Kobe scored 60 points to lead the Lakers to a comeback victory over the Utah Jazz at the Staples Center.

I had never seen this game before, even though it was shown right after Kobe's death.

* * *

"Play me a memory..."
—From Piano Man by Billy Joel

Sometimes I wonder how it works. When I am writing a book, like this one, things just happen to add to the final version. People I hadn't thought to write about appear out of nowhere. I find photos and hand-written notes on legal pads in my extensive files, in a storage room just to the left of my working space, just past photos of Muhammad Ali and Joe Frazier, from "The Fight of the Century" at Madison Square Garden in New York on March 8, 1971. It was the highlight of my sports-writing career and I had a ring-side seat to see it and feel the impact of the countless punches. I believe I am the only one still living who was in the ring or at ringside in the first row that night. I was 28 at the time. There is also a photo of the great Joe DiMaggio, taken when I was interviewing him in 1972 in Fort Lauderdale, Florida, where the Yankees conducted spring training. There is a photo of Babe Ruth (No. 3) before his final game at Yankee Stadium. I once had too much to drink, trying to keep up with Babe Ruth's wife, Claire, a former member of the Ziegfold

Follies, at an Old Timers' Game gathering at Yankee Stadium. So many memories...

I was looking for something to watch on TV that Saturday afternoon. There were no live sports offerings. Everything had been canceled as we were all challenged by the world-wide pandemic—the coronavirus—or as President Trump labeled it—"The Silent Killer." Perfect for tabloid headlines. In France, for instance, there was this headline: "The Yellow Peril."

I happened upon "Kobe Farewell," in time to view the fourth and final quarter of his career. He was unreal. His teammates kept feeding him the ball and Kobe never had to be encouraged to shoot the ball. He kept hitting unreal outside shots, but missed several easy layups. "He needed a puff of wind to get that one in," said NBA analyst Hubie Brown, working with Mike Tirico at courtside.

"We're seeing one of the greatest players in the history of the game," Tirico told us. Bryant shot the ball 50 times—5-oh—in this bow-out. Best of all, he led the Lakers to an uphill victory. "This is a dream way to end this," said Kobe after the game. "I was a Lakers' fan as a kid and I know the history of this team, all the great players. You couldn't write a better story."

He hugged all his teammates and former teammates such as Shaquille O'Neal, Byron Scott, Robert Horry, Lamar Odom, Derek Fisher, Gary Payton, Magic Johnson, and Frank Hamblen, an assistant coach I remembered well from his days in the ABA as an assistant to Doug Moe with the NBA Denver Nuggets and later in the NBA with Phil Jackson, and with the Lakers. Hamblen died on September 30, 2017 in San Diego. I am so glad I got to see Kobe's final game.

> *"Rosa Parks inspired me to find a way to get in the way, to get in trouble...good trouble, necessary trouble."*
> —Congressman John Lewis, 1940–2020

*   *   *

I saw "Pistol Pete" Maravich of the New Orleans Jazz score 68 points against Walt Frazier, Earl Monroe and Ticky Burden of the New York Knicks in a game one night—February 25, 1977—at the Superdome in New Orleans and Maravich could do things with a basketball that Kobe or anyone else couldn't do, but Kobe's final game was something special. Pete's dad, Press Maravich, was there to witness what is considered his son's greatest game.

I remember seeing Roger Brown score an ABA playoff record of 53 points for the Indiana Pacers in a 142-120 victory over the Los Angeles Stars in Anaheim, California in 1972. Brown hit 18 of 29 shots, had 13 rebounds, and passed out six assists, not bad for a 6–5 forward. Bill Sharman coached the Stars in that game and compared Brown's outburst to one he had seen Elgin Baylor achieve when Sharman was coaching the Lakers.

My seat for the seventh and final game of the Knicks-Lakers series in 1970 was the last one on the left side or the press row at Madison Square Garden, at the break where the ballplayers passed on their way to and from the locker rooms. *The New York Post*

Walt Frazier

"Pistol Pete"
Maravich

Roger Brown

had four courtside seats. That game is best remembered—legend has it anyhow—when Willis Reed, who was nursing a severe groin pull, limped onto the court and hit his first two jumpers from the top of the key over his taller adversary, Wilt Chamberlain—to get the Knicks going. Did I tell you that Reed pushed off my right shoulder as he stepped up onto the playing floor at the Garden? The floor was a few inches higher than the surrounding surface.

But it was Walt Frazier's fantastic performance that led the Knicks to a championship victory. "Clyde," as he was called (from the movie Bonnie & Clyde because he robbed opponents of the ball), scored 36 points, had an unreal 19 assists, seven rebounds. The NBA did not count steals back then. Not until the ABA did it. There were no 3-point field goals. Not until the ABA added it to its game.

Kobe's number with the Lakers was 24, the same as Willie Mays, Rick Barry and J.T. Thomas. Barry wore No. 24 because, growing up in New Jersey, he was a fan of Willie Mays. That's the way sportswriters think, I think.

They kept showing close-ups of Kobe's beautiful wife, Vanessa, in a stunning black outfit and their daughters, Natalia Diamante Bryant, and Gianna. They were so excited and joyful and proud, especially when Kobe smiled or winked their way. And you thought about the tragic ending of Gianna, just 14, and her dad, just 41. Rocky Marciano came to mind. Patsy Cline ("Crazy") came to mind. So did the "Big Bopper" and Richie Valens and Buddy Holly. I had just finished reading a memoir by Willie Nelson called *My Life,* in which he told the story how his friend Waylon Jennings had given up his seat to J.P. Richardson, aka "The Big Bopper," for that ill-fated flight, and lived to fight and sing another day.

I had heard Rod Hundley and Bob Leonard tell the story of how when they were playing for the Lakers their charter plane crash-landed in a farm field in Iowa—stopping just short of a steep precipice—and what a harrowing experience that had been. They lived to tell the story, and no one could do it better than "Hot Rod" Hundley, unless it was Leonard. Rocky Marciano, the great undefeated heavyweight boxer, wasn't as lucky when his small plane crashed in a pasture near Newton, Iowa on the eve of his 46th birthday on August 31, 1969. I had just moved to Miami, where Marciano had been living, to work for *The Miami News*. I would be covering the Dolphins and pro boxing on Miami Beach. Marciano's death was front page news.

Knute Rockne had coached Notre Dame's football team to back-to-back national championships when he boarded an airplane bound for Los Angeles to do a movie about the Notre Dame spirit back in March of 1931 when he was killed in an airline crash.

Kobe Bryant was into the book publishing and movie business and had even gained an Oscar for one of his productions, a short animated-film called *Dear Basketball*. He became, in 2018, the first pro athlete ever to win an Oscar. He was also publishing young adult books, and was reported to be worth $600 million. Now Vanessa Bryant is worth $600 million.

* * *

I had recently watched a wonderful movie, *As Good As It Gets*, starring Jack Nicholson and Helen Hunt. I thought about that and the time I introduced myself to Jack Nicholson in the media room at Staples Center. My daughter Rebecca O'Brien had surprised me and her mother Kathie with two tickets to a Lakers' game, and she and her beau, Juan Barrayo, had arranged through their connections at California Pizza Kitchen for me to get a go-everywhere pass.

I didn't know any of the writers who were in the media room, but I knew they were put off when they saw Nicholson enter the room. He wasn't a sportswriter. What's he doing here? In our private domain? That's how I saw it and sensed it, for whatever that's worth. I had a hard time understanding their dismissive attitude.

I was excited to meet Nicholson, still one of my favorite actors. "Jack, I have enjoyed your work," I said. He offered a handshake, and said, "Nice to meet you, big guy." And he gave me his best Jack Nicholson smile. Nicholson has had season tickets at courtside since 1970. In 43 years, he paid over $5 million for those two seats. His estimated wealth is $400 million so he can afford it. He should have a room of his own at Staples Center and sneer at any sportswriters who walked into it.

I remembered watching him on TV in the movie *One Flew Over the Cuckoo's Nest,* one of the great movies of all time, in my hotel room in New Orleans. I went to coach Red Holzman's room to tell him what a great life it was to be traveling with the New York Knicks

Movie star Jack Nicholson loved Lakers from his courtside seats.

to New Orleans. That was the night "Pistol Pete" Maravich scored 68 points—there were no three-point field goals at the time. Holzman said, "It would be a great life if it weren't for the damn games!"

Nicholson was McMurphy in *One Flew Over the Cuckoo's Nest,* a new inmate at a mental hospital. He organized a basketball game among the other defective individuals and was smart enough to pass the ball to Chief Bromden, a Native American Indian who was deaf and mute in the movie. He was 6–5 and appeared taller and made it look easy on the basketball court. One of the players was Danny Divito, who is 4–10, and played the part of Martini in the movie.

His Celtics' teammates dubbed Robert Parrish "Chief" after seeing the movie.

Hubie Brown is one of the giants of the basketball game, though just 6-feet tall. He has been involved in basketball in one capacity or another since he played ball at Niagara University in the early '50s.

Brown, at 86, was working with Tirico for Kobe's Farewell game. He was twice NBA coach of the year—26 years apart—and was the head coach of the Kentucky Colonels. His wife, Claire, was the culprit—I learned two years after the incident—who shoved a cream pie in my face when I was interviewing star Dan Issel outside the Colonels' clubhouse after a playoff victory. Issel kindly handed me his white towel. For that alone, he is deserving of his Basketball Hall of Fame honors.

Brown and Tirico were terrific in providing background music to Kobe's incredible send-off. No player ever scored more points in his last game, not even Michael Jordan.

I am rooting for Issel and his group to get an NBA expansion team for Louisville—one of the greatest basketball towns in America.

CONDORS' VERSION OF GUNFIGHT AT THE OK CORRAL

John Brisker and Nate Bowman were both volatile sorts, known to carry handguns in their travel bags when they were teammates on the 1971–72 Pittsburgh Condors. I knew Bowman because he had been a backup to Willis Reed and Dave DeBusschere two years earlier when I covered the Knicks in their playoff drive to the 1970 NBA championship. He'd played his college ball at Wichita State with the incorrigible Simmie Hill, a schoolboy sensation out of Midland, Pa. That helps explain this story.

Things got heated at a practice session conducted by Coach Jack McMahon, an amiable Irishman who grew up in Brooklyn, a real New York guy who had known plenty of tough guys in his boyhood neighborhood. The flare-up occurred at the South Side Market House, at 12th Street and East Carson Street.

Scene of the crime: South Side Market House.

28

**John Brisker drives by Indiana's Tom Thacker with Mike Lewis
at far left.**

When Brisker went hard to the hoop Bowman rejected him with a strong arm. "He wanted Brisker to know the inside was his space," a teammate once recalled.

Brisker was irate and stalked off the floor and went to the dressing room. He returned waving a pistol overhead. Brisker had often warned overzealous teammates that he'd be "bringing my piece" to practice the next day and make someone pay for their crime.

"A piece" was ghetto parlance for a handgun, whether in Brisker's boyhood hometown of Detroit or Bowman's hometown of Fort Worth, Texas.

When Bowman—known as "Nate the Snake"—spotted Brisker waving his gun, he, too, retreated to the locker room and hurried outside to the parking lot where he retrieved his sawed-off shotgun. A backup obviously believes in a backup. Seems like he thought he'd need more than his pistol to deal with Brisker. "They called him Nate the Snake for a good reason," said a former teammate. "Nate was not a nice person. Nate was evil."

All hell broke loose, and the rest of the Condors were diving here and there, to get out of danger, so they didn't end up nearly as extinct as their namesake. A reserve named Joe Kennedy got locked up in the dressing room and was discovered hollering for help from an upstairs window. No shots were fired.

Jim Eakins related this story to me on June 10, 2020 after I called him a second time to get some names and numbers for a story I was writing about him for this book. It's a tale that was told to him by Paul Ruffner, a teammate in 1968 at Brigham Young University, who was a power forward and center for the Condors. Two other former Condors, who wished to remain anonymous, certified this story in follow-up phone conversations.

Among the Condors scattering that day were Mickey Davis, Jimmy O'Brien, Arvesta Kelly, Dave "Big Daddy" Lattin, Charlie "Helicopter" Hentz, Walker Banks, Mike Lewis, Joe Kennedy, Skeeter Swift, Stew Johnson, Charlie Williams and Chuck Williams. Or so I thought, after checking out the team roster on the internet. They were a beautiful bunch.

"I was not there," said George Thompson. "I'd have remembered if there had been a shoot-out. Everyone knew that Nate and Brisk both carried guns in their bags."

"I'll never forget Paul's story," said Eakins, an exclamation point in his voice. "It is part of ABA lore. It was like our version of the Gunfight at the OK Corral.

"Paul told me he was crawling on his stomach on the basketball floor as fast he could, to get away from any gunfire, but he got passed by the coach, Jack McMahon, moving toward the same exit.

"As McMahon was crawling past Ruffner, he hollered, 'Whoever survives this, tell those crazy sons of bitches that practice is over!' "

Paul Ruffner   Jimmy O'Brien   Mickey Davis

Condors Publicity Photo

31

Jim Eakins of Virginia Squires goes up for layin against Warren Davis (32) and Jim McDaniels (1) of Carolina Cougars, as teammate Doug Moe watches from back court.

Jim Eakins
was equal to the task
every time out on and off the court

Jim Eakins recalls an exchange he had with Rick Barry as they were walking off the court when they were teammates with the Oakland Oaks during the 1968–69 season. Eakins had just missed a 15-foot jump shot.

As they neared the bench, Barry turned and said to Eakins, "Eak, who do you think has a better chance of making a basket, you from 15 feet out or me from 20 feet out?"

The story was aimed at pointing up the great confidence Barry had in his own ability. And that Barry was never sensitive about someone else's feelings. "He always called me Eak," said Eakins. "He was one of the greatest to ever play the game."

Eakins had a nice turn-around jump shot in the lane, turning either way, and had a career field-goal percentage of 50.44, better than Barry. No one shot free throws as well as Barry, who hit over 94 percent of his free throws in his last two seasons in Houston. Barry believed he'd always hit nine of ten free throws.

Eakins liked players who were confident and one of his favorites was Doug Moe. "We were coming off the court in one game," said Eakins, "and Moe was muttering to himself. I asked him what was wrong. He said his shot stunk. Only the way he said it was worse than what I just said. He said it over and over, and I told him he was just fine, not to let it upset him. He said, 'I'm going to start shooting left-handed.' I said, 'You can't be fooling around like that. We need to win this game. It's too important to be messing around like that.' We went back out on the court and Moe makes three shots in a row, all left-handed, and they weren't layups. They were jump shots. I guess he was ambidextrous. And confident. I admired that.

"He and Larry Brown were great together. Brown really studied the game. He was like a coach on the floor. He knew what would work best against any particular player or opponent. When we were on the road, I'd come across Larry having lunch with coaches and discussing strategy with them. He learned the game from everyone. The rest of us would be napping or reading a book or watching TV. It wasn't surprising that he became a coach, and such a successful one at that."

Eakins volunteered rich stories like that, a complete surprise to this writer. What had I missed all those years? Some of my favorite chapters in this book came from players I virtually ignored when I was covering pro basketball. That's scary. The stars often take interviews for granted; they've done so many of them. Lesser players have wanted to tell their stories for years. Someone just had to listen.

*   *   *

His birth name was James Scott Eakins, but his teammates called him Jumbo and Jimbo or, in Barry's case, Eak, which was funny because he was always so painfully thin, 215 pounds at best packed tightly on a 6–11 frame.

"I tried every off-season to put on weight and I'd work at it and get up to 240," recalled Eakins, "but after I'd come to training camp, and do all the running drills and scrimmages, I'd be down to 213. Always 213."

So, 215, which appears on his publicity photos, was a bit of a stretch. 6–11 was not. He wore a mustache at times, but it was scrawny, too.

"I always thought I had to give my best effort in order to succeed," he said. "I realized they were mostly interested in me rebounding and playing tough defense and getting the ball distributed to the shooters."

I interviewed Jim Eakins once during his ten years in pro basketball and I realized, after I was talking to him over the telephone in early June, 2020, that I had missed out on something special. He was an excellent story-teller and he told his stories with a slower-than-usual cadence that made it easier to take notes.

Eakins didn't remind me of Ryne Duren, a poor-sighted "Wild Thing" pitcher for the Philadelphia Phillies and New York Yankees, who made it easy to take notes because he followed each word with the F-word. That's hardly the way Jim Eakins examines his life.

When I told him his speaking cadence reminded me of a former University of Pittsburgh chancellor named Mark Nordenberg, Eakins said, "That's good to be put in the same company as a leading educator."

He repeated that line when he spoke briefly to my wife Kathie who I put on the line to certify that he sounded just like Mark Nordenberg. Kathie agreed.

When he was finished playing pro basketball, Eakins initially got into the banking business for five years, but he was not happy with his vocation. His wife urged him to find something he truly enjoyed, and he turned to teaching and coaching and never looked back. Except during our conversation.

He played pro ball in eight different cities, including Salt Lake City with the Utah Stars, and he settled in Salt Lake after retiring from the NBA.

He coached basketball at Mountain View, Mount Vernon, Granite and Cottonwood—all schools in Utah.

I had last spoken to Jim Eakins on the evening of Wednesday, January 23, 1974, after he had led the Virginia Squires to a 118–110 victory over the New York Nets at Nassau Coliseum in Uniondale, N.Y.

The Nets' starting center Billy Paultz sprained his left ankle after ten minutes of play, and was sidelined. He was replaced by Willie Sojourner. Sojourner had been shipped to the Nets the previous summer in a deal that brought Dr. J—Julius Erving—to his hometown Nets. Sojourner had been Dr. J's roommate on the road.

Jim Eakins tries to hold off Nets' center Billy Paultz, nicknamed "The Big Whopper" because he was 6–11, 250 pounds.

Eakins had beaten out Sojourner for the No. 1 pivot position with the Squires, and he put another beating on him this night in New York, driving at him and either shooting over him or drawing a foul.

Eakins scored 12 of his 24 points over a 6½ minute span in the fourth quarter, outscoring even Erving who was held to 23 points. I still have a copy of the tear sheet from the next day's *New York Post* that has a picture showing Eakins driving on Sojourner.

Eakins had survived for six seasons in the ABA at that point because of how dedicated he was to playing his best every time out. He had played at Brigham Young University when Sojourner was a star at Weber State, also in Utah.

He was always beating out people thought to have more natural ability than he possessed. His coach at Brigham Young, Stan Watts, said Eakins didn't have nearly the talent of another center on the same college team. That was Craig Raymond who managed to stay around the ABA for a few seasons mostly because he was white and seven feet tall.

I remembered Raymond well because Gabe Rubin was trying to recruit him to play for the Pittsburgh Pipers. Raymond had told Rubin he was interested in going to graduate school so Rubin asked me to take Raymond on a tour of the University of Pittsburgh. I must not have been a good recruiter because Raymond went elsewhere. After starting his career in the NBA with the Philadelphia 76ers, he moved to the Pipers for the start of the 1969–70 season.

Maybe someone tipped Raymond off in advance that he was never going to be the starting center for the Pipers who already employed an ABL refugee, Connie "The Hawk" Hawkins. The Hawk had gone to the NBA before Raymond returned to Pittsburgh. Raymond returned to Pittsburgh two years later, after

The Hawk had flown the coop in favor of the Phoenix Suns of the NBA, and the team was in need of a center.

I should have realized that Eakins was more than met the eye. He had been elected president of the ABA Players Association and was still in a leadership role, among those still pitching and pleading for a pension for ABA alumni by the NBA.

"That meant a lot to me," Eakins said of his election. "I knew the players respected me."

Artis Gilmore of the Kentucky Colonels was the only taller player at the ABA's 50th anniversary reunion in Indianapolis in April of 2018. "Gilmore was 7-foot-2 and about 240 to 250 pounds," said Eakins. "And his thighs were like those of a thoroughbred horse. I was always going up against guys who outweighed me. Zelmo Beaty was my toughest opposing center. He was so smart and knew how to gain position under the boards. We'd go at it pretty good, biting and scratching, whatever was necessary."

Eakins played ten seasons, the last two in the NBA with the Kansas City Kings, San Antonio Spurs and Milwaukee Bucks. He was a travelin' man.

He played in one ABA All-Star Game when he was with the Squires, and that was as a replacement for the still-injured Billy Paultz in 1974 at the Norfolk (Va.) Scope, one of four home courts for the Squires that season. They also played in Roanoke, Richmond and Hampton Roads. The Squires had some outstanding players in their time, such as Dr. J, George Gervin, Swen Nater, Fatty Taylor, Charlie Scott, Doug Moe, Ray "Chink" Scott and George Irvine, but were never on solid financial footing and, eventually, folded just before the merger with the NBA. They should have had Rick Barry, too, but Barry ruined that possibility by saying in a national publication that he didn't want his son coming home from school and saying, "Y'all." So the Squires sold Barry to the New York Nets for $200,000.

Jim Eakins
Virginia Squires

Al Bianchi, his coach with the Squires, had said after the Squires' victory over the Nets in New York, that he hoped Eakins would replace Paultz if he was not ready to play in the upcoming All-Star Game. "I'd like to see Jumbo play because he should have made it last year," said Bianchi.

I recalled that Eakins had sold a jersey once worn by Squires' teammate Charlie Scott when Eakins appeared at the ABA's 30th anniversary reunion in Indianapolis that included an auction. Scott's No. 33 Squires jersey drew a bid from a collector in Asia for $300. I sold about two dozen ABA press guides at the same event to a collector from Japan for $3,000.

When we spoke a second time in three days on June 10, 2020, Eakins told me how he got that jersey. "We were leaving a locker room after a game, and Charlie departed as I was leaving, and I saw his jersey laying on the floor," said Eakins. "I called that to Charlie's attention, and he responded by saying, 'You

Jim O'Brien

Some of ABA's best attended 30th anniversary reunion in Indianapolis, from left to right, James Jones, Tom Thacker, Charlie Scott and Willie Wise.

can pick it up.' And he left. He said goodbye to our trainer, Chopper Travaglini, and he was gone. I didn't learn until the next day that Charlie was jumping to the NBA's Phoenix Suns, just like that. So, I picked up his jersey and kept it all those years. It's the jersey he wore in his last game with the Squires."

Eakins, as mentioned earlier, had played with another high-scoring star in Rick Barry with the Oakland Oaks. He thought the Oaks might have been the best team ever in the ABA, succeeding the Pittsburgh Pipers as the league champions in the second season.

The Oaks posted a 60–18 record and won the ABA's Western Division title and then beat the Indiana Pacers 4–1 in a five-game championship series. The Oaks' roster included Barry, Moe, Larry Brown, Ira Harge, Gary Bradds, Warren Jabali and Henry Logan. I saw Harge, Moe and Logan at the 50th anniversary reunion.

The Nets' Billy Melchionni remembered Logan as a super-swift guard and Jabali, formerly known as Warren Armstrong, as a powerful backcourt man whose original name was more fitting.

The Oaks were coached by Alex Hannum. "He was the best basketball coach I ever played for," Eakins told me. He detailed how Hannum switched strategies in games to overcome huge deficits to put his team in position to win in the stretch run. He couldn't remember the opponents in these particular games, but he could still hear Hannum hollering instructions. He recalled how Hannum called time outs back to back in order to quiet an overzealous crowd in one contest, taking the crowd completely out of the game by the lengthier stoppage of play.

Eakins also did a brief stint with the New York Nets and said Kevin Loughery "really understood how the game should be played, and how to motivate his players."

Eakins was drafted in 1968 by the San Francisco Warriors, but signed instead with the Oakland Oaks on the other side of the Bay.

Altogether, he played for the Oakland Oaks, Washington Caps, Virginia Squires, Utah Stars and New York Nets of the ABA, and then with the Kansas City Kings, San Antonio Spurs and Milwaukee Bucks in the NBA. He had 8,255 points and 5,578 rebounds. His career averages were 10.8 points and nearly eight rebounds per game. At BYU, his career averages were 14.8 points and 10.1 rebounds.

He liked Art Becker of Arizona State and wanted to go there, but Arizona State was not interested in him so he went to Brigham Young University.

"I saw Art Becker on the hotel elevator in Indianapolis, and he was struggling," recalled Eakins. "That's what hit home with me about the last reunion. Everyone had gotten so old, and some were having such a difficult time getting around. Made me feel fortunate to be in the shape I'm in."

Jim O'Brien

Art Becker attended 50th anniversary reunion.

* * *

He's in the Hall of Fame at his high school in Sacramento, California and in the Northern Conference High School Hall of Fame.

As a schoolboy, he would shoot by himself at a playground near his home in Sacramento. "I was always Wilt Chamberlain and I was going up against Bill

42

Russell. There were six seconds to play, and we were down by one and I had the ball," he recalled.

I told him I could identify with that activity. "I was always Wilt, too," I said. "Why were you Wilt?" I asked.

"Because I was big for my age," he said. "So, I identified with the big men in the game."

"I was the smallest kid my age on our street," I said. "I used to emulate the way Wilt used that finger-tip roll shot and that made no sense, because you had to be above the hoop to do it."

I knew Eakins was smiling about that picture.

"My older brothers used to beat me up when I was playing," he said. He told me that his oldest brother, Richard, was 15 years older than him. He had a sister, Nancy, who was 10 years older than him, and a brother William, who was seven years older. Richard and his wife both died in an auto accident ten years earlier, and Bill was also deceased. Nancy was 84 and still alive.

Besides both us pretending we were Wilt Chamberlain as children, Eakin and I came from a similar family.

My oldest brother was also named Richard. He was 15 years older than me and was a baker on a Navy ship in the South Pacific when I was three and four years old. I had a brother Dan who was five years older, and a sister, Carol, who was ten years older. Our Mom had four children, one coming every five years.

I don't remember playing any sports with any of them. "My dad put up a hoop for me over the garage when he saw that I was seriously interested in playing basketball," said Eakins. "Before that, I went to a playground near our home. I think it disappointed him that I wasn't a baseball player. He liked baseball better."

Jim has been married to Jean for 51 years, and they have five children, Jim Jr., 50, Jeff, 47, Jill, 43, Jason, 37 and Jenna, 36.

* * *

When I asked Eakins how he was dealing with all the difficulties that had developed in 2020 with, first, the coronavirus outbreak and, second, the protests and riots that resulted from the killing of George Floyd in Minneapolis.

"I believe that Jesus Christ will see us through these difficult days," said Eakins. "I believe in spiritual healing. He is my savior. He will see us through this."

I asked Eakins if he was a Mormon, and he corrected me. "I am a member of The Church of Jesus Christ of Latter-Day Saints," he said. "There's a slight difference." I told him I had visited the Mormon Tabernacle Church in Tabernacle Square in Salt Lake City and heard its famous choir perform while traveling with the Nets. I'll never forget how small the bed that the prophet Brigham Young had reportedly slept in that was on display at a museum there.

Jim Eakins would have had to fold his body a few times to sleep in that small bed.

I knew some of the history of Mormonism. The church was founded by Joseph Smith at the age of 24 in western New York. He went west to get freedom of religion for his upstart religious movement and settled in Salt Lake. He said, "This is *the* place."

Jim Eakins echoed that thought. "This is definitely the place," he said, "for the Eakin family."

Walt Szczerbiak recalls his Condors' roommate Paul Ruffner trying to convert him from Orthodox Catholicism to Mormonism once during a road trip to play the Utah Stars. "He took me high on a hill overlooking Salt Lake City," Walt said, "and talked to me about joining the Church of Jesus Christ of Latter Day Saints. I didn't join him on that team."

Michael Jordan and
Red Mccombs combine
for great doubleheader

I feel like a police detective writing an incident report. I found a reporter's notebook over a weekend in mid-April, 2020, as I was writing this book. From top to bottom on the cardboard cover it read Chrysler Motors, The Big East Conference and 1986–87 Basketball Notebook with Dodge and Plymouth logos along the bottom.

Printed by hand were these notations, from top to bottom:

ABA
RED McCOMBS
MICHAEL JORDAN.

There were only eights sheets still in the notebook, held intact by a white spiral coil, with my scribbled hand-writing on both sides of each sheet, a total of 16 pages of notes. The notebook is filled with what Michael Jordan and then Red McCombs said to me in interviews I conducted at the Hemisphere Arena in San Antonio, Texas on Thursday, February 9, 1989.

That was quite a day, as it turned out, and it is proof of the enviable position or reporter's privilege that I enjoyed back then. I had one-on-one interviews with MJ and Red when they were at the top of their game in the professional basketball world.

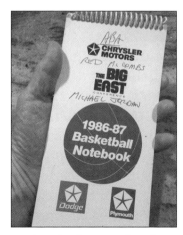

Here's the notebook.

45

They were two of the most powerful personalities in pro basketball. MJ was better known, of course. Kids kept saying "I like Mike," and were costing their parents a bundle in buying the AirJordan sneakers he endorsed for Nike.

McCombs had gotten richer than just about everyone in Texas—and that's saying something as Texans will tell you—selling automobiles. He owned 55 different auto dealerships at the peak of business and he was the principal owner of the San Antonio Spurs. He would later sell the Spurs and buy the Denver Nuggets and then sell the Nuggets to buy the Minnesota Vikings. To him they were just different models of owning a sports team of his own.

"And now we have Michael Jordan playing the Spurs in San Antonio," he told me at one point, summing up succinctly what the merger had meant to the former ABA teams when they were absorbed into the senior NBA circuit. "It will only get better."

This was only three days before the NBA All-Star Weekend in Houston on February 12, 1989. McCombs would later be joined at his table in a private club at the Hemisphere Arena by fellow NBA owners Sam Schulman of the Seattle SuperSonics, Irv Levin of the Boston Celtics and Carl Scheer was present as the general manager of the first-year Charlotte Hornets. Scheer would have a falling out with Hornets' owner George Shinn and depart Charlotte at the end of the season to return to Denver as general manager of the Nuggets. Angelo Drossos of San Antonio, one of the original owners of the Spurs, would show up later on at McComb's table. This was a round table of some of the most influential men in pro basketball, and I was there—the former founder and commissioner of the Sunnyside A.C. Basketball League (1955–56)—to hear what they had to say about the state of the game.

Levin was showing off the championship ring his Celtics had won in 1976. Schulman, who owned the Seattle SuperSonics from 1967 until 1983 when he sold the franchise to Oklahoma City investors, showed off the Sonics' NBA championship ring from the 1978–79 season. Schulman and Levin were both in the movie business. Schulman had the best line of the session when he told me, "Please don't remind me of John Brisker! Or Spencer Haywood or Jim McDaniels!"

Those were three outstanding ABA stars Schulman had signed for million-dollar contracts and they didn't work out for Schulman and the Sonics. They were all head cases of one kind of another. Most ABA ballplayers had a considerable chip on their shoulders. Someone had wronged them. Didn't want them in their game. Didn't pay them what they deserved. Any slight was seldom forgotten or forgiven. Bill Russell was excited when Schulman signed him to a big contract to coach those guys—Russell thought he'd have top talent to contend for a title, and there was talent for sure—but it all went south for Schulman and his money. "Even Bill Russell was afraid of John Brisker!" said Schulman in the San Antonio setting.

Made me think of just how far the NBA and its ownership had come over the years. Danny Biasone, who owned the Syracuse Nationals and gave us the 24-second clock, owned a bowling alley/restaurant in Syracuse and sold the franchise to Philadelphia interests because he did not have the bankroll to compete any longer. When I was writing this chapter, I checked Red McComb's net worth on the Internet. At age 95, he was reportedly worth $1.5 billion. That's b and not m in front of illion. Michael Jordan, age 57, is reportedly worth $1.6 billion. He is the principal owner of the NBA's Charlotte Hornets, and earned $130 million from Nike in 2019, four times as much as LeBron James, who has the richest shoe deal among active players.

I told an old friend, Dean Billick, about this meeting with McCombs. Billick had been the senior associate athletic director at Pitt when I was on the staff from 1983 to 1986, and later was the athletic director at Lamar University in Beaumont, Texas. He also served for 3½ years as the executive director of the U.S. Modern Pentathlon Association.

"I didn't really know Red McCombs," recalled Billick, "but I approached him for some funding for our pentathlon association and he gave me $50,000. The pentathlon wasn't that popular a sport, but McCombs came through for me. That makes him a good guy in my eyes."

People, or readers, who don't know me that well often ask, "How do you get to talk to these guys?"

Let me tell you how this came about. I went to the NBA All-Star Game every year for over 25 years when I was the founding editor of *Street and Smith's Basketball Yearbook*, the No. 1 selling annual of its kind, and eventually the NBA's official annual preview magazine. It was often referred to as "the bible of basketball." Everyone associated with the game was aware of *Street and Smith's*. I also wrote a column for *The Sporting News* and just about every weekly and monthly publication associated with the sport. I was treated well when it came to getting media credentials, photos and guides by Brian McIntyre and Terry Lyons of the NBA office. Rick Welts, more recently the president of the Golden State Warriors, was working in the NBA headquarters when, together, we oversaw the transformation of our basketball yearbook into being the official NBA annual.

About a week before the NBA All-Star Game in Houston, I received a telephone call from Wayne Witt, the publicity director of the San Antonio Spurs. Witt wanted to know if I planned on going to the All-Star

Game. I told him I was and he wanted to know what I would be doing the week before the game.

"Why don't you stop in San Antonio on the way to Houston?" asked Witt. It sounded like a line from a country song.

"Who are you playing?"

"The Chicago Bulls, Michael Jordan."

"I'll be there," I said.

Witt and the Bulls' publicity director, Tim Hallam, arranged for me to meet Michael Jordan in the visitors' locker room at the Hemisphere Arena before the game with the Spurs. It would be an exclusive one-on-one session. I can still see the scene.

While I was talking to Michael Jordan, Wayne Witt walked into the locker room and tapped me on the shoulder. "Pardon me, fellas," said Witt. "Jim, my boss, Red McCombs, would like to see you in our private club when you finish with Michael."

After my session with McCombs, I took my courtside press row seat. Witt came over and asked me how it went. "I don't remember Red ever having a sportswriter at his table like that," said Witt.

I thanked Witt for what he had done on my behalf. I felt special. It was a good feeling.

When it was just McCombs talking to me, he offered his thoughts about the future of pro basketball.

"I'm very proud of the players we have representing our league," commented McCombs. "Players like Dr. J, and Magic and Jordan. They set a good example. They want to be seen as more than just a ballplayer. They want to be the kind of person to set an example for the youth of America. They've gained some incredible honors, as college players in the Olympic Games."

McCombs was quite the flag-waver, but he might have gone a bit overboard on his evaluation of the top players in pro basketball. Even the good guys were led astray at times. NBA players didn't play in the Olympic Games until 1992.

He credited Angelo Drossos, one of the owners of the Spurs from the start, for helping him steer the Spurs' ship and to stay on course. "Angelo told me he'd work for nothing because he cared about the city of San Antonio. He attended all the league meetings. I was the president of the team—Angelo didn't carry the title—but he was our representative."

I actually was more familiar with Drossos. My wife Kathie and I had attended a party at his home prior to the ABA All-Star Game in San Antonio. His mansion was a local attraction right up there with The Alamo.

I had spent a special time with Sam Schulman on an earlier visit with him at his home in Beverly Hills, not far from the home of Wilt Chamberlain. I recall Sam had an Asian-American butler who wore a beige tunic jacket with matching slacks. Sam pointed out a framed photo of President Richard Nixon on the mantel above his fireplace. It was signed to Sam Schulman.

Best of all, I recall that some of Sam's friends were playing tennis on a court in his backyard. Peggy Lipton, the actress best known for her role as Barnes in the popular TV drama series, "The

Sam Schulman

Mod Squad," was out on the court. I didn't know it until I was working on this book

Peggy Lipton

that her father, Harold Lipton, was a high-priced LA attorney who invested in many of Schulman's ventures. He may have been playing in that tennis game I witnessed for a brief moment.

Jim O'Brien

ABA owners, from left to right, Joe Gregory of Kentucky Colonels, Gabe Rubin of Pittsburgh Pipers and Condors and Red McCombs of San Antonio Spurs and Denver Nuggets, enjoy reunion at ABA's 30th anniversary celebration in Indianapolis.

Schulman was the president of National General, which produced and distributed movies through a national chain of theaters. Gene Klein, who owned the NFL San Diego Chargers, was one of his partners. They had first met as fledgling figures in New York's garment district.

When I got home from that visit to Schulman, I purchased 100 shares of National General and it turned out to be a good investment. I sold it at a profit a year later. National General was liquidated in 1974.

The next time I met McCombs was at the ABA's 30th year anniversary reunion in Indianapolis. He was sitting with Max Williams, who had been an owner and coach of the Dallas Chaparrals.

McCombs invited me to join. "Let's catch up," he said.

The last time I saw and spoke to Michael Jordan was at the Mario Lemieux Celebrity Golf Invitational at The Club at Nevillewood from June 11–13, 2000. "Where have you been?" asked MJ.

Mario Lemieux and Michael Jordan

Kentucky owner John Y. Brown and Red McCombs

photos by Jim O'Brien

Doug Moe and Red McCombs of Denver Nuggets

Hands on coaching—
Connie's basketball clinics for city kids in Pittsburgh

The little boy kept walking back and forth, staring at the big man whose long legs stretched out before him. His stare seemed almost stern.

Cornelius Lance Hawkins—what a wonderful name—called Connie or "The Hawk"—was the big man. He was sitting with his broad back against the lowest section of a chain-link fence, as were a dozen or more little boys, watching a scrimmage game in the playground of the Northview Heights housing development on a hill overlooking Pittsburgh's North Side neighborhood.

Hawkins and his staff were conducting a clinic to teach the boys the fundamentals of basketball. The idea, of course, was to get the kids involved in a summer day program. Get them interested, keep them involved and off the streets.

His friend, John Brown, an offensive tackle and captain in his second season with the Steelers, had stopped by earlier to check out the action. Brown and his wife, Gloria, were living in Allegheny Center and she was teaching at Northview Heights Elementary School. I'd see Brown visiting his friend Gus Kalaris, "the ice ball man," at his iconic stand at West Park.

Kalaris can't remember Connie Hawkins ever stopping at his stand for an ice ball. Connie's loss. No better way to cool off on a hot summer's day.

All the kids, understandably, were somewhat in awe over Hawkins' presence. He was the star pivotman for the Pittsburgh Pipers who had won the ABA's first championship over that winter. He stood 6–8 and the hand which patted them on their head and back was an enormous one. He could hold a basketball the way these kids could hold a softball or baseball. But none stared as longingly as this little boy in the torn shirt who kept walking back and forth.

Hawkins is a hands-on coach. He knew he was holding more than a basketball when he held these little boys by the head or shoulders. Some of them didn't get that sort of attention at home. Hawkins had been one of those little boys as a youngster growing up like few others in his Bedford-Stuyvesant neighborhood in Brooklyn.

"I lived in the playground," he said when he would be inducted into the Naismith Memorial Basketball Hall of Fame on October 7, 2017. "I'd be there all day. That's where I learned my game, all that free-wheeling stuff."

He was as much a logo for the above-the-rim game of the renegade league that was the ABL and then the ABA as their red-white-and blue ball. He picked up a few more tricks when he played for the Harlem Globetrotters and Harlem Magicians over a two-year stretch between the ABL and the ABA.

* * *

Finally, Hawkins reached out and grasped the boy around his shoulders. "What's your name?" Hawkins asked.

"Michael," the little boy whispered.

"How come you're not playing basketball with us?"

"I don't know how to play," said Michael, again in a whisper so the other kids couldn't hear him. "I play baseball."

"So, you're a baseball player, huh?" said Hawkins. "Well, do you know who Jackie Robinson is?"

Michael shook his head sideways.

"How about Maury Wills?"

Again, Michael shook his head in a negative reply.

"Well, then where do you know me from?" Hawkins asked.

"From Charles Street," came the soft-spoken reply.

Hawkins had to laugh, and he rubbed his hand through Michael's head, and suddenly Michael was smiling. And then he walked away. Hawkins' home was on Charles Street. I'd been there, and recognized the name right away.

"I see myself out there," said Hawkins, pointing to the young boys on the court, playing basketball under the watchful eyes of such stars as Ed Fleming, Jim McCoy and Walt Mangham, all former pro players, in the National Basketball Association or the Eastern Basketball League. Fleming, a teacher and coach at Wilkinsburg High and Westinghouse High, had played

Connie Hawkins stood tall above the crowd at basketball clinic sponsored by City Parks and Recreation at Moore Field in Brookline in 1969.

with Maurice Stokes at Westinghouse, with Larry Costello at Niagara University, and five years in the NBA, two with the Rochester Royals and three more with the Minneapolis Lakers, and one of the classiest men you'd ever meet. He was an assistant to Jerry Conboy at Point Park College. I remember attending his funeral in the East End.

That was always disturbing. Connie was a month older than me so I hated to hear, from our friend Bill Neal, that Hawkins had died at age 75 in a senior residence in Phoenix. He had worked, after retiring from playing in the NBA, as an ambassador for the Suns and conducting, of course, summer basketball camps. Basketball was his life mission, and Connie converted a lot of kids to the cause.

"You remember that one drill we did early today? The circle with the one boy in the middle passing to the boys about him? It's good for passing and eye-ball control, but even more important, it gets them involved. That's my idea. I put it in the clinic. The kids enjoy themselves right away and they get interested. It's something they can handle. Right off the bat, they're a part of what we're doing."

Hawkins was such a good-hearted man who found amusement in the midst of a madding crowd. He had a knack for knowing who needs to be encouraged, who needs coddling, and who needs a quick reprimand or order. No one wanted to get on the wrong side of a man named for a predatory bird. His lengthy fingers didn't have talons at their ends, but they had a strong grip. Pirates' pitcher Steve Blass used to say he didn't know if he had a grip on baseball, or if baseball had a grip on him. The same could be said for Connie Hawkins and basketball. Bill Neal said Hawkins never asked for a dime for what he did.

He enjoyed being among these kids, mostly young blacks, but he was all business in the way he conducted his camp.

When Bill Neal formed a summer basketball league in later years, he called it the Connie Hawkins Summer Basketball League, and Hawkins lent more than his name to the program. He'd show up on occasion and entertain the crowd with some dunks and dribbling maneuvers, such as reversing to get free for a jumper. "Now you try that," he'd say with a smile.

I came to his clinic on the North Side and one earlier that he had done at a playground between the Pennley Park Apartments, where Maury Wills and Roberto Clemente, Juan Pizzaro and Alvin O'Neal McBean of the Pirates resided during the season, and the East Liberty Police Station on Penn Avenue.

Moe Becker, a member of the storied "Iron Dukes" of Duquesne University in the 1941–42 season and then as a basketball coach at Braddock High School and Greensburg High School, lived in the Pennley Park Apartments. We'd run into him on occasion at a mini-mart within the housing complex and he'd position Kathie as a center in one of the aisles as he explained some of his home-cooked basketball strategy.

The clinic at Northview Heights would be the last one of the summer camps sponsored by the City Parks & Recreation Department. Richard Caliguiri was in his first year as mayor of Pittsburgh after serving as director of City Parks & Recreation and president of City Council. Joe Natoli, who had a 40-year career with the department, was now in charge. Natoli also founded and coached the Morningside Bulldogs, one of the outstanding midget-football teams in the country.

"He's the draw," Fleming said of Hawkins' role at the summer camps. "He's great with these kids, and it's too bad he won't be doing any more this summer."

This was also the last summer for *Pittsburgh Weekly Sports. I* went to the clinic to write a feature story for our tabloid. Beano Cook went to ABC Sports as a publicist in New York, and I went to Miami to cover the Dolphins in their final season in the American Football League. We'd had a lot of fun, even if we didn't make much money, publishing that paper for five-and-a-half years. It led to a lot of great opportunities.

At the first clinic conducted by Hawkins that summer of '68, only seven kids showed up at a playground in the Glen-Hazel Projects. Hawkins had to send someone to knock at the door of the playground instructor to wake him up and get him over to the park for the clinic. Then other boys were rounded up.

Hawkins didn't have anything harsh to say to the tardy playground instructor probably because he had a reputation for sleeping late and coming to practice late when he played for the Pipers. Alex Medich, the team's trainer from Duquesne in the Steel Valley, was often sent to get a rise out of Hawkins at his home.

"Maybe they're too early in the morning," said Hawkins in reference to the 10 a.m. starting time for the clinics. "Maybe the kids aren't up yet."

It wasn't that way back in Brooklyn's Bedford-Stuyvesant area where Hawkins grew up. As James Baldwin has written, you couldn't stay in the house in the summer. Not those houses.

"It was a real ghetto," recalled Lenny Litman, who went there to sign Hawkins to a pro contract with the old Pittsburgh Rens (short for Renaissance). "I was shocked when I saw the inside of those places." They didn't look anything like Litman's home or neighborhood in Pittsburgh's Squirrel Hill community

* * *

ROGER BROWN

CONNIE HAWKINS
Forward 6–8

ABA's MVP in first season (1967–68) with Pittsburgh Pipers.

Jim McCoy

Hawkins was only 19 and had just left the University of Iowa during his freshman year. He had accepted money and favors from a man who was involved in point-shaving scandals in 1961. Hawkins was never accused of shaving points or dumping a game, but it was enough to keep him from varsity college ball or in the NBA for a long stretch.

"Connie slept in a bed with his brother in the living room," recalled Lenny Litman. "It was a real mess. I had to knock a roach off a dressing bureau to have a place for him and his brother to sign the contract."

"Sure, he slept with his brother," said Frank Martin, a 28-year-old boyhood buddy of Hawkins, who was visiting with Connie that week. He turned to another fellow who was at the clinic from Bedford-Stuyvesant and said, "Isn't that right? How about you?"

The fellow they called Mitch nodded. "You're not kidding," he said.

"I played basketball 26 hours a day," said Hawkins. "It was my life. You couldn't stay in the house. It was too hot. No one had air-conditioning. I didn't even come home to eat sometimes.

"I wasn't interested in anything else, and when someone told me I was good at basketball, I got more interested in it."

Hawkins was a hero at Boys' High, bigger than Sihugo Green and Lenny Wilkins, both pros, who had been there before him. He led his team to two straight City League titles. There are framed photos showing Hawkins as a schoolboy in a Legends' Room near the rafters at Madison Square Garden. I've seen them.

His family was still living in Bedford-Stuyvesant when I called upon Connie at the basketball clinics. He would go home from time to time.

Connie Hawkins was living on Charles Street, which I mentioned earlier. It was in the midst of a ghetto on the North Side. It was not a nice place to live. Connie lived there with his wife, Nancy, their children, Shawna, 5, and Connie Jr., a year-old and four sisters-in-law, and a brother-in-law who was deformed and retarded. You might want to read this paragraph again, and let it sink in.

The house was always crowded. The girls had their boyfriends calling on them, and Connie's pals were always at the door. He was making enough money to live elsewhere, but he chose to remain there. Hawkins didn't have to have an impressive address.

"I think I do more good here," he said. "Maybe I belong here."

The Pipers were scheduled to depart Pittsburgh in favor of Minneapolis for their second season in the ABA, and Hawkins wasn't sure whether he should move his family or stay in Pittsburgh.

"I hope he stays for selfish reasons," said his friend, Father Jack O'Malley, a former basketball star at St. Francis of Loretto (Pa.) who rated a tryout with the Detroit Pistons, and was now serving as a priest at St. Joseph's Church in Manchester. "He's great for those kids. He even came down to our school this past year and signed 295 autographs, and talked to the kids, and told them to stay in school, and talked about his own school years. It was something. They understand him, and they pay attention. I'll miss him."

It is this way...Hawkins has the ear of the ghetto kids. He gains their attention and respect where a doctor with a degree in child behavior might fail. That is why the loss of the Pipers was more than just a loss of a basketball team.

Gale Sayers, Lamar Lundy, Lonnie Sanders were some of the pro athletes who went into the ghettos, be it the South Side of Chicago or Watts in LA, and they could talk to the kids and tell them to cool it.

Those days, more than ever, fellows like Connie Hawkins are needed in the long, hot summer.

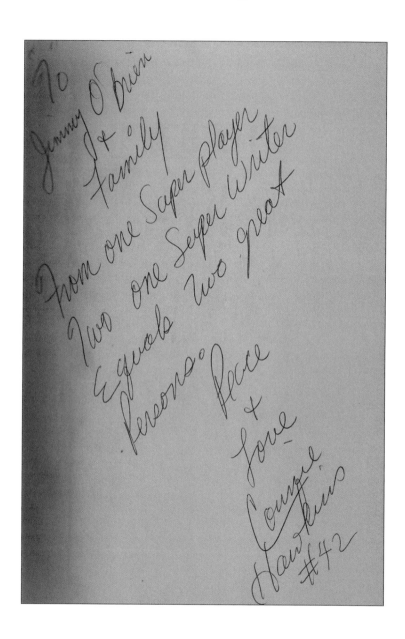

Hands On approach by Connie Hawkins got their attention at City Parks clinics.

Bill Neal of Champions Inc. tells a story about when Julius Erving came to Pittsburgh to be the featured speaker at a Willie Stargell Awards Dinner. "Dr. J pointed to Connie Hawkins in the audience and said, "If it weren't for Connie Hawkins there'd have been no Dr. J. He was my model, my inspiration." Neal met Dr. J the next morning to escort him from a downtown hotel to the Pittsburgh International Airport. "I'm sitting in the back of a limo with the greatest basketball player in the world, and I was feeling pretty special," related Neal. "Dr. J said, 'If Connie ever needs anything, and I mean anything, you call me.'"

John Havlicek
Hondo is still a Bridgeport boy
who helped Celtics win championships

As the 1976–77 NBA season approached, some fans were wondering whether it would be John Havlicek's last season. Could the Boston Celtics win another championship, a last hurrah for Hondo?

Only Havlicek and the Celtics knew the answers. "He might go on forever," said Red Auerbach, the general manager of the Boston ballclub and Havlicek's former coach.

Havlicek had never stopped running during his playing days and maybe he had no intention of quitting. Some felt he had slowed down, but then he seemed to find a second breath and new legs, and he would leave everybody behind him and blow to the basket for two points.

"I saw him at a get-together this summer," said Nets' coach Kevin Loughery, who put in 11 years himself in the NBA, "and played some tennis with him. He still looks in great shape. He still looks like he could beat you on a fast break.

"He's such a super guy," volunteered Loughery. "There's absolutely no pretension about him or his wife Beth. They're both super people."

That's a large part of Havlicek's charm. According to a survey I've seen, he's not only supposed to be one of the most recognizable and, even more important from an advertising point of view, the most believable pro basketball player, as far as the fans are concerned. He's always been one of the top vote-getters in the annual all-star game balloting by the fans.

He's been a marvelous athlete, competitor and person. "When he stops playing," wrote Bob Ryan of

The Boston Globe, an unabashed fan of Havlicek, "one thing will be certain: in terms of combined skill, dedication and character, we may not see his likes again."

Red Auerbach perhaps paid him the highest tribute, as he once said, "John Havlicek is what I always thought a Celtic should be."

And the beat goes on...

Everybody loves John Havlicek, don't they? Ever heard anybody rap him? Never.

He was 36 years old in 1976 and he would be 37 by the time the next NBA playoffs rolled around—April 8 was his birthday, if you wanted to send him a birthday card or, if his knee acts up again, a get-well card.

He sustained a knee injury on March 3 of the previous campaign, and it bothered him the rest of the schedule. But he still played a big role in the Celtics winning another NBA title, their 13th in league history.

This would be Havlicek's 15th season, a milestone reached only by Dolph Schayes, who put in 16 years in the NBA, and Lenny Wilkens and Hal Greer. (Years later, others would top these numbers. Havlicek's teammate Robert Parish would play 21 seasons, as did Kevin Willis and Kevin Garnett. Kareem Abdul-Jabbar played 20 seasons.

Havlicek still ranks as one of the Top 20 scorers in NBA history with 26,395 points.

Havlicek played 16 seasons with the Celtics, eight on NBA championship teams. The Celtics were champions during his first four seasons with the team. Hondo was one of my favorites too. I was saddened to hear he had died, at age 79, on April 25, 2019.

*   *   *

In 2015, I traveled to the St. Florian Hall in Wintersville, Ohio with my friends, Lee and Roger Glunt and George Morris to see Havlicek honored as an inductee into the Lou Holtz/Upper Ohio Valley Hall of Fame. Steve Blass of the Pirates and Jerome Bettis of the Steelers were both speakers at the banquet that night. I had a chance to interview Havlicek before the dinner.

I reminded him, as I always did, that my mother, Mary Burns, was from his hometown of Bridgeport. My oldest brother, Dick, lived his entire life in Bridgeport. Havlicek remembered Dick as one of his coaches when he was a youngster. Dr. Joseph Maroon, one of the Steelers' team doctors, is also from Bridgeport, and spoke glowingly about my brother Dick's influence on him as a coach.

I never needed to soften up Havlicek, however, because he was accommodating to everyone who ever approached him for an interview. "You get tired of answering some of the same questions," he said, "but I was raised to be nice to people. That's the way I was brought up."

The 6–5 forward/guard was a holdover from another era. He was there when Bill Russell and Sam Jones were winning titles in Boston, and bridged the gap during some pretty bad years, until Jo White, Don Chaney and Dave Cowens came along and comprised another title team.

"One of these days John will collapse on the floor and fall apart," said his coach and former teammate Tommy Heinsohn, "and nuts and bolts will fall out. It's inhuman how he runs."

It's okay for Heinsohn to say something like that, but when a reporter asked Havlicek is he had slowed down, Heinsohn interjected, "The older he gets the more he runs."

John Havlicek and Bill Russell

Another former teammate, Bill Russell, once cracked over an ABC telecast, "That Havlicek is going to find out someday what it is to be tired. And he's just going to drop dead."

Havlicek heard about Russell's remark, and said, "I admit it pleased me, because it was recognition that year-round preparation and the precautions I take pay off in my ability to continue to contribute to the Celtics' success and permit me to continue my living as an athlete."

It's for that same reason that Havlicek had been eager to surpass Hal Greer for most games played in the NBA. "It would signify," said Havlicek, "that I've always been talked about in terms of stamina and endurance. People say I'm a scorer more than a shooter.

"One of the things that I'm proudest of now is that I played in more games (1,270) than any other player when I retired." He has since been surpassed in that respect by many players. He now ranks 33rd all-time in that regard going into the 2020 season. Former teammate Robert Parish was in first place with 1,611 games played. LeBron James of the Lakers passed Havlicek in 2020 for the 32nd spot.

Havlicek had a simple philosophy which he tried to live by: run as hard as you can for as long as you can. "If you're going to do it," he says, "do it right."

Cowens says, "He has to enjoy making people think, 'How does he do it?' He likes people to try and analyze him. But you have to ask a doctor how he does it. Something drives him."

"Havlicek is the only
true superstar."
—Rick Barry

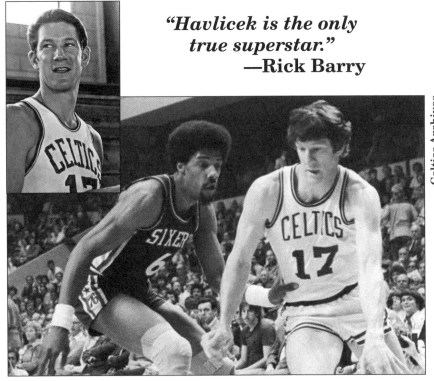

Hondo drives on Dr. J. These are two of my all-time favorite players and personalities in pro ball.

Alex Groza
He was one of the greatest players in college ball back in late '40s, early '50s

Alex Groza was a great example of a guy who was given a second chance at reclaiming his life in pro basketball by the American Basketball Association.

So many players who had been tainted one way or another found a home in the ABA after being banned from the NBA such as Tony Jackson, Doug Moe, Charlie Williams and, of course, Connie Hawkins and Roger Brown. There were so many others who were cut by NBA teams and ended up playing in the Eastern Basketball League or semi-pro circuits in the Midwest.

The ABA was a haven for the homeless, none more than in the case of Alex Groza, one of the nicest, upstanding men this author ever met in his travels in sports. He was six-feet-seven and called "Beak" because of his prominent nose.

He was first-team All-America in 1948 and 1949 when Adolph Rupp's University of Kentucky team won consecutive NCAA championships. Groza was captain and the leading scorer and rebounder for the Wildcats and in 1949 he was named the National Player of the Year.

He played two seasons for the Indianapolis Olympians, and was the 1950 NBA Rookie of the Year, an award that is no longer recognized by the league. Groza and the University of Kentucky team were caught up in the CCNY point-shaving scandal in 1951. Groza paid dearly for his crime, and it was, indeed, a crime.

Maurice Podoloff, the commissioner of the NBA at the time, banned Groza and his UK teammates Ralph

Beard and Dale Barnstable from playing in the NBA for life.

Beard and Groza were the stars of the Indianapolis Olympians. That team was founded in 1949 and folded, from the fallout of Beard and Groza being banned, in 1953. They had played their home games at Butler Field House—now called Hinkle Field House—on the campus of Butler University.

I would learn from reading a book called *We Changed the Game*, an enlightening look-back (2018) at the Indiana Pacers in their ABA days, that the Pacers were not permitted to play their home games at Butler when they were formed in 1967 because of what happened to the Olympians. I read that 174-page book in a single day in mid-May 2020, after Bob Netolicky had sent me a signed copy. Indianapolis did not get back into the NBA until 1976 when it was one of four ABA teams to be admitted to an expanded NBA.

The former Pacers star, along with one of the team's original owners, Richard Tinkham, and a sportswriter Robin Miller had co-written the book. It was signed "To my good friend Jimmy, Bob Netolicky, 24." Whenever someone calls me Jimmy, I know they like me.

Alex Groza was the general manager of the Kentucky Colonels when I first met the man in the early '70s. Mike Storen was the team president, Jack Ankerson and Bud Olsen were his top assistants, and Dave Vance was the team publicist. It was the best front-office in the ABA.

The Colonels' offices were located in the Executive Inn, a hotel across the road from Freedom Hall, where the Colonels and the University of Louisville played their home games. I recall interviewing Denny Crum of the University of Louisville, a Hall of Fame basketball coach, one day in the stands after a practice session at Freedom Hall.

That was also the sight of my worst night of covering the ABA for *The New York Post*. This was in the spring of 1975 and I was covering a championship playoff contest between the Colonels and the rival Indiana Pacers. I was interviewing the game's star player, Dan Issel, outside the Colonels' clubhouse.

Suddenly, I was blinded. Someone had shoved a cream pie into my face. Issel handed me his white towel to clean up the mess. I didn't discover, until two years later in Las Vegas of all places, that the person who slammed the pie into my eyes was none other than Claire Brown, the wife of Kentucky coach Hubie Brown. She did not like a story, it seems, that I had written about her husband.

I didn't feel much like writing a story when I returned to my hotel room after that. It got worse. Whenever I entered the lobby of the Executive Inn, an old geezer spotted my *New York Post* label on my press badge, and came after me, waving his cane menacingly, shouting at me as he neared my frozen figure.

"You New York writers screwed up things for the University of Kentucky with your scandal stories!"

"I had nothing to do with that!" I replied. "I wasn't in New York at the time!"

It was 24 years later, but the scars of the scandal still were plainly evident. The University of Kentucky had to cancel its 1952–53 season, the first school to be hit with the NCAA's so-called "death penalty."

That incident at the Executive Inn should have prompted me to write a story about Groza and the point-shaving scandal that rocked the New York basketball world from its foundation in 1951.

The Colonels came on strong and won 23 of their final 26 games of the regular season, and won four of five games in the ABA Finals with the Indiana Pacers to win the 1975 ABA title.

*   *   *

I realize now that I should have written an in-depth story about Alex Groza for *The Post* and other basketball-related publications I contributed to in those days. It had strong New York as well as national ties.

Four New York schools were implicated in the point-shaving scandals of 1951. They were CCNY, the only team ever to win both the NIT and NCAA Tournament in the same season, Manhattan College (now University), New York University and Long Island University. Sherman White of LIU, the best player in the city, was also banned for life by the NBA. Another LIU player, Julius Kellogg, turned down an offer to shave points, and helped the district attorney Frank Hogan in the investigation.

Bradley, Toledo and Kentucky were also implicated in the scandal, and Kentucky is the only school involved that managed to restore its place among the nation's outstanding basketball programs.

Groza, Beard and Barnstable had been set up by a former University of Kentucky football player named Nick Englisis with his gambling associates, and the players confessed to point-shaving—fixing the final score according to the betting point spread on the game. They were each paid $500 to do so. They kept the score too close in an NIT game against Loyola of Chicago and ended up losing the game.

That all came out during the investigation of the New York schools getting caught in 1951. I remember something that Vince Boryla once said to me when that subject same up for discussion. Boryla was then the president of the Utah Stars. He had played for the Knicks in the NBA and before that he was a consensus All-America in 1949 at the University of Denver.

"I'm just glad," said Boryla, "that no one approached me with a money offer to shave points back then." The implication was clear. Boryla might have been tempted. Money was hard to come by for a college kid in those days, especially one who had grown up in the hard-scrabble Chicago streets.

* * *

Dave Vance was always advancing story ideas and notes, quotes and anecdotes, but he never suggested I do a story about how things had turned out for Alex Groza.

Groza wanted his sin to be forgiven and forgotten. Who could blame him? I knew he had been a great player and that he had been banned from playing in the NBA, but I didn't know the full story.

Researching it now, I realize that Groza was even a greater ballplayer than I had originally thought. I also better understand why the New York police officials came down so hard on Connie Hawkins and Roger Brown when the story broke that they had both accepted money gifts from gamblers, even though they were never charged with any wrong-doing.

They were never guilty of point-shaving, or fixing the final scores of games. They were in their first year in college, when freshmen were not eligible for varsity competition, at Iowa and Dayton, respectively. But the stain remained on the college game.

The 1949–50 CCNY team starting five consisted of two blacks and three Jewish players, all from local high schools. They were the first team to win an NCAA title with blacks in the starting lineup. Their first six players were Ed Warner, Norm Mager, Irwin Dambrot, Alvin Roth, Ed Roman and Floyd Lane. Dambrot was the uncle of present-day Duquesne University coach

Keith Dambrot. Keith's father Sid played basketball at Duquesne and that's one of the reasons Keith left Akron to coach at his father's alma mater.

* * *

I visited the University of Kentucky campus in July of 2018, at the invitation of John Calipari, the coach who was a grad assistant at Pitt when I was the assistant athletic director for public relations, in the mid-80s. "You're always welcome to pay a visit," Calipari wrote on his personal stationery, a card I still keep in my files. I was taken on a tour of Memorial Coliseum, where the Wildcats still conduct their practices, by basketball publicist Eric Lindsey. I recognized a lot of the faces in the framed team photographs, including Groza.

He was from Martins Ferry, Ohio, the same as John Havlicek. My mother was from neighboring Bridgeport, where they went to high school, so I was familiar with all the great athletes from the Ohio Valley. Alex Groza's brother was Lou Groza, an All-Pro offensive tackle and a great place-kicker who's honored in the Pro Football Hall of Fame in Canton, Ohio. I was showing off when I identified Lou Tsioropoulos,a sophomore forward on UK's 1951 title team who played three seasons with the Boston Celtics.

The Niekro Brothers, Phil and Joe, are from Martins Ferry. Phil is in the Baseball Hall of Fame. So is Bill Mazeroski, from nearby Rush Run, Ohio.

Joe Niekro   **Phil Niekro**   **Bill Mazeroski**

George Morris, a friend of mine and one of the proof-readers for this book, asked me if Alex Groza was in the Basketball Hall of Fame. Morris thought I had failed to mention him in a paragraph about Hall of Fame players.

Morris is a graduate of Ohio Wesleyan where he played varsity baseball, and grew up in as a fan of the Cleveland Indians and Cleveland Browns.

I have seen a list of the greatest basketball players from Ohio and Groza is not on the list. He should be. Ohio has produced the likes of Havlicek, Jerry Lucas, LeBron James, Stephen Curry, Jimmy Jackson, Larry Jones, C.J. McCollum, Nate Thurmond, Neil Johnston and Gus Johnson. Add Alan Hornyak to this list.

Groza first gained attention as the star center for the Martins Ferry Purple Riders. He led them to two undefeated regular season records and to the Ohio state high school tournament. The Purple Riders went 24–1 in 1943 and 26–1 in 1944. In 1944, he scored 41 points in one game and was named All-Ohio.

At Kentucky, he was one of the "Fabulous Five," that won national championships in 1948 and 1949. He was the leader scorer on the U.S. team that won the gold medal in the 1948 Olympic Games. (That's the same Games in which my friend and boyhood hero Herb Douglas won a bronze medal in the long jump.)

He was all-SEC and All-America for three varsity seasons, and a two-time Final Four Most Outstanding Player. Get the picture now? Yes, Groza was that good, that great.

He was drafted in 1949 by the Indianapolis Olympians. He led the team in scoring with 23.4 points a game, and was named the NBA Rookie of the Year. The NBA does not recognize that honor, saying it was because sportswriters voted for the award. OK, how does that nullify the feat?

Because he was banned from further play in the NBA, he was the first NBA player to end his career with a season in which he averaged at least 20 points per game. Only three players have since averaged 20 or more points in their final NBA season: Bob Pettit (22.5 ppg in 1964–65 season), Paul Arizin (21.9 ppg in 1961–62) and Drazon Petrovic (22.3 ppg in 1992–93).

One of his teammates on the Indianapolis Olympians was Bruce Hale, later the father-in-law of Rick Barry, who played for him at the University of Miami. Hale was hailed in one of the Olympians' game programs as "The Handsome Bruce Hale."

See how these things go round and round?

After his playing days came to an end, Groza became the basketball coach at little Bellarmine College (now University) in Louisville, Kentucky.

In 1963, he led the Knights to a Kentucky Intercollegiate Athletic Conference (KIAC) title and was named KIAC Coach of the Year.

He left Bellarmine in 1966 to take a front-office position as business manager for the Colonels. In 1969, he left Louisville to be the general manger of the San Diego Conquistadors. The Q's, owned by an ultra-successful dentist named Dr. Leonard A. Bloom, had big plans but a small arena and a big payroll and gave way to the San Diego Sails. Groza was in charge of personnel and player development with the Sails.

Wilt Chamberlain came over from the Lakers— it said in his fat contract that he didn't have to come to practice if he didn't want to so his assistant Stan Albeck did most of the coaching. Finally, Wilt walked away from the job, and Groza took over as the coach. Groza could always say he replaced Wilt Chamberlain in the pro basketball world.

Groza had a 2–0 record for coaching the Colonels and was 15–23 with the Conquistadors. When the franchise was moved to Houston, Groza gave up the ghost. He went to work as a marketing manager for Reynolds until his death from cancer at age 68 in 1985. He and his wife Jean had been married for 42 years. She thought he was a good man.

Another Ohioan who can understand the pain of Alex Groza is Pete Rose, "The Cincinnati Kid," who was one of the greatest baseball players in history, but has been banned for the Baseball Hall of Fame for gambling on baseball games as a player and a manager, never admitting his guilt or saying he was sorry. I'd have voted for Rose in a heartbeat but his name has never appeared on a Baseball Hall of Fame ballot.

Alex Groza was NBA Rookie of the Year in 1950 while playing for the Indianapolis Olympians.

Martins Ferry playgrounds
drew top talent

Completely out of the blue, I received a telephone call from Ed McGlumphy Sr., from Stone Creek, Ohio who had been a highly-successful athlete at Washington & Jefferson College and as a coach at high schools in Ohio and Pennsylvania. He ran a top-notch summer basketball camp for many years and has authored how-to basketball books and guides.

His son had given him a copy of my book *Looking Up*, and he wanted me to know how much he enjoyed it. Now into his 80s, McGlumphy still likes to keep a hand in sports. He ordered five more copies for friends.

He had played three varsity sports at Martins Ferry (Ohio) High School, and recalled summer basketball activity there when he was younger. Martins Ferry had several playgrounds near each other.

I told him I had just written a chapter on Alex Groza, the greatest basketball player ever to come out of Martins Ferry. McGlumphy told me that Alex and Lou Groza, his brother who became a Pro Football Hall of Fame lineman and place-kicker for the Cleveland Browns, both used to show up for summer night games under the lights. John Havlicek of Bridgeport and some of his Ohio State teammates would show up from time to time, as did Jerry West, an All-America standout at West Virginia University. Imagine watching those games...The Niekro Brothers, Joe and Phil, would play as well as Bill Mazeroski, who had been the second leading scorer, behind only Jerry Lucas of Middleton, Ohio. Mazeroski was a 5-10 center for Warren Consolidated High School, since absorbed by Buckeye Local High School, near Rayland in Warren County. They say Maz could dunk a basketball.

McGlumphy got inducted into the Martins Ferry Hall of Fame Class of 2015, the same year the 1941 football and basketball teams were honored. The Groza Brothers, who were on those teams, were honored individually in 2014. I recognized two other names on the Class of 2014, namely Bill Van Horne, who became the sports editor of *The Wheeling News Register* for 28 years and was the favorite sports writer in the region during that long span, and Fred Bruney, who starred in football at Ohio State and later played six years in the National Football League with three different teams, including the Pittsburgh Steelers.

I learned from the Hall of Fame program booklet McGlumphy sent me that the 1941 Purple Raiders basketball team captained by Lou Groza posted a 27–2 record and won the Ohio Class A State championship. The football team outscored its opponents 333–19—read that again—including seven shutout victories and were declared state co-champions after tying Toledo Libbey in "The Glass Bowl" in Toledo.

George Kalinsky/Madison Square Garden

Imagine what it must have been like when Jerry West, seen here driving on Oscar Robertson and Willis Reed of East team in NBA All-Star Game, showed up to play with John Havlicek and Alex Groza on basketball courts in Martins Ferry, Ohio.

Kentucky Colonels' correspondence:
CONFIDENTIAL and personal

When I was getting my files in order to write this book, I came upon many treasures, cards from my mother and father I didn't know I had, and letters from people I dealt with when I wrote for daily newspapers in Pittsburgh, Philadelphia, Miami, New York and, once again, Pittsburgh.

Best of all, for this book, I found several letters on Kentucky Colonels' official stationery, from one of the owners and team president and ABA president Wendell Cherry, general manager Mike Storen, coach Gene Rhodes and several from Colonels' publicist Dave Vance.

Vance, one of the best in the business, is the only one still living as I write this sentence. He was always writing to me, suggesting story topics and with notes, quotes and anecdotes for my ABA columns in *The Sporting News*, *The New York Post* or the next issue of *Street and Smith's Basketball Yearbook*, or *The Complete Handbook of Pro Basketball*.

As I read this correspondence, I realized that it represented an era that no longer exists in pro or college sports. Today, no one in the media gets friendly letters from front-office executives or story suggestions. The public relations task today is to keep the media at a distance and to keep the owner and head coach happy.

This correspondence makes me realize how lucky I was to cover pro basketball, the ABA and the NBA. Today's players make so much money they have lost touch with reality and they don't need any allies in the newspaper business.

I received a letter from Wendell Cherry dated October 27, 1971. It was attached to a copy of a 16-page typewritten memo that he had sent to ABA Commissioner Jack Dolph.

"Per our recent conversation when you were in Louisville, I am enclosing herewith in confidence the memorandum I wrote on January 20, 1967, concerning my participation in the original organization meeting of the American Basketball Association. I say I am delivering this in confidence because, as you can see, I make some highly personal observations (perhaps dangerous ones) about certain of the persons who attended the meeting."

Wendell Cherry

I have never reprinted the contents of this letter heretofore. If Cherry's phrasing sounds like an attorney's, I can continue in kind.

"If you have any questions, give me a call. Looking forward to seeing you soon, I am Cordially, KENTUCKY COLONELS. Wendell Cherry. He signed his signature. Just Wendell.

I knew it wasn't from Wendell Ladner.

The first ABA organizational meeting took place at the Beverly Hills Hilton Hotel on January 1, 1967. The franchise fee was set at $1,000. Eight cities had paid that money: New York, Pittsburgh, Oakland, Anaheim, Dallas, Houston, Minneapolis and Kansas City. Cherry was checking it out on behalf of Louisville interests.

He and other Louisville businessmen were already in a consortium to support the early pro boxing career of Cassius Clay, the Olympic champion, who would later change his name to Muhammad Ali.

He mentions in his memo that a former New York stockbroker and West Point athlete named Mark Binstein was at the meeting. I have a critical letter from Mr. Binstein, written after he had gotten involved with ownership and management of the Pittsburgh Condors. I had blamed Binstein for being one of the reasons Pittsburgh didn't have a pro basketball team. Two sports editors, Chester L. Smith and Al Abrams, were also on that list. Smith once wrote "If they played the NCAA basketball tournament in my driveway, I would close the blinds."

The Village Smithy, as he called himself, was no basketball fan, for sure. With Binstein at the original meeting was Connie Seredin of Professional Sports Management in New York, whose favorite words, according to a *Sports Illustrated* story were "concept" and "divine." His associate was Art Brown of ABC Forwarding Company, who would get the New York-New Jersey franchise.

"Mr. Seredin is a memorable, if not unbelievable, prototype of a person who plays the Madison Avenue game, both in appearance and manner and in terms of what he says," wrote Cherry. "He may know his business, but when he gets into areas of finance and other business aspects, he would scare you to death. Some of his statements made me wince."

Cherry continues later on:

"There was a great deal of loose talk, I think, as to present NBA player dissatisfaction, and Mr. Binstein (a high school classmate of Wilt Chamberlain, he claimed) stated unequivocally that he had gotten the agreement of Wilt Chamberlain to join the New York franchise both as a partial owner and a highly-paid player, and that Mr. Chamberlain would assist in contact and recruitment of existing NBA players into the new league. On this note, the morning session ended.

"In the afternoon, Mr. Binstein announced that the eight teams that had paid in $1,000 would meet in closed session, and later would be joined by prospective members from Louisville, Memphis, New Orleans, Indianapolis and perhaps St. Louis.

"Frankly, I am skeptical," Cherry continued later in the memo, "based unfortunately on impressions and feelings rather than fact, that this group is made up in the main of people who are promoters and who have very little financial muscle."

One of the people who turned off Cherry the most was the combative little theater owner from Pittsburgh, namely Gabe Rubin. Rubin was in favor of cities such as Cleveland and New Orleans and St. Louis, but viewed Louisville, Memphis and Indianapolis as "bad situations."

And further, "His remarks, quite frankly, grew even more personal in the sense that he was considering the Louisville situation as having some wealthy person just playing around with a franchise which he (Rubin) thought was doomed to failure because Louisville had not supported any big league athletic venture or even semi-pro league venture."

It gets better.

"An argument then developed between Mr. Dennis Murphy and Mr. Rubin as to the relative merits of Louisville and, after letting it go for a few moments, I addressed myself to Mr. Rubin's remarks.

"I told him that I was there to gather facts and that I was quite interested in his conclusions as to the prospects of Louisville in the league. I stated that we would withhold any decision on Louisville pending the League settling its affairs as to which cities it wanted. I further pointed out that I was not there to sell Louisville, but to be sold on the ABA."

Later in memo...

"And Mr. Rubin holding steady that he did not think Louisville was a big-league town. To some extent, his remarks touched on personalities. I resented them and expressed myself accordingly. Mr. Rubin is one of those individuals who prefaces a remark with the statement that there is nothing personal in what he says, but then he gets personal. It was quite a performance. Mr. Rubin's position troubles me a great deal, particularly when I have obviously reached some skeptical conclusions as to the present credibility of this group, and their ability to bring this thing off."

Cherry said that several men at the meeting, especially Chuck Barnes (a soulmate) of Indianapolis, and that he was urged to continue to pursue prospective owners for Louisville, and not to take Gabe Rubin's remarks personally.

Cherry left the meeting around one o'clock, still convinced that there was an opportunity for Louisville in a new league, but that "leadership was lacking to pull the whole thing together."

I have put Wendell Cherry's letter back in my Kentucky Colonels' file.

Jim O'Brien

Connie Hawkins with Braddock's Billy Knight, both all-ABA performers.

Mike Storen and his daughter, Hannah Storm of ESPN fame.

Here's an excerpt from a brief letter sent over the signature of club general manager Mike Storen, that was sent in early January of 1974:

Dear Jim:
"I look forward to seeing you at the ABA All-Star Game in Norfolk, later this month. I hope you will bring your wife Kathie to enjoy some of the pre-game social activities. I have made all arrangements for your hotel stay and for game credentials. We can sit down and discuss what's happening around the league. I hear you are going to be named president of the ABA Writers Association, so congratulations in advance."

Mike Storen, Kentucky Colonels

From *Newsweek*, February 28, 1972:
    In the early slightly zany days of the ABA, Storen was one of the few front-office executives with a knowledge of nearly every facet of the basketball business, from selling tickets to scouting players. "I was shocked," said Storen, "at how little the ABA owners knew. At one of our meetings, we had a lengthy discussion about doubleheaders. One guy was vehemently opposed, so I finally asked him why. He said 'Have you ever talked to a player after he's played two games in one night?'"

A letter on Kentucky Colonels stationary dated January 11, 1974, from Gene Rhodes, General Manager

"I have been following your column on the ABA in The Sporting News, and I certainly appreciate all the nice things you have to say about the Kentucky Colonels and the American Basketball Association. If there is anything that we can do for you to help you in any way, please feel free to call on us. Looking forward to visiting with you during the All-Star Game on January 30 at Norfolk."

Gene Rhodes

A letter from David M. Vance, Director of Publicity, Kentucky Colonels, dated June 10, 1971:

"I hope you find the enclosed material on the Kentucky Colonels useful. I have taken the liberty of enclosing additional pictures of Artis Gilmore. We sincerely feel that the addition of Artis will provide us with an excellent complement to the talents of Dan Issel. It also offers potentially the finest combination in basketball.

"If you want to interview Artis, Dan or any of the other players—as well as Coach Frank Ramsey or President-General Manager Mike Storen—please give me a call and I'll be happy to make the necessary arrangements. Thank you for your interest, and if I can be of any assistance at any time in the future, please let me know."

As I said, Dave Vance was in a class by himself as far as publicists were concerned, as the following letter (dated July 5, 1972), definitely attests:

"Thought you might be interested to know that there is now a Mrs. Artis Gilmore. Alex Groza and I attended the wedding Saturday at Shelby, North Carolina.

"The new Mrs. Gilmore met Artis when he played at Gardner-Webb Junior College (now a four-year college) in Shelby. Harold Fox and Chip Dublin, former Jacksonville players, and Joe Williams, who coached at Jacksonville but now is at Furman, also were at the wedding.

"By the way, Artis' wife's name is Enola Gay. Her parents (Mr. and Mrs. James Maddox) saw a movie about the bombing of Hiroshima when her mother was expecting. The name of the bomber, of course, was the Enola Gay. Couldn't a publicity director have fun with that one?

"Also, it might be inter-esting from a column stand-point that while Artis and his attorney, Herb Rudoy, were visiting Europe this summer, they decided to leave London for Tel Aviv three hours ear-lier than previously planned.

"Exactly three hours after leaving the Tel Aviv airport by rented car, that big shooting took place in the airport. In other words, had they followed their origi-

Col. Paul Tibbets who piloted the Enola Gay.

nal plans, they would have been at the airport when the shooting took place. And it would have been difficult to miss a guy like Artis (7-feet two-inches tall) with a machine-gun. Artis and Enola are spending their hon-eymoon at the Riviera Hotel in Las Vegas."

Is it any wonder I miss the ABA?

Artis Gilmore
The Big A is still the tallest man in the room, also the quietest

Ask Artis Gilmore a question and he will look deeply into your very soul and think awhile before answering. He is considerate, accommodating and available, even today, but he doesn't rush to reply.

Artis Gilmore is just the way you remember him when he was playing basketball and you were writing about the ABA, and he was the most dominant man in the other league. You both have exceeded your playing weight in the interim. But who's going to tell Gilmore he's gotten a little heavy? He was no match for George "Ice Man" Gervin or Julius "Dr. J" Erving in the flash and flair air above the hoop, but no one dunked with more authority than Artis Gilmore. Unless it was Wilt Chamberlain or Bill Russell.

Gilmore never rushed to reply on the basketball court, either, but he got there—planting legs anchored by tree-trunk thighs to hold his spot—and then toss that accurate hook shot, or a put-back off the glass, into the basket. He was right up there with Chamberlain, Russell and Kareem Abdul-Jabbar in that respect, though a tad lower in the all-time ratings for centers. Gilmore never got the attention he deserved because, first, he was playing his best ball in the ABA and, second, he was not one to boast about himself or to attract the media. He was never an easy interview, but he's less intimidating today.

Gilmore was often referred to as "a gentle giant."

He wrapped those long arms around a lot of former teammates and opposing players, friends and foes alike, and held them close at the reunion. For the most part, their heads were buried in his chest. Gilmore greeted them all with his own under-the-radar enthusiasm and smile. He may be a shade under 7–2, but everyone at the reunion looked a little shorter than the size listed in the game programs of that era.

I was glad Gilmore was comfortably seated in a well-cushioned mauve chair in the lobby of the JW Marriott Hotel in downtown Indianapolis as I spoke with him. Frankly, I was tired of craning my neck and *looking up* at him during interviews after games in the ABA and the NBA.

When I saw him the next day and gave him some photographs of himself when he played at Jacksonville University and with the Kentucky Colonels, he thanked me in a sincere, but almost silent manner. Artis never had to raise his voice to get attention in a room or a lobby or at courtside or in the locker room. Artis signed his autograph to a card, the same autograph that appears with this story, and it's a fancy one, calculated much like that of Steelers' Hall of Famer Jerome Bettis. It's a studied sketch.

He was well-liked for his easy manner. I reminded him of a time in his life when he was the star attraction at a party in the palatial—make that plantation-like—home of John Y. Brown, the owner of the Kentucky Colonels who bankrolled the franchise with money from his Kentucky Fried Chicken, Inc., then and still one of the largest purveyors of fast-food in the world. Right up there with McDonald's.

I can still picture, and my wife Kathie, who came with me to Louisville that All-Star Game weekend, remembers a scene at the Brown home that stays with both of us. She has assured me it's an honest recall, not something I made up.

Artis Gilmore, an All-America center at Jacksonville University, would soon be signing a record high-paying contract with the Colonels, and was—forgive me here—the center of attention in the crowded hallway of the home. This was in 1969.

He had to be uncomfortable with the mostly white crowd, invited there by John and his wife, Ellie. It was like visiting Tara, the O'Hara home in the movie "Gone With the Wind." John Y. later traded Ellie in exchange for the former Miss America, Phyllis George. John Y. blamed working together—and often disagreeing about what was best to do—for ruining the relationship. Phyllis George passed away at age 70 in May 2020. I thought Brown made a bad move when he folded the Colonels. But Brown understood business better than basketball and, as usual, through some maneuvers over franchises in Buffalo and Boston, made even more money, but he cost Louisville and Buffalo their pro basketball franchises. Both the Colonels and Braves deserved better. The Silna Brothers, Ozzie and Dan, by comparison were eventually paid over $800 million by the NBA for folding the Spirits of St. Louis in what is often referred to as "the best sports deal of all time."

Moving among the guests that night when Gilmore made his first appearance in Louisville were four black female servants, dressed for their roles in attire of a, thankfully, bygone era. I couldn't believe it. I thought it was insensitive, and definitely not what I would have done in the way of welcoming the newest star in town. I always wondered what Artis Gilmore thought about that antebellum scene.

"I don't remember that," he calmly told me at our Indianapolis meeting on April 7, 2018.

"You were the tallest man in the room and you had the best view of the guests and servants," I said.

"I've always been the tallest man in the room," said Gilmore. "I'm still the tallest man in the room."

A photo in my extensive files came to mind showing Gilmore looming over Pat Livingston, my former boss at *The Pittsburgh Press*, when both were in attendance at a fund-raising golf tournament for Pittsburgh Children's Hospital that was held at Arnold Palmer's Latrobe Country Club in the early '70s. It was coordinated and hosted by former Steelers' all-pro linebacker Andy Russell, who continued to host such a fund-raiser for 40 years and remains a consultant for the event.

Michael Chakiris

Artis Gilmore talks to Pittsburghers at one of Andy Russell's Celebrity Golf Invitationals at Arnold Palmer's Latrobe Country Club on June 7, 1979. Pat Livingston, the gentleman in the white blazer, was my boss at *The Pittsburgh Press*. I had just returned from nine years in New York to cover the Steelers for my hometown daily that was sponsoring the event for the benefit of the Press Old Newsboys Fund.

Gilmore remembers games and other slights or lack of sensitivity, but not the one about the Aunt Jemima look-alike maids. Maybe that's why I'm a writer and he is in the Basketball Hall of Fame in Springfield, Massachusetts (Class of 2011). He just remembered there were big numbers on that contract, especially for someone who came from where he came from, and he could still smile about that.

Gilmore's net worth these days is reported to be $5 million, but I didn't ask him about that. So, his wife Enola Gay Gilmore, whom I recall as a beautiful woman, must be able to go shopping whenever she pleases.

"He's come a long way," said Joe Hamilton, a former teammate with the Colonels who still resides in his hometown of Louisville. "I visited the big man in his hometown of Chipley in the Florida panhandle. Chipley...you talk about a *God-forsaken* town. I grew up in Smoketown here, and that was pretty humble. But it was a lot better than Chipley. That man comes from humble beginnings, believe me!"

I reminded Gilmore of some other things and he smiled at each comment. I had not done any special homework before attending the ABA's 50th year reunion. I just remember things. People remark that I have such a great memory, but I admit I remember events and exchanges of 50 and 60 years ago like it was yesterday. I just have difficulty keeping track of yesterday and this morning.

Dr. Joseph Maroon, a famed neurosurgeon and professor and vice chairman at UPMC's Neurology Center, and an author and triathlon competitor, who serves as one of the team doctors for the NFL Steelers, told me our older memories are etched deeper in our cranium than current ones and that's why they stay with us longer. Check out Dr. Maroon's book *Square One: A Simple Guide to a Balanced Life.*

"You were from Chipley," I said, maybe showing off a bit.

Gilmore just grinned.

"That was in the Florida panhandle."

Another Gilmore grin, framed by a dark mustache and goatee, as dark and painted-looking as Tom Selleck in his role as Commissioner Frank Reagan on TV's *Blue Bloods* series, if that helps to get the picture.

"You also grew up in Dothan, Alabama, about 30 or so miles north of Chipley, with relatives."

Another acknowledging grin.

"You played at Jacksonville University with Rex Morgan and Pembroke Burrows III." You can't forget names like that. They sound like names from one of Hall of Fame LIU basketball coach Clair Bee's books in his Chip Hilton series.

Dallas Frey, a friend and an ABA fan in his teenage years in Edgewood, a suburb east of Pittsburgh and the Civic Arena and its Pipers and Condors, interjected the name of another teammate at Jacksonville U., namely Vaughn Wedeking. I have since learned that Wedeking died at age 60. Frey knows his facts, and was an invaluable aide as a proof-reader and fact-checker for this book.

Frey served as my navigator on the six-hour drive from Pittsburgh to Indianapolis and back, and we never stopped talking to and from. Frey was more excited about meeting George Thompson, a former Condors' backcourtman, who drove to the hoop like a speedy running back, even if the likes of Artis Gilmore stood tall between him and the hoop. Frey knows his hoops and filled in some blank spaces.

Tom McGuire, another one of my proofreaders, wanted equal time with our friend Dallas Frey. Tom remembers when in December, 1971 one of his new friends, Paul Ruffner, a journeyman center from Brigham Young University, had the best game of his pro career. "Ruffner scored 17 points and had 12 rebounds against Artis Gilmore and the Kentucky Colonels. I'm sure Ruffner has probably told his grandchildren about that game so many times."

I didn't need any help in giving Gilmore a snapshot of his life when we spoke in the Marriott lobby.

"You were married to a college sweetheart named Enola Gay."

"Still am," said Gilmore, proud to report that they had been married for 47 years. They are nearly at the 50-year mark as I write this sentence.

It's hard to forget a name like Enola Gay, though my wife Kathie held out for her favorite ABA player's wife, Slick Neumann, who was married at the time to Johnny Neumann, who was billed as the second-coming of "Pistol Pete" Maravich when he starred at Mississippi. Slick's real name was Carolyn, but Slick sounded more interesting and the perfect partner for the crazy kid that was Johnny Neumann.

The arrival of Artis Gilmore, along with Dan Issel, upgraded the talent level of the Kentucky Colonels and the ABA at large.

In its early days, the NBA was able to still get the big men when it came time to signing star college players, but Gilmore and Issel, as well as Jim McDaniels,

Artis Gilmore
maneuvers for
position against
Billy Paultz of New
York Nets and, as a
collegian, against
Steve Patterson
of UCLA, in 1970
NCAA Basketball
Tournament. The
Bruins won 80–69 in
championship final.

Maurice Lucas, Marvin Barnes and Moses Malone enabled the ABA to stand nearly as tall as the established league.

Gilmore was a giant determined to be the greatest basketball player ever—"you have to have a goal to be the best," he said whenever he said something, which was rare—but Gilmore was the real thing.

They couldn't make fun of the ABA anymore. Louisville had some major league sportswriters such as Dick Fenlon, Billy Reed and Dave Kindred, who could all write with the best of them.

Kindred, who would move on to *The Washington Post*, captured the perception of the ABA, in a lengthy article for the Sunday edition of *The Courier Journal*:

"The ABA was a funny league. Funny red, white and blue basketball. Funny names. The Amigos, the Muskies. Funny players. Dexter Westbrook and Dewitt Menyard and where have you gone Orb Bowling? Funny coaches. Jim Harding was fired when he won a fist-fight with the owner (Gabe Rubin). The LA Stars had a belly dancer to lead the team in calisthenics."

Now they needed a new script. Gilmore wasn't laughing. He seldom smiled. He was serious. After all, the Colonels had committed $2.7 million on multi-year contract to get Gilmore. Issel had signed a $1.4 million contract. They had an NBA-like frontline.

Billy Cunningham, an NBA all-pro player who had jumped to the ABA with the Carolina Cougars, said of Gilmore, "He's a man among boys. This guy was just unmovable under the boards." That was after the Colonels had swept the Cougars in four games in the 1974 playoffs.

Wendell Cherry, one of the principal owners of the revamped Colonels, was a 35-year-old attorney who made millions owning a chain of extended care residences for seniors. He was serious, too. When he wooed Mike Storen, the most able ABA executive away from the Indiana Pacers for a bigger paycheck, he was criticized by Pacers owner for robbing their store. They questioned his ethics. The franchises were rivals to begin with, located just 120 miles apart.

"Indiana was hot about it," recalled Cherry, "saying I violated ethics. Well, I didn't give a _____ about ethics. I didn't know their ethics. I was never in the game. I just wanted the best man to run the team."

In Storen, the Colonels replaced the Pacers as the best organization in the ABA, in my opinion.

Gilmore was a good man in many ways. He went about his work quietly, perfecting a lethal hook shot, paying more attention to defense, and setting a proper tone for all the Colonels.

When most players got their first pro contract or first paycheck, they rushed to the nearest Cadillac or Corvette dealer to buy themselves some hot wheels.

The first thing Gilmore did when the Colonels signed him was to take his mother, Mattie, to the dentist and he bought a pick-up truck that his father had wanted. His parents never had those things. His mother had eight children to raise and could be forgiven if she hadn't tended to her teeth as much as she should have. Someone wrote that his father didn't work much after that, unless you consider fishing as working.

The Big A didn't always give his best effort, and there were nights when he appeared to be sleep-walking, but not in the playoffs. Gilmore's on-court demeanor drew this description from Barry McDermott of *Sports Illustrated*. Yes, *Sports Illustrated* was now paying more attention to the ABA, even assigning ace writer Frank Deford to do pieces about the upstart league.

McDermott described Gilmore as "the malevolent center with the docile demeanor." There were a lot of pro basketball players that wouldn't know what McDermott meant by that, but Gilmore wasn't going to change the mask he wore to keep inquisitors away.

I always liked talking to Gilmore. He looked down his nose at me most of the time when I was interviewing him, but he took me seriously, too, and still does.

Gilmore had a standing reach of 8 feet 7 inches. No wonder he could dunk the ball with the best of them. He was a physical specimen. He had a 30-inch waist— what man had a 30-inch waist after high school?— 27-inch thighs and size 16 shoes. Is it any wonder that he was unmovable, as attested by Cunningham who was called "The Kangaroo Kid" because of his leaping ability and living proof that "white men *could* jump."?

In his early days, Gilmore was awkward and Gilmore fouled out of a lot of games. Wilt Chamberlain never fouled out of a pro game, which might be a statistic even more unreal than his 100-point game.

When the Colonels folded after the merger, the Chicago Bulls got Gilmore in a draft of the players left behind in Kentucky, Utah, St. Louis and Virginia. A Boston newspaper pictured the prize ABA players now available to NBA teams in this special draft, and the list started with Artis Gilmore and included Moses Malone, Marvin Barnes, Ron Boone and Bird Averitt.

Two players who weren't pictured were Maurice Lucas and Dave Twardzik who were in the starting lineup, along with Bill Walton, when the Portland Trailblazers won the NBA championship the following season. Willie Wise was also worthy of mention.

Louie Dampier of the Colonels, one of the ABA originals still in the game along with Freddie Lewis and Byron Beck, was signed by the San Antonio Spurs after the dispersal draft.

The Colonels had dealt Dan Issel to the Denver Nuggets the season before the merger.

Had the Colonels remained intact, they would have been a force in the NBA. "With Gilmore," said Bill Sharman, who had coached successfully in three pro leagues—the ABL, ABA and NBA, "the ABA has someone who can play up there with Kareem Abdul-Jabbar. The Colonels will be able to compete with anyone."

Jim O'Brien

GIANTS OF THE GAME—George McGinnis and Artis Gilmore enjoy reunion.

THE STORY OF ENOLA GAY

I was always fascinated by the name Enola Gay and Enola Gay Gilmore. Enola Gay was the name painted on the nose of the Boeing B-29 super-fortress propeller-driven bomber that dropped the atomic bomb—or A-Bomb—on Hiroshima to help bring an end to World War II's action in the Pacific Theater. That airplane was named in honor of Enola Gay Tibbets, the mother of Col. Paul Tibbets, the pilot of that plane. He had personally picked it for himself when it came off the assembly line.

This story became even more personal when I learned that the Tibbets family was from Bexley, Ohio, a small well-preserved portion of Columbus, Ohio where our daughter,

Col. Paul Tibbets is the man in the middle with the pipe in his mouth with the men of the Enola Gay.

Dr. Sarah O'Brien, resides with her family. Dr. Sarah, who met Dr. J and Connie Hawkins in their heyday, is an assistant professor at The Ohio State Medical School, and a pediatric hematology/oncology specialist at Nationwide Children's Hospital in Columbus. She has season tickets for Ohio State basketball.

I have walked past the Tibbets home while taking my grandchildren for walks in the Bexley neighborhood. Chicago columnist Bob Greene, who grew up in Bexley and still shows up on occasion at The Top and Giuseppi's Ritrovo on Main Street, across from Capital University, wrote a wonderful book about Paul Tibbets called *Duty,* and I recommend that you read it, along with some of Greene's other books.

Bob Greene had beseeched Paul Tibbets several times, but Tibbets told him he was not interested in talking about his World War II experiences, and then one day Tibbets called Greene and said he was ready to share his story and that they could meet and talk.

I introduced myself to Greene a few years back when my wife recognized him in front of Giuseppi's Ritrovo. Kathie and Sarah were sitting across from me, when Kathie leaned forward and whispered to me, "I think that's Bob Greene behind me." She had heard some of the conversation at her back.

So, I looked and recognized Bob Greene. I stood up and introduced myself as a big fan of his writing. I said I was a writer from Pittsburgh and had written some books myself. Greene was less than impressed. He just blew me off, I mean blew me off. He just turned away.

Dr. Sarah made a quick diagnosis. "Don't feel bad, Dad," she said. "He's a jerk."

Greene's great run as a nationally-syndicated columnist for the *Chicago Tribune* and an author came to a swift end when he was caught having an affair with a young intern at the *Tribune*. And you thought that Bill Clinton, Donald Trump and Joe Biden were the only ones who fooled around with women. The owner of the Ritrovo, Giuseppi himself, later told me on a return visit to his restaurant that Greene sat alone at the end of the bar when he came to town, didn't want to say hello to anyone, shake hands or sign autographs. Just kept to himself. Told me he wasn't always like that.

In the books by Bob Greene that I have read, he always came off as a sensitive, caring person, but that was not the Bob Greene who said hello and goodbye in the same swift rejection that day in Bexley.

Three other book recommendations: *Hiroshima* by John Hersey, and *The Wild Blue—The Men and Boys Who Flew the B-24s over Germany*, by Stephen Ambrose, and *Once Upon a Town—The Miracle of the North Platte Canteen* by Bob Greene. Check the Internet for a transcript of an interview of Col. Tibbets by Chicago's iconic author Studs Terkel.

The signing of Artis Gilmore was a milestone in ABA history. It represented a major breakthrough in talent acquisition with the rival and more established NBA. "So goes the myth that the NBA always gets the big men," said Wendell Cherry, one of the owners of the Kentucky Colonels and, at that time, the president of the ABA.

Gilmore signed a contract with the Colonels even before the NBA conducted its draft of college players. The Colonels were awarded the rights to Gilmore simply because they were the only ABA club willing to put up as much money—over $2 million—as it was thought necessary to sign him.

The announcement was made in New York City at Toots Shor's saloon in order to get the best national coverage. The Colonels were playing in an ABA doubleheader at Madison Square Garden the next night, and they were making the most of this showcase event.

Dan Issel, the scoring star of the Colonels, was at the press conference and he said he felt he'd be able to make the adjustment of moving from center to forward now that Gilmore would be on the frontline with him.

He thought life in the ABA would be a lot easier with Gilmore on his side. Most other people in the ABA knew it was going to be mighty difficult to compete with the Colonels from that day on.

After the Colonels extended the Utah Stars to seven games in the ABA championship series, winning coach Bill Sharman, later with the Los Angeles Lakers, said, "I predict they'll be the first team in the ABA to battle the Milwaukee Bucks on even terms. Artis Gilmore will be to the Colonels what Bill Russell was to the Boston Celtics. He'll give them an intimidating defensive player who can set up fast breaks and allow a great player like Dan Issel to concentrate more on offense."

Gilmore had made a name for himself and the University of Jacksonville in the two previous seasons. The school had been a little known junior college just a few years before Gilmore made the scene, arriving there after two seasons at Gardner-Webb Junior College in North Carolina.

Joe Williams was his coach, a flashy dresser and outspoken man who could recruit. At the 2018 50th season reunion of the ABA, one of its former players, recalls talking with other coaches and Williams at a conference. "He said, 'you guys worry about getting caught doing something wrong when you're recruiting. Here's all you have to do. Take cash with you when you're after someone. They can't put a tracer on cash. Just don't write checks." Who knows if that strategy helped Williams woo so many terrific players to Jacksonville.

Jacksonville is the largest city in the country in land mass, but the school, with Williams and Gilmore leading the way, was the smallest school ever to play for the national championship. The Dolphins advanced all the way to the NCAA finals on March 21, 1970 before bowing, 80–69, to John Wooden and his UCLA team. Artis was just a junior that season. The previous year, few people north of Waycross, Georgia had ever heard of the Jacksonville Dolphins.

Gilmore and his teammates were called The Mod Squad for their flashy attire.

I hadn't realized until I did some research upon returning from the 50th year ABA Reunion just how dominant Gilmore had been as a college and pro performer. His numbers are numbing.

At Jacksonville, he led the nation in rebounding as a junior and senior, compiling a career average of 23 per game. As a senior, he averaged 22.3 points, and in two seasons he connected on 58 percent of his shots.

He blocked about ten shots a game, and was truly an intimidating force.

He was the first collegiate giant signed by the ABA, unless you would classify a muscular 6–9 Spencer Haywood as a giant.

With Gilmore manning the post, the Colonels became the first ABA team to beat an NBA team in inter-league exhibition play. While Issel topped everyone with 24 points, Gilmore had 16 points, 16 rebounds and blocked seven shots, as the Colonels clipped the Baltimore Bullets by an unbelievable 111-85 score.

"He's awesome," exclaimed Coach Gene Shue of the Bullets. "He's fantastic."

"I don't see anything to hold him back," said Wes Unseld, the Bullets' big man whom the Colonels tried to get to jump leagues because he was a hometown favorite in Louisville.

Kevin Loughery of the Bullets, who would later coach the Philadelphia 76ers and New York Nets, called Gilmore "one of the five best players in pro basketball right now. Some people said last year that he wasn't a No. 1 draft choice, but they must've been watching someone else," allowed Loughery.

From the Inception of the ABA until the end, Jim was there writing and being part of not only the good times But also the bad.

No One else is more suited to tell our story. Charlie Scott

Louisville
Bisquit and Little Joe led me
on a journey in Smoketown

B isquit Porter was sitting with his back against a wide gray garage door, a can of beer between his outstretched legs. He took another sip of beer as we approached him and two other men who were standing nearby. He smiled, and there were missing teeth, when he was introduced to us. His beer was from a Louisville brewery called Apocalypse Brew Works, which had a slogan, as I learned later, "Drink beer till the end." Seemed to suit the occasion.

"Bisquit was some ballplayer," said Joe Hamilton. "Basketball, football, you name it; he could play it. He was special."

Bisquit kept smiling in acknowledgment of the praise. It went well with his beer. It was only a little before 10 a.m. on what would be a warm day in July, 2018. Beer for breakfast, secreted in a brown paper bag was a fine way for Bisquit to begin his day. I asked him to shed the bag so I could read the label. Always looking for "concrete details," as they told us in a writing class at the University of Pittsburgh.

It was the first time I had ever heard of Bisquit Porter. He had been a star cornerback at Eastern Kentucky University. He dropped out, after getting caught with drugs. I shook his hand, and told him it was great to meet him. "I've heard about you," I lied. "Yes, you must have been quite the ballplayer."

I was with my traveling companion and auto navigator Alex Pociask, and Joe Hamilton, often called Little Joe Hamilton because he's about 5–9 at best, now a burly 5–9. I knew Hamilton when he was playing a mean guard in the ABA. He was listed at 5–10 but that was a stretch.

Alex Pociask

GUARD

SPURS

JOE HAMILTON

Joe Hamilton hosts Jim O'Brien at Los Aztecas Mexican Restaurant on Market Street in downtown Louisville.

"So many of *our* guys got sidelined by booze, drugs and women," said Hamilton.

James Hamilton Jr., his real name, had come out of Smoketown, the black section of Louisville, where workers once rolled cigars at local cigar-making factories. Little Joe could play basketball with the best of them. After he was caught stealing an ice cream cone at a neighborhood market, his irate mother sent him to live in Lexington with relatives and he earned high school All-America honors there at Dunbar High School. He matriculated to North Texas State University during the same period (1968–1970) when future NFL standouts Joe Greene and Cedrick Hardman starred for the school's football team—the Mean Green of Canyon, Texas. That's how Mean Joe Greene of the Steelers came by his nickname, and it suited his style of aggressive play.

That purloined ice cream cone may have been a turning point in his life, which turned to be a positive story. All he needed was a second chance, and the ABA, an outlaw league, as it was often called, offered that.

Simmie Hill, one of the ABA's legendary players, and Mercury Morris and Duane Thomas were standout athletes at West Texas State during the same span. They were all characters. "If the Super Bowl is supposed to be the ultimate game," asked Thomas, a recalcitrant running back for the Dallas Cowboys, "how come they play it every year?"

They put a snake in Simmie Hill's room because they heard Hill was afraid of snakes. Nice friends and classmates.

* * *

Bisquit Porter went to Eastern Kentucky University, but no one knows him anymore, just Joe Hamilton and the guys that grew up with him in Smoketown. There's a humble pink house on Grant Street near Smoketown, but in what is called the West End, with a simple steel plaque implanted in the front yard identifying it as the boyhood home of Cassius Clay, who grew up to become Muhammad Ali. We walked by it and took pictures of it. There was a colorful mural nearby with Muhammad Ali in the middle of a lineup of local favorites.

Photos by Alex Pociask

"I knew the young Cassius Clay and he didn't forget who I was when he became the biggest star in the sports world," said Hamilton. "He came upon me with some friends of mine in a Miami restaurant when I was playing against the Floridians, and he came over and greeted me as 'Li'l Red.' That's what he called me. Another time, when I was playing for the Chaparrals in Dallas, he saw me. He picked up my son and held him up high, and called him Li'l Red Junior. You don't forget things like that."

There's a super-sized mural of Ali on the side of the LG & E Building at Third Street and Main in downtown Louisville, and one of Diane Sawyer, the TV newscaster with Louisville roots, can be seen on the side of the Starks Building, between Muhammad Ali Boulevard and Fourth streets.

Dwayne Woodruff, a proud University of Louisville grad, meets Muhammad Ali at campus event.

There are murals to be found on other downtown buildings of golfer Bobby Nichols, of such basketball figures as Denny Crum, Darrell Griffith, jockey Pat Day, baseball's Harold "Pee Wee" Reese with his friend and teammate Jackie Robinson, football's Paul Hornung, and George Garvin Brown, who began to distill whiskey in 1870 and was the first to bottle bourbon. Louisville is home to many bourbon distilleries and bars that serve such whiskey.

There are murals of actor Victor Mature, actress Jennifer Lawrence and football's Phil Simms, Colonel Sanders, Bud Hillerich, who turned out Louisville Slugger bats at his factory. Alex and I got a personal tour of the bat factory by Rick Redman. Steve Higdon, a former Chamber of Commerce president, introduced us to Redman and paved the way for us to have a great tour of Louisville.

We had the honor of holding the bats once used by Babe Ruth, Henry Aaron, Willie Stargell, Willie Mays, Ralph Kiner and Stan Musial, some of my favorites.

Rick Redman shows author Louisville Slugger Factory product.

Alas, there are no murals to be found of Bisquit Porter or Joe Hamilton, or Dan Issel, Artis Gilmore and Louie Dampier of the Kentucky Colonels, or Howard Schnellenberger who was a terrific football coach in college and the pros, and grew up near Hornung's home on the outskirts of Smoketown in the city's West End. "This was a better neighborhood," said Joe Hamilton, pointing toward a stretch of still well-preserved homes. "Hornung lived there and Schnellenberger lived there," said Hamilton. Bisquit and the ABA stars never got the sort of respect they might have deserved. George Tinsley grew up in Smoketown and starred at Kentucky Wesleyan and was a member of the Louisville Colonels' ABA champion basketball team. He became successful in the restaurant business, where he was mentored by Colonel Sanders of KFC fame, another Louisville legend.

Every town has somebody like Bisquit Johnson, nursing a beer at a local bar or at curbside in good weather, wondering what might have been if things had turned out differently for them. Their pitching arm went bad, their knee got ruined, their girlfriend got pregnant somehow, some misfortune kept them from stardom. And big money.

I can name more than a dozen hometown heroes in Hazelwood and Glenwood, where I grew up in the inner-city of Pittsburgh, but only Herb Douglas, who won a bronze medal in the long jump in the 1948 Olympic Games in London, starred on the big stage. Regis Toomey made it as an actor in Hollywood. Bill Cullen and Rege Cordic became big-time radio and TV hosts. August Wilson, better known as a Hill District product, lived in Hazelwood for a few years, on Sylvan Avenue, next to Gladstone High School, which he attended briefly. Johnny Kirsch came from Pittsburgh Central Catholic to be a halfback at University of Louisville in early '60s.

*　*　*

I was traveling through Indiana and Kentucky with my pal Alex Pociask. He did the driving in his cream-colored Cadillac. He arranged for our hotels and provided a detailed plan for our excursion, as he did for several of our sports journeys.

We met Joe Hamilton, as Hamilton suggested, at the Los Aztecas Mexican Restaurant at 445 East Market Street, within walking distance of Holiday Inn Express Hotel and Suites at 800 West Market Street.

We started off with frozen margaritas. Mine was a 12-oz. glass and Alex got a 16 oz. glass. I think he confused the concoction with a milkshake. Mine left me tired and ready to go to bed early that night. The burritos were great, too.

Jim O'Brien

Alex happy with super-size frozen margarita.

I recommend Louisville as a great place for a sports fan to visit, especially Churchill Downs and the Kentucky Derby Museum, with a side trip to Lexington. Be sure to dine at Los Aztecas Mexican Restaurant.

I have a personal history with Louisville. I spent ten weeks in basic military training at Fort Knox in the winter of 1964, but I never got a pass to go to town during that spell.

I learned how to shoot a rifle—an M-1—during that span. I had never touched a rifle before I was inducted and I have not shot a real rifle since then. I don't like guns and I would never think of shooting a deer or quail. I fired "expert" three times. I have recently read a book in which it says it is easier to teach someone to shoot a rifle well if they have never touched a rifle before than it is to teach someone who has handled a rifle and may have picked up some bad habits.

112

I was startled when someone dropped shells into storage boxes and I couldn't believe it when I hit targets 300 yards away. That, too, was scary stuff.

My worst night of covering pro basketball occurred in Louisville. I was interviewing Dan Issel of the Kentucky Colonels after he had starred in an ABA playoff game with the Indiana Pacers at Freedom Hall.

Someone shoved a cream pie in my face and forced it into my eyes and nostrils and mouth. I learned two years later, in Las Vegas of all places, that I had been assaulted by the wife of Colonels' head coach Hubie Brown that night. Her name was Claire Brown and Larry Donald of *Basketball Weekly* was the one who revealed that Claire was the culprit in my embarrassing experience.

My favorite hotel on the road was the Executive Inn in Louisville. The beds were so high you had to do a "Fosbury Flop" to get onto the mattress surface. I was in a hotel once in Annapolis, sharing a suite with Myron Cope, where they had similar high beds. I remember hearing a loud thud when Cope fell out of bed in the next room of our suite. We were both bachelors and we had picked up a pair of sisters—not nuns mind you—at the Red Bull Inn. There had to be 30 men and two women at the bar that night, and our chances of connecting seemed hopeless at best, yet Cope kept talking to the women and wooed them to our rooms. When they went to the rest room before we left the Red Bull, Cope started thumping his shoe on the floor. I later learned he did that when he got excited. Some called him "Thumper" after a Disney rabbit of that name. The thump I heard when he fell out of his embrace was the sound of his head or cranium, as he called it on his radio show, hitting the hard floor.

During the most recent visit, I entertained my buddy Alex in the summer of 2018 and had a grand time retelling my stories of life on the road in my days working for afternoon daily newspapers in Miami, New York and Pittsburgh.

We saw International League baseball games in Indianapolis and Louisville. When I was checking out of our hotel in Indianapolis the morning after the game, I saw a young man carrying a bag with a Pirates' insignia on it. I thought it was Adam Frazier but I wasn't certain. Frazier was friendly when I asked him if he played for the Pirates. "I hope so," he said, explaining that he'd gotten a call the previous night to report to Pittsburgh. He was going to the big leagues and he was still there, as I wrote this. I became a big fan of Frazier after meeting him in Louisville.

Adam Frazier
of Pittsburgh
Pirates

We stopped in Bardstown at the Stephen F. Foster Museum. I told the folks there that they had just removed a statue of Foster from its pedestal near the Carnegie Museum in Oakland, just across the street from Stephen Foster Memorial Hall on the campus of the University of Pittsburgh. The big objection to the statue was the presence of a black banjo player at the feet of Foster. It was demeaning to blacks, we were told. I told the staff at the museum in Bardstown, where a cousin of Foster's once lived in an estate that still stands there and is the site of a stage show featuring all the southern music written by Foster, one of America's first composers.

I told the staff that Foster was treated better in Kentucky than he was in his hometown of Pittsburgh. They had heard the news about his statue being removed and were dismayed by the news.

There was a large mural of Foster playing the piano in the museum display and, sure enough, it had four black minstrels at his feet. I thought Pittsburgh and Pitt officials refused to stand up for something that deserved to be preserved. It was a different time. It was never meant to mock anyone. Those are my feelings, for whatever they are worth.

There were probably a few objectors to the Muhammad Ali Museum in Louisville considering that he had given up his Christian name in favor of a Muslim name and that he had refused to report for military duty when drafted.

The South is better than the North when it comes to preserving its history, even defeats more so than victories in the Civil War.

* * *

We drove through horse country farms on the road to Lexington. We included a lot of special activities on our journey through Indiana and Kentucky. It was a wonderful sports and history odyssey.

I plan a return trip to Kentucky. I want to see Paris, where Duquesne's Jim Tucker grew up. I want to see Hopkinsville, the hometown of Bird Averitt, and Bowling Green, where Donna and Darel Carrier have a farm that has a basketball gym built on the grounds. Carrier can still shoot a basketball from the foul line with the best of them. I plan to take my wife. She'd enjoy seeing the Muhammad Ali Museum, Louisville Slugger Bat Factory and the Kentucky Derby Museum, I think. And we'll get Joe Hamilton to give us a tour of Smoketown. We'll have a few frozen margaritas.

Muhammad Ali

Darel Carrier
Fieldhouse of Dreams in the hills of western Kentucky

Darel Carrier

It all began with a basketball, a goal and a dream, as Darel Carrier describes a boyhood scene that stays with him, as he approached his 80th birthday in the summer of 2020.

He stands by a big hay barn on his farm not far from the defunct Bristow High School in Warren County, Kentucky where he was a three-time all-state basketball player in his teen years. It's also close to the campus of Western Kentucky University where he starred in the early '60s.

He converted the barn into his own field house, with a full-length basketball court with glass banking boards where he schooled his sons, Jonathan and Josh, into basketball players good enough to earn college scholarships. Josh played for Tubby Smith at UK.

There was a time, long after his playing days, when he liked to go out to his own gym and shoot from the

Darel Carrier shooting basketball in the gym on his Kentucky farm.

foul line. He was always good at it. Like Rick Barry, he always thought he could make nine of ten free throws, and often did at summer basketball camps when he toured with "Pistol Pete" Maravich and "Easy Ed" Macauley, both Basketball Hall of Famers.

He and his attractive wife, Donna, are happy here, both easy company as we learned from spending time with them in Louisville during the days before the Kentucky Derby in 2018, won by Justify on a muddy track, the first jewel in the thoroughbred's Triple Crown season.

The bucolic scene brings to mind the 1989 movie "Field of Dreams," starring Kevin Costner and Amy Madigan, in which a man builds a baseball diamond on his land after having a dream in which he heard a voice telling him, "build it and they will come."

It was based on a book I loved by W.P. Kinsella called *Shoeless Joe*, about "Shoeless Joe" Jackson, a great player who was banned from baseball and its Hall of Fame for cheating. In the movie Shoeless Joe and the ghosts of other baseball players emerge from a corn field in Iowa to play ball on that diamond. It was Burt Lancaster's last movie, in a cameo role as Archibald "Moonlight" Graham, who played in one game in major league baseball in 1922 and became a doctor in Chisholm, Minnesota, I believe.

They could make a movie about Darel Carrier's life, but in the meantime, we'll have to settle for some YouTube offerings on the Internet about when his No. 25 jersey was retired in 2014 at Western Kentucky University. Check it out; it's worth your time if you're really into basketball, and you wouldn't be reading this book if you weren't a big basketball fan.

* * *

Life is funny. I never interviewed Darel Carrier when I was covering the ABA from the late '60s into the early to mid-70s. I talked to everyone in the front office of the Kentucky Colonels, coaches Gene Rhodes and Frank Ramsey and Joe Mullaney, Dan Issel, Artis Gilmore, Goose Ligon, Wendell Ladner, Louie Dampier and Jim O'Brien of Boston College fame, but never Darel Carrier. Don't know why. I must have missed the games when he scored in big numbers.

He and Dampier were the most dynamic duo in the formative years of the ABA, a backcourt combination that could score from anywhere, especially behind the 3-point line. Carrier was a three-time all-ABA player, a member of the league's all-time team, and had the best 3-point field goal percentage (.377) in the league's nine-year run. He played five years with the Colonels and 16 games with the Memphis Tams in 1972–73. He averaged 20.8 points per game for his pro career. He and Dampier are friendly when they see each other, but they always went their own way, embracing different lifestyles.

Randy Mahaffey, Mike Gale and Louie Dampier

There was a night in the 1971–72 season, against the Denver Rockets, for instance, when he hit seven of eight field goals in the first half, backing up behind the 3-point line to hit one of those shots.

* * *

We're in a lobby of the Marriott Hotel in downtown Indianapolis in April of 2018 and Carrier is chest to chest with me, and he lowers his left shoulder into me, knocking me back a step or two, and then he leans back and fires up an imaginary jump shot. "That's how I'd get free for my jump shot," he explained. "That's all I needed, an opening."

Carrier caught me by surprise because he hadn't told me what he was about to do to get my attention. He held on to my wrist a lot over a two-day span, so I wouldn't get away, and told me one story after another about his basketball days with the Colonels and at Western Kentucky University and at Bristow High School.

His recall was as accurate as his shooting touch. He also had the "people touch," the affinity for people that made the late Art Rooney Sr., the owner of the Pittsburgh Steelers, so special.

Rooney made annual road trips with his buddies to Louisville and Lexington for big races, and loved the blue grass country. His Shamrock Farms was in Maryland, and he loved the horses maybe more than his Steelers back in the '40s, '50s and '60s. He named horses after some of his favorite Steelers.

Art Rooney would have loved the Carriers. "We've become close friends; we're buddies now," Darel said to explain our newfound fondness for each other. His wife, Donna, a retired schoolteacher he married when he was in his 40s, hit it off with my wife Kathie as well. Donna lent Kathie one of those fancy hats familiar to anyone who has attended or watched a televised report on the Kentucky Derby.

I met Joe Gregory and his daughter, Evalyn, at iconic Churchill Downs on a Wednesday before the Saturday Derby. Gregory and his late wife, Mamie, were the original owners of the Kentucky Colonels. Mamie's prize show dog Ziggy was the Colonels' mascot and often had a front-row seat at home games.

They were especially happy to see Darel Carrier. When he played for the Colonels, Carrier

Artis Gilmore is flanked by Kathie O'Brien and Donna Carrier, both 5–8, at Churchill Downs in Louisville, Kentucky.

also managed a farm for the Gregorys. Darel can do it all. He owned an auto wash for awhile, he was in the antiques business and he was an auctioneer. He looks more like a farmer than a former basketball player, but he has a smile that lights up a room, and it's obvious Donna Carrier is mighty fond of her fella.

Just to prove his auctioneer ability, and he didn't have to lower his shoulder into me to get my attention this time, he did one of his rapid-fire rickety-tickety auctioneer's chants for me on the telephone in one of our long-distance conversations over a two-year period. Unreal! It's the first and only time someone spiced up an interview with me by soliciting a bid on an antique piece of furniture. Do I hear two hundred? Do I hear three hundred?

Darel Carrier is flanked by former Colonels' owner Joe Gregory and his daughter Evalyn, at Churchill Downs in Louisville. "What did your mother think of me?," he asked Evalyn. "She absolutely loved you," she replied.

Former Phillips 66ers teammates, from left to right, Tom Kerwin, Darel Carrier and Bobby Rascoe at ABA reunion in Indianapolis.

Darel Carrier could always draw attention. He and his twin brother Harel had a lot of people staring at them as look-alike kids and teammates on high-scoring high school and college basketball teams. He came to Western Kentucky after Bobby Rascoe, and he credits Rascoe for much of his early development as a basketball player.

"When we started out, Bobby would beat me 20-to-4 and scores like that in one-on-one games," recalled Carrier. "It took me awhile before I made the scores more respectable, and finally caught up with him."

The Carriers are still close friends with Bobby Rascoe and his wife Nancy. They were always together at the Colonels' 50th anniversary celebration in Louisville. Rascoe was good enough at Western Kentucky to have his jersey retired. Darel had the same honor with his No. 25 jersey in 2014, joining the likes of Coach Ed Diddle, Coach John Oldham, and players such as Jim McDaniels and Clem Haskins high in the rafters at the E.A Diddle Arena (capacity 7,600).

"Bobby was an All-American at Western Kentucky when I was in high school. We later played together with the AAU Philips 66ers and with the Colonels."

Bobby Rascoe grew up in Owensboro, the hometown of Cliff Hagan, one of his basketball heroes. "When I was playing in the ABA," remarked Rascoe, "I was guarding Hagan once and he liked to muscle you to get inside. I knocked him down and I must admit it felt good to do that, even though he had been my hero."

"Of the Kentucky schoolboy basketball players, the University of Kentucky wanted me and Jeff Mullins and Tommy Harper," recalled Carrier, "but Mullins went to Duke, Harper went to UK and I stayed close to home at Western Kentucky. Plus, they offered my brother Harel a scholarship, too. And Bobby Rascoe, my friend, was there.

"It's a good thing I did. I wouldn't have been happy in Lexington. I would have been homesick. I came home most weekends at Western Kentucky and enjoyed my mother's home-cooked meals. I could walk home from the campus. I was 15 minutes away."

* * *

Darel scored 62 points in one game as a freshman in high school. He likes to share a story about how he got started in basketball.

He grew up on a farm in Warren County and milked cows before and after school. As an adult, he had a farm with 100 head of cattle, and ten acres of tobacco. He still has a vegetable garden, just enough to have a steady stream of healthy salads with their meals. They pass some produce along to their neighbors as well.

He bought his first ball for $3.99 and attached a hoop to a corn crib and started firing away at it as a third grader.

It was a rare miss that turned things around for him in a hurry. "Harel and I played with that ball, but we only had that ball for three days. There was an opening in a fence about six feet high and the ball went through it. Some sow pigs got it and chewed it to pieces.

"Money wasn't easy to come by in those days, but my mom and dad came up with $9.41 for us to buy a better basketball. We put a hoop up on a backboard. We were in business. We'd just shoot, shoot, shoot. With the gym we have now, my brother-in-law extended it, and it's a pretty impressive place to play ball. As a kid, the coach gave me a key to our school gym and I'd go there on my own and shoot. Now I have my own gym.

"I have vertigo now, and get off balance easily, so I quit shooting. We had some shooting camps in there,

Billy Keller of Indiana Pacers pushing the ball to get by Darel Carrier of Kentucky Colonels.

and a couple of kids have come to improve their shooting technique. My son and I have some drills we use. I followed my older brother, Roy Lee, who liked to play basketball, too.

"When I was young, I had a burning desire to play. You don't find that in most kids these days. They don't have the same passion to play the game, to get better."

In a story in the Bowling Green *Daily News*, written by Chad Bishop on February 22, 2014, Carrier captured his attitude in these words: "Every time I played, I wanted to do as well as I could do. I wanted to play hard. I wanted to do a good job. I wanted the coaches to be pleased. I wanted my teammates to be pleased. I would give it my all."

When we talked on the telephone, Darel said, "I played on a dirt basketball court as a kid, and there'd be soot all around my eyes. My mom would call us for dinner, and I'd keep on shooting. 'Just a few more shots, Mama,' I'd holler to her. She holler back, 'Darel, I have supper ready.' I had a good meal every night. We grew up like the Amish people. Lots of hard work and family was important. We had a couple of mules, and we milked cows. When I was an adult, I had a dairy farm, and still had to milk cows. We'd have from six to 12 cows. Then I got equipment to milk them; made it much easier and more efficient. My dad had a heart attack, and that was a real setback. We've gone through some tough times in this part of the country, farmers losing their homes and their land.

"I don't keep up much with basketball these days, just the local high schools."

He was rooting for Dan Issel, his former Colonels' teammate, in his bid with local investors to get an NBA franchise for Louisville. "It's a great basketball town," said Carrier. "The Colonels could have been successful in the NBA."

Dan Issel

*   *   *

Darel shared a funny story about a not-so-funny incident in the life of his Colonels' teammate Jim "Goose" Ligon,

125

a high-jumping, hard-rebounding forward. The ABA was definitely a "second-chance" league for Ligon.

He had spent three years in the Indiana State Penitentiary as a penalty for an alleged rape case. As a senior at Kokomo (Ind.) High, he led his basketball team to a state scholastic championship and was a big man on campus. He was fooling around with a teenage girl in the back seat of a car. When she got home late, looking a bit disheveled, her mother frisked her and found her underpants in her small hand purse and called the police.

"It wasn't rape," said Carrier, "according to what Jim told me about the incident." Even so, Ligon spent the next three years in the pen instead of college.

"When Jim and I made some appearances for the Colonels, someone would ask where we went to college, and, of course, I'd say Western Kentucky, and Jim would say Penn State." Carrier continued to tell me why he was a lucky man. "I got married late in life," he said "But I've had the best wife. I had the best mother that ever lived and my dad was pretty good, too.

"My wife is a lot like my mother. She has people over to our house, and she likes to cook something special for them. I had the best boss in basketball in Mike Storen. He was shaking some trees, he told me, trying to get me into the Basketball Hall of Fame. He thought he had me in. Now he's died and he won't be shaking the trees anymore.

"From the time I signed with the Colonels, Mamie Gregory took a liking to me," said Carrier. "She and Joe hired me and Kendall Rhine, a Colonels' teammate who'd gone to Rice, and we looked after her farm for them. We had maid service, women who'd come in and clean for us and cook us meals. We had a swimming pool and horses to ride. We had it made. Mamie loved us as much as she loved her show dog Ziggy, I swear."

William Averitt
A wounded Bird

Poor Bird Averitt. His life has been difficult in his post-basketball career. It never gets easier. Now 68, he had two toes amputated from his foot in June 2020, and while he was rehabilitating in the hospital, his home in Hopkinsville, Kentucky was condemned and leveled by local government officials.

"So he'll be homeless when he comes out of the hospital," reported Steve Higdon, who has taken a special interest in the care of William Rodney "Bird" Averitt, so called because of his slight build during his ballplaying days.

"His daughter, Alesha, is looking after his care," said Higdon, who was the catalyst for organizing the Colonels' reunion. Higdon had twin beds in his hotel room in Indianapolis and Louisville and he allowed Averitt to share his room.

Higdon had grown up in Louisville as a big fan of the Colonels, and was later a mover and shaker in the Louisville business community, a Chamber of Commerce-type leader. Bird Averitt was one of Steve's favorite players.

"He told me that the reunion was the best night of his life since the Colonels won the ABA championship in 1975," said Higdon. Averitt averaged 13 points and four assists for that title team.

Higdon has been an advocate for the care of Bird Averitt, and has managed to get him

Bird Averitt and former Colonels' backcourt man Darel
Carrier.

monies from the NBA, from the Dropping
Dimes non-profit in Indianapolis, headed by
Scott Tarter and Dr. Joe Abrams, which raises
funds to help out former ABA players and personnel in need.

Back in 1995, Bird and his former wife
were both injured badly in an auto accident.
They both suffered a broken neck and he
had injuries to his left arm. In 2020, he suffered at least two mini-strokes. His left side is
paralyzed.

The sight of Averitt struggling to get
around at the 50th anniversary reunions of the
ABA and then the Kentucky Colonels in the
summer of 2018 is an image that stays with me.

Averitt could have moved around in the
electric wheelchair that was provided him,
but he chose to walk in a parade of past
ABA players across the floor at Bankers Life
Fieldhouse in Indianapolis, looking as proud
as a peacock, a wounded peacock.

He was swinging his arms, dragging his left leg along the floor. Once upon a time, no one moved quicker on a basketball court than this talented left-handed guard. When the ABA's four teams were merged into the NBA in 1976, a story appeared in *The Boston Globe* about the ABA players who would be available to the NBA teams in a dispersal draft.

The Globe had head shots of the ABA players thought to be the best available players and they included Artis Gilmore, Moses Malone, Marvin Barnes, Maurice Lucas, Ron Boone and Bird Averitt.

As a sophomore at Pepperdine University he averaged 28.9 points per game, and as a junior in 1973, he led the NCAA in scoring with 33.9 points per game. As a freshman, when first-year players were not permitted to play varsity ball, he twice scored 50 points in freshman contests with UCLA led by Bill Walton. He turned pro after his junior year.

I spoke with George McGinnis in the summer of 2020 and he was aware of Averitt's many ailments and challenges. "Getting older is no fun," said McGinnis, his voice still cheerful despite some setbacks of his own. "I had serious back surgery this year," he said, "and I lost my wife. She died too young. That was a real setback. The ABA was fun while it lasted, but it's not fun anymore."

Bird Averitt
at high school
homecoming
ceremony

Jim Tucker
His story merits attention of the basketball world

I always remembered that Jim Tucker was from Paris, Kentucky. There was something enchanting and appealing about that home address, like Vinegar Bend, Alabama being the hometown of Hubert Mizell, a Pirates' pitcher on the 1960 championship team who became a U.S. Congressman.

Paris, Kentucky is 373.1 miles or a six-hour drive from Pittsburgh. It's 91 miles—an hour and a half drive—directly east of Louisville. I wish now that when I took a trip in the summer of 2018 with my buddy Alex Pociask to Indiana and Kentucky for basketball, baseball and boxing stories that we'd gone to Paris. Just to see what it's like.

A boy who collected basketball cards and baseball cards and listened to Joe Tucker—no relation to Jim—who broadcasted Duquesne University basketball over WWSW Radio back in the '50s knew all that stuff.

I was really into the Dukes in those days and planned to go to college there and major in journalism, but a Senatorial Scholarship to Pitt changed all that, and it worked out well for me.

Jim Tucker was a slender 6–7 forward for the Duquesne University basketball team from 1951 to 1953. The Dukes were one of the greatest college basketball teams in those days, the 1955 champions of the NIT when that was a more prestigious basketball tournament than the NCAA version. Tucker was in the pros that season.

On a Sunday in February 2020, by serendipity I suppose, I was checking the TV listings for the day when I discovered a 20-minute documentary about Jim Tucker's story on WQED. That is an education television station in Pittsburgh and I learned some things about Jim Tucker I didn't know. The Tucker story was followed by a documentary (2014 vintage) about Westinghouse High School—"The House"—by my friend Chris Moore and that, too, was compelling.

The double feature was part of a Black History Month tribute by WQED.

Jim Tucker's story is a fascinating story.

He was a star at Paris High School who caught the attention of Adolph Rupp, "The Baron of Bluegrass," and the famous coach at the University of Kentucky, came to see him play. "I like the way you play basketball," Rupp reportedly told Tucker. "I wish I could have you on my team, but you know our situation at Kentucky."

When an all-white Kentucky team was beaten in the NCAA championship game on March 19, 1966 by an all-black Texas Western team—the first time an all-black five accomplished that feat—Rupp and other southern coaches responded by recruiting black players to keep up with the competition.

Tucker had the right nickname to play for Kentucky—"Tuck"—but he wasn't the right color. It was their loss.

Rupp recommended Tucker to his friend Dudey Moore at Duquesne and Tucker accepted Moore's scholarship offer.

*　*　*

Jim Tucker played for the Dukes in the days when there were limits on how many black players a school might recruit and how many black players—no more than three—could be on the floor at the same time. I'm not making this up.

That's why Fletcher Johnson became known as "one of the best sixth men in college basketball." He should have been a starter. I got to know Johnson in the '70s when I was working at *The New York Post*. He went to Europe to play pro basketball and went to medical school in Cologne—learning French, the language in medical school—and became a highly-regarded heart surgeon in New York City.

I called him "the real Dr. J." He, too, is worthy of a TV documentary. He was a teammate of Jim Tucker on a team that won 26 games (26–3) in one season (1953–1954).

So were Dick Ricketts and Sihugo Green, both All-American players. Ricketts was from Pottstown, Pa., and Green from the Bedford-Stuyvesant section of Brooklyn, also the hometown of Connie Hawkins, the greatest player ever to play for a Pittsburgh pro basketball team. Duquesne is the answer to a sports trivia question. What school had the first player picked in the NBA draft in consecutive years? Ricketts and Green. I recall that Lou Iezzi and Mickey Winograd, who became a lawyer, were guards on that team. So was Sid Dambrot on that Duquesne team. He was the father of Keith Dambrot, the current coach at Duquesne who is delivering on what he promised to do when he took the job.

The Dukes posted a 21-9 record in 2019-2020, the first 20 wins season in the last 48 years at Duquesne.

* * *

Tucker was taken on a later round by the Syracuse Nats in 1954. He and Earl Lloyd were the only two black players on that team that was the last of the small market teams in the NBA. Danny Biasone was

132

the owner of that team. His main business was running a bowling alley and a restaurant so he wasn't a millionaire. He sold the team to Philadelphia interests and it became the 76ers.

Biasone was best known for introducing the 24-second clock to basketball. Biasone believed that the games were getting tedious, and less interesting because of the slow and low-scoring games.

The Nats, led by Dolph Schayes and Johnny Kerr, won the NBA championship in 1955, and Lloyd and Tucker were the first blacks to play on an NBA championship team. Lloyd was the first black to play in the NBA. Lloyd and Tucker were often booed and called names by fans when they played on the road.

Just because they were black.

Chuck Cooper of Duquesne was the first black player drafted by an NBA team, and Nat "Sweetwater" Clifton of the Harlem Globetrotters was the first to sign a contract, with the New York Knicks. So there are three "firsts" relating to black basketball pioneers in the pro ranks.

When Walter Brown, the owner of the Boston Celtics, was about to draft Cooper, a fellow owner said to him, "You know he's colored?" To which Brown famously replied, "I don't care if he's striped or plaid or polka dot. Boston takes Charles Cooper of Duquesne."

Tucker was with the Nats for four seasons (from 1954 to 1957). His claim to fame for many years was that he accomplished a triple-double—double digits in points, rebounds and assists—in the fastest time, 17 minutes. I was not aware of this before I watched the TV show and I pride myself on what I know about basketball.

Michael Jordan is on the list, with a triple double in 22 minutes. Tucker's record was broken in 2018 when Nikola Jokic of the Denver Nuggets had a triple double in 14 minutes and 33 seconds on February 15 against the Milwaukee Bucks. Most players are delighted if they have a triple double in 48 minutes.

Tucker has been dealing with Alzheimer's Disease in recent years and doesn't remember so well the highlights of his life but he knows it's been a good one. "I've done my best," he says to his wife, Jan Tucker, also his caregiver, in the documentary. "You know that." He and Lloyd were much admired by their teammates for what they did on the court and in the clubhouse, and for what they accomplished after their NBA days.

Tucker became a corporate executive, a rarity among black athletes back then. Jackie Robinson and Joe Black of the Brooklyn Dodgers are cited as two other black athletes who became corporate executives.

My boyhood hero, Hazelwood's Herb Douglas, an Olympic bronze medal in the long jump in 1948, was able to do the same. He is an emeritus member of the board of trustees at his alma mater, the University of Pittsburgh. Tucker said his parents preached to him that he should "let 'em know you're there," as he progressed through life and that became his personal mantra. In other words, Jim Tucker left his mark wherever he went.

Duquesne Dukes dominated Pittsburgh sports scene

We lived in an apartment with no private entrance. My bedroom was on the third floor. Very cold in the winter and so hot in the summer. I slept on a glider on the front porch with vinyl covers. During the winter in the '50s, Duquesne basketball on the radio was a favorite time for me. I listened to every game in that attic bedroom. To this day, I still remember all the players: Dick and Dave Ricketts, Mickey Winograd, Lou Iezzi, Jim Tucker, Sihugo Green and the best 6th man in the country, Fletcher Johnson. Because he was black, he couldn't start as there was a quota. What a man. He went to Europe and became a doctor, taking the courses in a foreign language. He became a highly-respected heart surgeon in New York City.
—Pat Santelli, Allison Park, Pa.

When George Brown of the Dukes
outscored Oscar Robertson, 19–13

One special night stays with George Brown forever, and it was a night that Pittsburgh basketball fans 70-years-old and over won't soon forget. It was a game in which Brown, starring for the Duquesne University basketball team coached by Red Manning, was credited with "holding" Oscar Robertson of the University of Cincinnati to 13 points.

That's right, 13 points, an all-time low in his collegiate career. "The Big O" was one of the nation's outstanding basketball players, averaging in double figures in scoring, rebounding and assists for the Bearcats. Brown scored 19 points. "I think even our most loyal fans thought they were in for a Roman holiday with Cincinnati expected to score over 100 points," said Manning in the aftermath.

It was "the night George Brown won an Oscar," screamed a headline in the *Pittsburgh Sun-Telegraph.* The Dukes played a slow-down game, but still lost by 61–58. They had been an 18½ point underdog to the No. 1 nationally-rated Cincy club, thought to be one of the most talented college teams in history.

The game was played before 5,300 fans at the Pitt Field House "who could hardly believe what they were seeing," according to one newspaper report.

The UPI report of the January 23rd game said Robertson "appeared listless," in a game in which Duquesne often froze the ball. It was the lowest scoring effort for Robertson and the Bearcats all season. Robertson entered the game needing 46 points to break the three-year scoring record held by Frank Selvy of Furman. The Big O had only nine rebounds, four field goals and hit five of six free throws.

Dick Forbes of *The Cincinnati Enquirer* thought the Pittsburgh papers over-glorified the Dukes and George Brown. Forbes said the Dukes were "a mediocre team" and that Cincy simply played an "indifferent" game. This made me think of something the legendary boxing trainer Angelo Dundee once told me when I worked at *The Miami News*. "I tell my boxers never to berate an opponent after a loss," declared Dundee, who worked the corner with Muhammad Ali among other champions. "If you say the guy's a bum, what does that make you?"

Robertson's scoring average was reduced but not nearly as much as Brown's body. Brown lost 14 pounds chasing after Robertson, going from a pre-game 212 to 198 pounds in a post-game weigh-in.

"I had to be on the go every second," said Brown. "I think it was partially emotional and partially physical. I practiced on the freshmen (earlier in the week), and I thought about it all week, how I'd do it. I planned it. I know he's the best player in the country, but he was going to have to prove it.

"I spent all week convincing myself that maybe he might make a fool out of me, but he'd have to be great. I figured if I do my best, I can walk out of there knowing I played the best game."

Brown was named to that week's All-East basketball team along with the likes of Lenny Wilkens of Providence and Sam Stith of St. Bonaventure.

Brown, who now resides in Houston, came out of North Catholic High School to star for the Dukes. Dudey Moore was the coach at the time but left to coach at LaSalle and left the Dukes' program in the hands of his assistant, Red Manning. That's when Duquesne, Pitt and Carnegie Tech all fielded fine basketball teams stocked with local talent, homegrown greatness. It will never be that way again.

George Brown with his wife Colleen.

Coach Dudey Moore with, from left to right, Dick Ricketts, Sihugo Green, Jim Tucker, Mickey Winograd and Sid Dambrot on the 1954 Duquesne University team. Sid was the father of current Dukes' coach Keith Dambrot.

The Dukes played in two national championship games and won the NIT in 1955. Dave Ricketts of Pottstown, Pennsylvania, the kid brother of Dick Ricketts and later a catcher for the Cardinals and Pirates, was a holdover from that NIT team when Brown came to The Bluff. Duquesne is the only college in the country to claim the No. 1 draft choice in the NBA in consecutive years (Dick Ricketts in 1955 and Sihugo Green in 1956). Those were the days my friend; we thought they'd never end. Duquesne University was a 12.5-acre campus atop Boyd's Hill in those days and it has since been expanded to a nearly 50-acre complex in the Uptown section of the city, abutting the Pittsburgh Paints Arena where the Penguins play.

Brown's performance on defense against Robertson gained national attention, according to Fred Landucci of *The Pittsburgh Press*, and the NBA's Detroit Pistons said they wanted to talk to Brown about pro ball after the college season was completed.

Landucci's "Sports Stew Served Hot" column also contained notes about Ed Fleming, the former Westinghouse High and Niagara College star, who scored 29 points for Wilkes-Barre in a game against Allentown in the Eastern Professional Basketball League (EPBL). He also mentioned that former Duquesne standout Jim Tucker was playing in the same minor league for the Easton entry.

It caught the attention of Mel Cratsley, the often feisty and outspoken head coach at Carnegie Tech, who hoped that Brown's newfound fame would have an impact on his players. Cratsley called for more of an effort on defense from his Tartans.

He tacked newspaper clippings calling attention to Brown's sterling defensive play on a board in the Tech dressing room. "Playing defense is a lot of fun," claimed Cratsley. It also was a lot of work.

"You can't turn this thing on and off like a light switch," continued Cratsley. "I think George Brown exemplified this by starting to get ready for Robertson a few days before the big game.

"I think George Brown took up this challenge against Oscar Robertson. If we get a few more kids like Billy Mauro and George Brown and Mike Flynn we'll get basketball back where it should be."

Roy McHugh of *The Pittsburgh Press* quoted Cratsley as saying, "I think this thing George Brown did is wonderful for our game."

Cratsley often stole the show at the weekly sportswriters and coaches gathering at Gustine's Restaurant on the Pitt campus, which I attended regularly during my student days at Pitt. I learned as much from Frank Gustine St., a former infielder for the Pirates who owned and operated a restaurant near Forbes Field for over 30 years, as I did from the Pitt professors.

I could say the same about Doc Carlson, a charter member of the Basketball Hall of Fame, who went from being the basketball coach at Pitt to running the student health service in an office within walking distance of Gustine's.

Red Manning was more soft-spoken than Cratsley, but he was still drawing great satisfaction from Duquesne's strong showing against Oscar and the Cincinnati team.

"For the first time this season," Manning told the basketball writers, including Jack Sell, who always referred to the Dukes as the Bluffites and Pitt as "the Jungle Cats" or "Skyscraper U," we had to open our bottle of merthiolate and paint skinned knees of our players.

"They were finally hitting the deck to get the ball."

Merthiolate, by the way, is a mercury-containing antiseptic.

Cincinnati Nips Duquesne, Big 0 Is Held to 13 Points

PITTSBURGH, Jan. 23 (UPI).
—Oscar Robertson was limited
to only 13 points to match the
lowest total of his career and his
Cincinnati teammates had to resort to a freeze near the end of
the game to squeeze past Duquesne, 61-58, Saturday night.

It also was the lowest total for
Cincinnati this season.

Entering the game, Robertson
needed 46 points to break
three-year scoring record
held by Frank Selvy, of F
But the Big 0 appeared
and had only nine rebou
scored four field goals an
good on five of six free
GUARDED SUPERBLY

George Brown guarded
son superbly and also m
to wind up as the game
scorer with 19 points. Pau
was high for the Bearca
17.

Cincinnati was ahead
with four minutes left. Du
scored eight straight po
make it 56-56 with 1:48
Then Cincinnati froze the
about a minute.

BENE', HURT

Duquesne's chances for
set dimmed when Paul
fouled by Hogue, went spin
the floor with a knee inji
had to be carried off.
twisted knee. At that tim
had scored 13 points.

Cincinnati, beaten day b
ley, now shows 14 victorie
tain its high national rati
hapless Duquesne team
enced its ninth defeat in
10 games.

Cincinnati Enquirer
Monday, January 25, 1960

Cincy Wins S
As Duques

Pittsburgh, Jan. 23—(UPI)—
Oscar Robertson was limited to
13 points tonight to match the
lowest total of his career, a
his Cincinnati teammates h
to resort to a freeze near t
end of the game to squeeze pa
Duquesne, 61-58.

It also was the lowest total
for Cincinnati this season.

Entering the game, Robertson
needed 46 points to break the
three-year scoring record
set dimmed when Paul Bene,
2,338 held by Frank Selvy of
Furman. But the Big "O" appeared listless and had only nine
rebounds. He scored four field
goals and made good on five out
of six free throws.

George Brown guarded Rob-
ertson superbly and also managed to wind up as the game's

Guard The Big O
And Lose Weight—George Brown
Did It And Lost 14 Pounds

PITTSBURGH, Jan. 25 (P)—
Ever wonder how to lose 14
pounds in a hurry? You might
ask George Brown's, reducing
plan and chase the Big O.

The Big O, in case you don't
know, is Oscar Robertson

So Do National
Title Aspirations

By Dick Forbes
Enquirer Reporter

Any team with championship aspirations, and rated as a
champion is normally considered to have the requisites that
go along with such a label.

These include the obvious things—good personnel and
good coaching. They also include the spirit, the want, the
hunger to call it whatever you may

PITTSBURGH
Oscar Robertson
yesterday went overboard in
praising Duquesne's effort
against Cincinnati.

Paul Hogue, who played the
game in his career. With-
Bearcats would

said the Sun-Telegraph, in
part: "Other teams have used
trick defenses, gang defenses, to
doubles whither Cincinnati deserves the No. 1 spot.

The Bearcats didn't play
like No. 1 Saturday night.
From a standpoint of desire,
teamwork and obedience to
instructions, they didn't play
like No. 1, Fifty or even No.
100.

A strong indictment? Yes, it is.
Where these professional players, names, chapter and verse
could be recited. Being amateurs,
they had not been pinpointed, but
they know who they are and so
do their teammates.

"I practiced on the freshmen,"
said Brown, "I thought about it
all week how I'd do it. I planned

some 6500 persons had strict
try to step Oscar Robertson.
They've failed. He'd still get his
30 and 40 and more. Last night
one guy put the muzzle on
Oscar.

"George Brown was all over
him like a new suit of underwear and had a hand wig-wag-
ging in Oscar's face constantly.
The result was a bad shooting
night for Oscar.

"Brownie not only held Oscar
to 25 points less than his 33-
point average, the nation's best,
but also outscored the 'Big O'
and everybody else in the game,
getting 19 points.

"The 'Big O' had only nine

Manning also cited the fine play of Dukes such as Billy Stromple, Ron Cygrymus, Bob Slobodnik and Paul Benec as well as Brown. Those are names that still resonate warmly with senior Dukes' fans. They were all western Pennsylvania products.

Brown may have been the best basketball player to come out of North Catholic where the 6-foot-4 forward played for the legendary Don Graham from 1952 to 1956. Brown once scored a school record 51 points against Langley High of the City League. Earlier, he scored 45 points against Greensburg High, 41 against Kittanning, 40 against both Central Catholic and Charleroi.

"Of the ten highest scoring games at North, I have ten of them," Brown likes to point out. He and Matt Szykowny, the school's all-time leading scorer, and Fritz Binder are regarded as North Catholic's finest basketball players.

Brown drew interest from Duquesne, Pitt, Penn State, Toledo, Dayton, St. Bonaventure, North Carolina State and Notre Dame. He still has a hand-written letter from John Jordan, the basketball coach at Notre Dame, dated April 4, 1956, offering him a scholarship that included room and board, tuition and books. "I can assure you," wrote Jordan, "that you would do well at Notre Dame in athletics and studies. Please let me know soon as to your interest."

Brown said Rip Scherer was his coach on the freshman basketball team at North Catholic and his football coach. Brown played end for the Trojans. Scherer felt that Brown, who had good hands, could have been a terrific football player, but Brown gave up the sport as a senior to concentrate on basketball, when Scherer left North Catholic to coach at nearby Millvale High School.

Brown still has fond memories of scoring the game-winning touchdown in a 30–27 upset of Boys Town of Nebraska at South Stadium. One of the Steelers' future owners, Tim Rooney, was a starting back along with Larry McCabe, a brother of Richie McCabe, a future NFL and AFL player and coach.

Brown also scored a game-high 27 points in pacing North Catholic to a 70–56 win over PCIAA defending champion Erie Cathedral Prep in the Western Regional final before 1,200 fans at Pitt Field House, according to a report by Fred P. Alger of the *Post-Gazette.*

* * *

Brown, who came from Etna, was a contemporary of Walt Mangham of New Castle.

"Mangham is the better jumper," said Graham, "but Brown has more shots. His best is a jump shot, but he can also drive and hook. And he's tough on defense."

Mangham set a PIAA high jump mark of 6–5¾, and also cleared 6–6¾ in the New Castle Invitation, according to sportswriter Ray Kienzl. Mangham played for the Pittsburgh Rens and I once saw Mangham, Connie Hawkins and Jim McCoy play for the Porky Chedwick All-Stars in a game at the YMHA in Oakland. Tickets went for 50 cents.

Brown started out his professional career at Esso after turning down an invitation to attend the Detroit Pistons tryout camp.

"I thought I could play professional basketball," Brown said. "I had played against some top pros at Mellon Park. But I had to go into the service." He was commissioned as a second lieutenant after completing ROTC at Duquesne. went on to become an industrial sales coordinator for Esso in Houston, Texas, which in 1972 became known as Exxon.

The Night Wilt scored 100 points
There was a sweet smell
in the air in Hershey, Pa.

Wilt Chamberlain nearly missed the team bus that took the Philadelphia Warriors from Philly to Hershey, Pennsylvania the night he scored a record 100 points.

This is a story behind the story on his scoring outburst against the New York Knicks when he hit on 36 of 63 field goal attempts and 28 of 32 free throws, which was impressive in itself because Wilt was a notoriously bad free throw shooter.

PHILDELPHIA (169)	FG.	FT.	F.	Pts.
Arizin	7	2-2	0	16
Meschery	7	2-2	4	16
Chamberlain	36	28-32	2	100
Rodgers	1	9-12	5	11
Attles	8	1-1	4	17
Lareso	4	1-1	5	9
Conlin	0	0-0	1	0
Ruklick	0	0-2	2	0
Luckenbill	0	0-0	2	0
Totals	63	43-52	25	169

New York	26	42	38	41—147	
Philadelphia	42	37	46	44—169	
Attendance—4124.					

He shot over Knicks' 6–10 center Darrall Imhoff most of the game, extending his right arm over Imhoff's head again and again. Imhoff referred to Wilt's shot as the "Ban roll-on shot" because Imhoff's head was in Wilt's armpit most of the night.

The night was a Friday night, March 2, 1962.

There is a constant aroma of chocolate in the air outside the Hershey Sports Arena, now relabeled the Hersheypark Arena, because the factory that makes that internationally-beloved chocolate is located there. There is also an amusement park and we used to meet friends from New York there so our kids could ride the rides together, and Hershey was a midpoint on the highways.

It was a two-hour drive at the time from Philadelphia to Hershey.

I had visited the Hershey Sports Arena to check it out. It was the home venue for the Hershey Bears of the American Hockey League. It was a smaller version of Maple Leaf Gardens in Toronto. The Pittsburgh Hornets had just rejoined the American Hockey League in 1961 after a five-year absence. They were folded after Duquesne Gardens was leveled in Oakland, and the franchise was resurrected when the Civic Arena was built.

There is still a plaque on the wall inside the Hersheypark Sports Arena citing the accomplishment of Wilt Chamberlain's 100-point effort. It doesn't tell the whole story.

Wilt was a man of great appetite and he loved to love women though he never married. He said he didn't want to make that kind of commitment. He had been out partying with a woman friend the night before in New York City and he didn't drop her off until 4 a.m. He had to get up early to catch a train to Philadelphia that morning.

He had a long lunch with friends in Philadelphia and was late for the bus to Hershey. It wasn't the first time the team waited for Wilt at a bus station, train station or airport. Who wouldn't wait for Wilt?

He had a hangover and didn't feel so good. After all, he didn't get much actual sleep.

Wilt Chamberlain of Philadelphia grabs rebound away from teammate Luke Jackson and Willis Reed of Knicks in 1967 action at Madison Square Garden.

The Hershey Sports Arena held nearly 7,000 seats and the attendance for the game that night was an announced 4,124. Eddie Gottlieb, the crusty and canny owner of the Warriors, was known to exaggerate the crowd numbers. It was the third game the Warriors would play in Hershey that 1961–62 season. They farmed out games because they wanted to attract new fans and because they couldn't sell a full schedule of tickets in Philadelphia.

Many in the crowd that night were there mainly to see a preliminary exhibition game between the Philadelphia Eagles and Baltimore Colts basketball teams. Many left after that game.

They missed what Wilt would do that night. There were no New York sports-writers covering the game. Paul Vothis brought a camera and took a posed photo for the Associated Press of Wilt holding up a sign that said 100.

Al Attles scored 17 points that night for the Warriors and Paul Arizen added 16 points. Richie Guerin and Willie Naulls were the top players for the Knicks, who were not a good team that season.

"Some times you just get lucky," said Chamberlain. "I wasn't a good free throw shooter, but they went in this time."

"That 100 points is still an NBA record. Somewhere in there you should mention that Wilt holds 72 NBA records, 68 by himself. That's pretty amazing."
—Tom McGuire

Wilt Chamberlain beats Walt Bellamy to the ball in 1967 action.

Travels with Wilt and
some other hoop greats

I had a dream about Wilt Chamberlain last night. Wilton Norman Chamberlain, his full name came to me when I was still half-asleep. In my dream, I was hanging out with Wilt, hearing his stories as we sat at a bar at Kutsher's Country Club where I first met him in the summer of 1970. I thought Wilt was so cool, always have, always will. Or should that be always wilt?

I liked his real name, just as I liked Ferdinand Lewis Alcindor more than Kareem Abdul Jabbar and Cassius Marcellus Clay more than Muhammad Ali.

Wilt was there to play, as he did every year, in the Maurice Stokes Game, a fund-raiser to help a former NBA foe. Stokes had played at Westinghouse High School in Pittsburgh and at St. Francis of Loretto (Pa.) near Altoona. He had struck his head falling to the floor in the last regular season game, and was knocked unconscious. A few days later, in the opening play-off game against the Pistons in Detroit (in which he scored 12 points and had 15 rebounds), Stokes became ill on the flight home to Cincinnati. He had a seizure and a brain injury left him paralyzed the rest of his life. Teammate Jack Twyman, also from Pittsburgh, became his guardian and created fund-raisers such as the game at Kutsher's to raise money for Maurice's care.

Stokes and Wilt Chamberlain were the biggest and most fearsome players in the league, and the sight of Stokes in a wheelchair—for the rest of his life—was a sobering scene.

Stokes was born in Rankin, Pennsylvania and his father worked in the nearby mill and his mother

That's Wilt Chamberlain at far right in lineup of pros playing in the Stokes Game at Kutsher's Country Club in Catskill Mountains. Others, left to right, are Harold "Happy" Hairston, Al Bianchi, Adrian Smith, Wayne Embry, Walt Bellamy, Johnny "Red" Kerr, Jerry Lucas and Tom Gola.

cleaned homes for other people. The family moved to Homewood when Maurice was eight years old. He did not start on the basketball team until his junior season but then led Westinghouse to consecutive City League championships in 1950 and 1951. Ed Fleming, who later played at Niagara University and in the NBA, was a teammate at Westinghouse.

So why was I dreaming about Wilt Chamberlain at 5 o'clock on a Wednesday morning, May 6, 2020? I woke up at 5:15 a.m., trying my best not to wake up my wife Kathie.

After thinking about Wilt, I was thinking about some of the great experiences I had while writing about basketball in the '70s and '80s.

I wasn't in Hershey, Pennsylvania the night Wilt Chamberlain scored 100 points against the New York Knicks. No member of the New York press was present that night at the Hershey Arena. There's no video of the feat.

I was in New Orleans the night "Pistol Pete" Maravich scored 68 points against the New York Knicks. I was in Anaheim, California the night Roger Brown of the Indiana Pacers scored an ABA playoff record 53 points against Bill Sharman's LA Stars.

* * *

Wilt Chamberlain was my favorite athlete when I was a kid growing up—oh so slowly—on Sunnyside Street in the Glenwood section of Pittsburgh. That's just southeast of Greenfield and Squirrel Hill and before you hit Hays, West Homestead and Homestead.

I was a teenager and my reading was limited to *Sport* magazine, *The Police-Gazette, True* and *Classics Illustrated* comics. Wilt was a wunderkind at the University of Kansas, a 7–1 center for the Jayhawks, and a definite standout on the school's track and field team.

He could run the quarter-mile with the best of them, toss the discus and shot—he threw a 16-pound shot 47 feet in high school—glide over the hurdles, a true decathlon man. When he matured, he even considered boxing Muhammad Ali. He weighed 275 pounds when he was playing pro basketball and he was the best-proportioned big man I ever saw.

When George Kiseda was covering the Philadelphia Warriors for *The Philadelphia Bulletin*, he conducted a test with Wilt Chamberlain as a willing participant. He had Chamberlain run up and down steps and then had a doctor check his heart rate. Unusually tall men in those days often had heart problems. Not Wilt. He passed the test with flying colors. Kiseda, one of the best and most enterprising newspaper reporters of his time, knew he had someone special to write about.

I read magazine stories about Chamberlain and became fascinated with him. He was from Philadelphia, at the other end of our state, but we had little in common. He was black and I was white. He was a giant—called "Wilt the Stilt" and "Goliath"—and I was a midget called "Scoops" because of my newspaper interest. He hated both of those nicknames, by the way, and preferred "The Big Dipper." That was given to him by boyhood friends because he had to dip his head or duck when he passed through most doorways. I remember him dipping to enter my room at Kutsher's.

Over 100 schools sought his services while he was a junior in high school. He scored 42 points to lead the freshmen to a first-time ever victory over the varsity at Kansas, and the first-year players drew more fans to their games at Allen Field House than the varsity did. In his first varsity game, Chamberlain scored 52 points and brought down 31 rebounds.

I was one of the smallest kids in the freshman class (1956–57) at Central Catholic High School and I had been at the front of the parade at St. Stephen's Grade School when I made my First Communion and later my Confirmation. The smallest kids were in the front of the procession and the tallest kids, mostly the girls, brought up the rear.

Maybe I loved Wilt because I wanted to be tall like him and stand above the crowd. I read somewhere that short people have a great perspective on life because they are always looking up. Wilt boasted that he had a view unlike most people.

Vernon J. Biever/Street and Smith's Basketball

JERRY WEST

Lew Alcindor of Milwaukee Bucks challenges Wilt Chamberlain in Western Conference finals in 1971, with Gail Goodrich in background. Alcindor (later to be called Kareem Abdul-Jabbar) and Oscar Robertson teamed up to beat Lakers in four of five games. The Bucks were the first Western Conference champions to win NBA title since the St. Louis Hawks in 1958. The Bucks swept the Baltimore Bullets in four games in the championship series. That was an incredible feat since Bullets' lineup included Earl Monroe, Gus Johnson, Wes Unseld, Kevin Loughery, Fred Carter and Jack Marin. It was the first time in ten years that NBA finals were not played in the state of California. Alcindor led the league in scoring (31.7 ppg) and Chamberlain in rebounding (18.2 pg), with 20.7 points per game.

Rick Barry
No wonder he still has a place in my heart

Rick Barry gets an assist for setting me up to score successfully in the sports-writing business. Beano Cook and I were struggling to publish *Pittsburgh Weekly Sports,* a brash tabloid ahead of its time, and Barry was coming to town for a pro game at the Civic Arena. This was in late summer of 1968, into our sixth year with the paper.

I wanted to do a story on Barry for *PWS* and I needed a photo to illustrate the story. One of our subscribers and contributing writers was John Crittenden, the sports editor of *The Miami News.* Barry had played his college ball at the University of Miami. I had never met Mr. Crittenden, but he was familiar with my work.

I wrote a nice note to Crittenden asking if he could send me a photo of Barry. Crittenden complied and sent me a photo with artist's markings, blanking out the background as newspapers did in those days.

He added a note of his own. "What will it cost me to get you to come down to Miami and write for our paper?" he asked.

Turned out the cost would be $200 a week. It doesn't sound like much, but it was twice what I was making, and more than anyone else on the sports staff at *The News*, the afternoon daily in Miami, was making at the time. A fellow named Art Grace covered horse racing and he'd been on the paper for 17 years. His salary was $175 a week. Crittenden told me not to tell anyone what I was making. I can reveal it now.

I made some attempts to find reasons to remain in Pittsburgh, but my wife Kathie said, "It's time to go."

My assignment would be the Miami Dolphins, set for their final season in the American Football League. Crittenden had already promised the beat to Al Levine and Jim Huber, which made me a real popular fellow when I got there. I had a steel gray desk overlooking Biscayne Bay and Miami Beach, and that was worth something.

The Pittsburgh Pipers and Minnesota Muskies were both moving that season (1968-69), the Pipers to Minnesota and the Muskies to Miami where they became the Floridians. The Pipers would return to Pittsburgh a year later, and then they were called the Pipers for a season, then the Pioneers for a week, and, finally, the Condors and, soon enough, they were an endangered species just like the California condors.

In Miami, I could still see and write about the ABA, and before I left Miami a year later in favor of *The New York Post*, I landed the assignment to write a weekly column in season about the ABA for *The Sporting News*.

I had also been hired in 1970 on a free-lance basis as the editor of *Street and Smith's Basketball Yearbook*, which was being resurrected after not publishing a magazine for a few years after it had published two annuals and ceased doing any more.

Charley Tyra of Louisville and Tommy Kearns of North Carolina had been featured on the first two covers. So, I was writing for *The Post*, editing *Street and Smith's Basketball,* and before I even stepped foot in the Big Apple, I had a deal to publish another annual, *The Complete Handbook of Pro Basketball* and *ABA All-Stars*, a paperback book, for Lancer Books. I was a busy boy the summer of 1970, running back and forth from the East Side to the West Side in Manhattan, and covering baseball games in the evening at Shea Stadium and Yankee Stadium.

This is the photo, still in pristine condition on a cardboard backing, of Rick Barry in his University of Miami days.

RICK BARRY

No wonder it took us six years before our first-born Sarah arrived, Rebecca arrived less than three years later. Both like to tell friends they are New York girls.

I worked for *Street and Smith's* for over 30 years, as an editor and then editor emeritus, and managed to save enough money—$125,000—to pay for college tuition and room and board for our girls at the University of Virginia and Ohio University respectively. Our greatest gift to them was that they came out of college with no student loan debt.

Rick Barry was the star for the Nets when I covered them and the Knicks from time to time in the early '70s. Barry was one of the best basketball players in the land. In one brief stretch, New York could have claimed four of the best-passing forwards in the game, namely the Knicks' front-line combination of Dave DeBusschere and Bill Bradley, and the Nets with Barry and then Julius Erving. They could also shoot and rebound rather well.

I remember Billy Crystal, then a comic newcomer from Long Island, saying, "Julius Erving...finally, New York has a great Jewish ballplayer!" Crystal used to come into the city to lighten up things at writers' luncheons at Mama Leone's Italian Restaurant. He also played, as did Buddy Hackett and Phil Foster, at Catskill Mountain resorts.

The Catskills were called "The Jewish Alps" and the "Borscht Belt," and comics such as Crystal cut their eye teeth there, as did Sid Caesar, Jackie Mason, Buddy Hackett, Henny Youngman ("Take my wife...please!) and Don Rickles. One of the popular resorts, Kutsher's Country Club & Resort, was a big basketball mecca for summer time activity, where Wilt Chamberlain came into national notice, where the Stokes Game was held each summer in the '70s. And the matzo ball soup and lox and bagels were to die for.

None of this happens, as I realize now, if I don't write a note to John Crittenden asking for a picture of Rick Barry. I just got up from my writing desk and opened a fat file of photos on a nearby table and—lo and behold—I found that photo of Rick Barry. I always say strange things happen when I am working on a book.

Don Shula died the other day. I interviewed him once before I moved from Miami to New York in January of 1970. For openers, Shula said, "You're the guy who cost George Wilson his job." Shula had a scowl on his face when he said that. And I said, "And you're the guy who took his job while he still had it."

Good thing I was moving to Manhattan. Shula was smart. After a game, Shula started talking—filibustering, really—until many of the media had to run and meet deadlines, not giving them much of a chance to ask him any questions. He managed the news.

I once told Bill Cowher, when he was coaching the Steelers, how Shula handled the press and personal interviews. A flushed-faced Cowher kicked me out of his office at Three Rivers Stadium. Cowher is now honored in the same Pro Football Hall of Fame as Shula. Neither of them needed my help.

Bill Cowher, the former Steelers head coach, was voted into the Football Hall of Fame in 2020. Here he is talking to the author backstage at Cowher's Carlynton High School in Crafton, Pa. not far from Heinz Field, or the former Three Rivers Stadium where Cowher and Chuck Noll coached the Steelers to Super Bowl triumphs. Mike Tomlin also has one championship effort to his credit.

Eleanor Bailey

Leonard still Slick, but now
a Pacer of a different color

B ob Leonard was lying in bed, a white ballcap, with a small American flag on the front of it, down over his eyes. There was no answer when I had knocked on the door of Room 115 at the Westfield (Ind.) Rehab Center, so I pushed the door back and I let myself in.

"Slick," I said loud enough to rouse him.

Leonard pulled his ballcap off his face and looked over my way, smiled, and said, "Long time no see." And he smiled. Slick still has that smile that makes anyone feel comfortable from the start. If he had been a doctor, they would have said he had a good bedside manner. He still had that raspy voice, still an Indiana accent, still a great story-teller. He didn't need much prodding, never did.

Still reminded me of Gene Hackman, the actor who played the part of basketball coach Norman Dale in the iconic movie "Hoosiers."

That's just the way he's always been, back in his playing days at Indiana University, with the Minneapolis Lakers at the start of his seven-year NBA playing career, and when he was coaching the Indiana Pacers to three ABA championships in the early '70s.

Two former NBA players and ABA coaches I knew well, Kevin Loughery and Rod Thorn, both credit their long pro careers to Leonard giving them a chance to play when he was coaching the Baltimore Bullets, his first pro coaching position.

Slick Leonard was looking forward to another year at courtside for the Pacers, providing expert analysis and color to the team's broadcasts. Leonard is famous for shouting "Boom, baby!" whenever one of the

Bob Leonard was a look-alike for Coach Norman Dale, as played by actor Gene Hackman, of "Hoosiers" movie.

Pacers hits a three-point field goal. Even some of his best friends didn't think he'd be up to task, but Slick Leonard had been counted out before, and got off the mat to work another day.

I'd seen him look a lot better. He didn't have any covers on and his body was black and blue, "eggplant purple blotches over his entire body" was the way a writer named Gregg Doyel of the *Indy Star*, who had been an earlier visitor, described his appearance in a newspaper feature I found on the Internet, looking like someone had taken a baseball bat to him in great anger.

Out of pure affection for a fellow ABA traveler and a love for Leonard, who was always so kind to me, so approachable, I decided not to take any photos of him in his rehab bed. Better to remember him at his best. Get the picture?

My buddy Alex Pociask sat in on my interview with Bob Leonard and enjoyed every minute of it.

"Now I know why you loved the ABA so much," said Alex when we were driving the following day to Louisville from Indianapolis.

On the way home from this odyssey, after Alex and I went our separate ways when I picked up my car in the driveway of the Leonard home in Carmel, Indiana where I had left it, I stopped at the Indiana Basketball Hall of Fame in New Castle, Indiana where Leonard and the likes of Larry Bird and Oscar Robertson and so many others are enshrined.

Leonard has also been inducted into the Basketball Hall of Fame in Springfield, Massachusetts, along with Mel Daniels and Roger Brown.

*   *   *

Leonard had suffered a broken right hip and then, when going to the hospital to get a check-up on that injury, he had slipped and fell and broke his left arm in several places. It was a compound fracture, as if someone had dropped a vase in that parking lot. He was a color man all right.

"Those legs don't look so good," I said matter-of-factly.

Leonard looked at me like there was a fly in his soup and smiled and said, "Those legs did some pretty good jumping in their day." I hope I didn't upset Slick with my observation, but I think I did.

A man who seldom got an inch off the floor playing basketball had to give points to the Pacers' color man on that quick comeback.

There was a black hard-shell brace on his left elbow. It still hurt and he'd been taking a lot of pain-killers in recent months. It didn't slow his speech any. He could still out-talk anyone. You had to write notes in a hurry because he had observations you didn't want to forget.

"The NBA still has an attitude toward us ABA guys, but the NBA is playing the ABA game— fast-breaking, free-wheeling, high-flying basketball," allowed Leonard. "Red Auerbach never had anything good to say about us, but they play the ABA game, no doubt about it. They got the three-point basket from us. Everyone on every level has a three-point basket, but we had it first. They took everything from us but the red, white and blue ball."

Leonard looked like hell, but he still had that fire, that same determination, and he remembered where he came from, and how fortunate he has been in his lifetime. He had great success in sports and he had overcome many health challenges.

There was the heart attack in 2003, cardiac arrest in 2011, and then a year later he fell in Larry Bird's driveway and suffered broken ribs. He injured his hip early in 2018, requiring a cane at the ABA reunion in Indianapolis in April, and then he had a second fall in mid-June and broke his left arm. It was propped on a pillow once he used the bottom to raise the top half of his bed so he could sit up and talk to me easier.

When he was playing for the Minneapolis Lakers, he survived a crash of a DC-3 on a snowy night in January of 1960 in a farm-field in Carroll, Iowa, coming to a stop just short of a steep ravine. Eleven months earlier, a plane crash in Iowa took the lives of rock & roll headliners, Buddy Holly, Ritchie Havens and J.P. "The Big Bopper" Richardson. Former heavyweight boxing champion Rocky Marciano perished in a small plane crash in an Iowa farm field. Leonard was luckier than those other stars. What is it about Iowa that it was the scene of so many plane crashes?

Not that he was a safety-first guy. He was known to stay out late and have a good time with the boys, but he reformed a few years earlier and stopped smoking. He still enjoyed a stiff drink.

"I'm still here because of my wife, Nancy," allowed Leonard. "She's kept me on course and kept me out of trouble for the most part. Yes, Nancy is the secret to my staying power."

Indiana Pacers publicity

Nancy and Bob Leonard have always been a winning team.

Nancy and Bob Leonard had been married 66 years, as I was writing this. I had not seen either of them for more than 20 years yet Nancy received my telephone call with instant recognition, and didn't make me feel like some stranger or spam caller.

She helped Bob and the Pacers stay the course through some difficult challenges, helping to raise money for the Pacers when they were in debt after buying their way into the NBA. She worked in the front office of the Pacers when her husband coached the team.

"Health and happiness are the name of the game," Bob said. "My health needs a little work. But I have happiness."

Nancy said Bob was "quietly romantic."

He shared the secret of their marital success with Gregg Doyel of *The Indy Star.* "Every day," he said, "every day…every day, we say 'I love you' to each other. If I forget, Nancy nudges me before we fall asleep."

Nancy said, "There were some nights I didn't feel like saying it, but I said it just to keep him happy."

* * *

He mentioned some magic names, oh so casually, in his story-telling: the likes of teammates Elgin Baylor and Jerry West, Hot Rod Hundley, Larry Faust and Jim Pollard and not many men in America could make such a claim. He had coached the likes of Bob Netolicky, Mel Daniels, Roger Brown, Freddie Lewis, George McGinnis, Billy Keller and Billy Knight. He played and coached the best. None of them ever offered anything but praise for Slick Leonard. He was fun to be around, if you could keep up with him.

"Slick is still Slick," Bob Netolicky noted. "We still get together regularly for lunch and swapping stories with George McGinnis and Tom Thacker. Mel Daniels used to join us when he was well."

Leonard wasn't the only Slick in the ABA. Johnny Neumann, who left Ole' Miss after he averaged 40.1 points a game as a sophomore to sign with the Memphis Tams, had a wife named Carolyn who was also called "Slick." She was a show-stopper.

Neumann was called "Johnny Reb," and was often compared to another SEC sensation, LSU's "Pistol Pete" Maravich. Neumann, by the way, died at age 68 after a long illness. He never lived up to his college feats in the professional ranks.

Leonard told me that Larry Bird was coming to visit him the next day. Bird always feared dying young because he knew big men often died prematurely. I'd have loved to have been a fly on the wall when those

To Jim O'
a good member
of the A.B.A.
Fromily. Best wishes

Mel Daniels
34

Indiana Pacers

Mel Daniels fires up a jump shot for Indiana Pacers, with teammate Don Freeman at far left.

two got together. Bird was much more introverted than Leonard, but Leonard liked him and said they got along just fine. When Nancy came to visit with their daughter, Terryl Grembowicz, I thought it time for us to leave. I had spoken to Nancy on the porch of her home when we first arrived, and her granddaughter, Katie Claeys, was visiting at the time. Nancy came out on the porch because the house was in disarray because she was packing to move to a new home.

She showed me her championship ring with three diamonds, one for each ABA championship her husband and the Pacers had won.

"Hey, let's face it," her husband told me when it was time for us to leave. "I was a street kid and look what basketball has done for me and my family."

Leonard had some great influences as a kid in Terre Haute when he was an outstanding basketball and tennis star at Gerstmeyer Technical High School in the late '40s. Terre Haute was also the hometown of Duane Klueh, a star in basketball and tennis, the same size—6 feet 3—as Leonard. Klueh was a record-setting coach at Indiana State University in Terre Haute long before Larry Bird showed up.

Leonard and twelve of his buddies all joined the military service. "I got to play basketball in the service. We were sent to Okinawa and the South Pacific action, and, unbelievably, they all made it back. I thank God for looking after us," allowed Leonard.

At Indiana University, Leonard played for the highly-respected Branch McCracken. Leonard was impressed when I said I remembered Don Schlundt, a three-time All-American, as the star of that Indiana team. They were a fast-breaking team and they were hailed as "the Hurryin' Hoosiers." I remembered reading about McCracken and Schlundt in sports magazines I kept on a bedside table in by boyhood bedroom.

Indiana U. archives

Branch McCracken was coach of Indiana U.'s NCAA championship team in Leonard's junior season.

Kentucky Colonels publicity

JOHNNY NEUMANN
Ole' Miss sensation, but
something less as an
ABA player.

Indiana Pacers publicity

Indiana Pacers coach Bob Leonard was a sight on the sideline with polyester white suits and others that were the fashion in 1974–75 season. His sideburns rivaled those of Elvis Presley. His assistant, Jerry Oliver, is seated behind him.

That team beat Kansas by one point for the NCAA title. IU always had great swimming teams, too, with Jim Counsilman as coach (1957–1990). He coached our Olympic swim team.

"I got to play pro basketball with George Mikan as my teammate on the Minneapolis Lakers," said Leonard. "We also had Vern Mikkelsen and Jim Pollard on that team. Does it get any better?"

Mikan, of course, was the ABA's first commissioner and Pollard was the coach of the Minnesota Muskies and Miami Floridians.

"I'm proud of my long association with the ABA and the NBA," said Leonard. "The ABA changed the game. The NBA is now playing the ABA game, but no one ever did that better than Dr. J with Virginia and New York. Can you imagine him and George Gervin playing on the front line together with the Virginia Squires? No team in the ABA did it better than our championship teams in Indianapolis."

I told Leonard that when I had stopped at his home in Carmel, I spotted two basketball hoops in his driveway. "We had some pretty good basketball games there," said Leonard. "Ask Neto. He and Mel and Tom and Billy and Roger and some others played a few games there. There were some elbows and heated exchanges, but it was all in good fun. We were doing everything but jumping."

Bob Leonard completed his seven-year NBA playing career as player-coach of the Chicago Zephyrs. The Zephyrs became the Baltimore Bullets the following year and Leonard continued as coach.

Bobby Plump has been living
off one shot all his life

The game-winning field goal by Bobby Plump in the 1954 Indiana State High School Basketball Championship finals was the inspiration for the classic movie "Hoosiers." The movie, starring Gene Hackman as the basketball coach at Hickory High School, was often shown to basketball teams on all levels to get the players pumped up for an important game.

Milan High, a little school in Indianapolis, overcame all odds to win the state title and Bobby Plump was named "Mr. Indiana Basketball" after that 1953–54 season. Plump has been living off a last-second shot ever since. Plump was from Pierceville, a tiny town with a population of 45, near Milan.

"That last shot was one of the few things that were true in that movie," said Plump. "Most of it was just made up. There was never the kind of tension in our town that was in that movie. But I've watched it a few times."

His game-winning shot was like Bill Mazeroski's game-winning home run in the seventh game of the 1960 World Series when the Pirates upset the heavily-favored New York Yankees, and the "Immaculate Reception" by Franco Harris in the 1982 AFC playoff contest with the Oakland Raiders.

Bobby Leonard led me to a meeting with Bobby Plump on the front porch of the bar-restaurant he has owned for many years, called "Plump's Last Shot" in neon lighting, best seen on a summer's night. It reminded me of a scene from another movie I liked, "Picnic," starring William Holden and Kim Novak. Remember how there were strings of different colored

169

lights in an outdoor picnic area in a memorable scene from that movie? When I talked to Leonard on the telephone in the spring of 2018, he mentioned that he'd see Bobby Plump from time to time.

* * *

Leonard and Plump had a basketball bond. In his senior season at Indiana U., Leonard scored two free throws in the last seconds of the game as the Hoosiers defeated Kansas in the 1953 NCAA championship game. Basketball is still the biggest game in Indiana, and Plump and Leonard have lived off their heroics ever since.

I called Bobby Plump on the telephone to introduce myself and to tell him why I wanted to see him, and I knew within two minutes that he would be a good interview, warm, friendly and so eager to share stories of his heyday. In some of the reviews of his restaurant, he is often referred to as "one of the nicest guys in town." I was told he was a shy kid in his days at Milan High, but that was no longer the case. I knew I'd like Bobby Plump. He sounded a lot like Bob Leonard.

If you were casting for a movie, you would have Gene Hackman play the part of Bob Leonard and Robert Duvall as Bobby Plump.

Plump, at age 81 when we met and 84 come September of 2020, leaves running the restaurant to his son Jonathan these days, but he agreed to join me there on a summer afternoon, July 24, 2018. Bob Netolicky, a 6-9 forward for the Indiana Pacers in their ABA championship seasons of the early '70s, joined Plump and my pal, Alex Pociask, on the porch for some roundtable discussion. It was Netolicky who provided me with Plump's cell phone number. (I checked in again with Plump by phone on August 3, 2020 and he said he was doing fine.)

170

There's a place next door on Cornell Avenue called Brews and Books, and I had to check it out. They have shelves of books you can read while enjoying a beer, and there is even a kids' play area for anyone who wants to have a beer while baby-sitting, a scary thought. There are lots of interesting-looking restaurants and bars in the Broad Ripple section of town.

We were near a CSX railroad track and the haunting sound of a train whistle would punctuate our story-telling now and then. There's nothing more eerie than the sound of a train horn in the dark of the night. Plump turned down scholarships at Michigan State, Purdue and Indiana University because they were "just too big," and played for Butler University in his hometown of Indianapolis. He felt comfortable with legendary coach Tony Hinkle, for whom the school's Field House has since been named.

Plump later played for the Phillips 66ers, one of the best teams in the National Industrial Basketball League. It was an amateur circuit and the players had good-paying jobs with the sponsoring companies. Darrel Carrier, Bobby Rascoe, Tom Kerwin and Larry Brown, who all later played in the ABA, got their starts with the 66ers in the NIBL.

*   *   *

I told Bobby Plump a story about a friend of mine from Pittsburgh. He is a retired fireman known as "Jonesy," "Lump Jones" and "The Lumper."

Charles Jones has a constant red glow in his face, like a man who stared down too many fires. He carried adults and babies out of home fires and was cited for heroic acts more than once in his career. But he was best known, as a Notre Dame football fan all his life, for being able to do a flawless imitation of Joe Boland

171

broadcasting a football game for the Fighting Irish. Jones got into more than his share of arguments, if not fights, in the "Rhoid Room" at The Jamestown in the Dormont section of Pittsburgh. It was a popular bar owned by a guy named Jimmy Breen, that attracted sports figures from the Steelers, Pirates and Penguins. Breen liked to start arguments among his customers. Go figure that.

Steve Blass and Dave Giusti were regulars, as were Steelers' assistant coaches, Dick Walker, Woody Widenhofer and George Perles, members of Chuck Noll's staff. Noll drove by the Jamestown every day on the way to and from practice, but never stopped. There were always Penguins in the place, and sportswriters such as Myron Cope and Pat Livingston, and yours truly.

Jones came by the nickname of "Lump" Jones or "The Lumper" because he had missed two critical free throws in an important high school basketball game in his teen years.

"Imagine If you missed that last shot," I said to Bobby Plump. "You'd be known as Lump Plump."

"And you wouldn't be here talking to me!" he said with a big smile.

Plump provided me with the largest tenderloin sandwich I have ever seen, and a story I wasn't expecting—about a missed free throw that haunted the great John Wooden throughout his life.

Wooden won 11 NCAA titles at UCLA. He had been a star player at Purdue. He is one of only four men in the Basketball Hall of Fame both as a player and as a coach. The others are Bill Sharman, Lenny Wilkens and Tommy Heinsohn. Yet, Plump told us that Wooden dwelt on a missed free throw all his life, and that was a few days short of being 100. It happened in a state final game in 1928. "He talked about that missed shot till the day he died," Plump once told a writer named Al Lewis from *The Denver Post*. He repeated the story, unsolicited, when we spoke on his restaurant porch that afternoon.

* * *

There is a sidebar story to my day on the porch of Plump's Last Shot. Later in the day, when we got back to our hotel in downtown Indianapolis, I could not find my car keys. I was in a panic mode. My car was sitting in the driveway of the home of Nancy and Bob Leonard in Carmel and I had no keys for it. I knew I could call my wife Kathie back in Pittsburgh and have her overnight a spare set, but I was reluctant to do that.

Kathie had her concerns about me going on this trip in the first place. She thought I'd get lost. I admit to making more U-turns than I had in earlier years. I got off on a bad note on this trip, as Kathie feared I would. I brought two suitcases with me and I left one of them, the one that contained my toiletries, my shaving kit, my medicinal pills, at my daughter's home in Columbus, Ohio where I had stopped overnight before driving the next day to Indianapolis.

I had to buy undershorts and shaving materials at a store in Indianapolis. When I finally got home, it took Kathie five minutes before she asked me "where'd these cheap underwear come from?"

Alex told me he remembered seeing my keys on the table where we sat in the afternoon. I called Bobby Plump on the telephone and told him of my dilemma. He said he could check the bar and get back to me. He did, about ten minutes later. No luck, he said. No one found them.

That night, Alex said we should go back to the bar and check for ourselves. There were young women, four of them, sitting at a table next to the one we had occupied earlier in the day. There was a young man sitting at a table next to them, attracting their attention because he had a cute French bulldog. Having a cute dog has always been a good way to attract positive attention if you're also a cute guy.

I went directly to the bar inside. There was a big burly man behind the bar, with lots of facial hair, and he looked like he'd spent the day in a deep forest. I asked him if he had found any car keys. He reached behind him to the back bar and fetched some car keys. "Are these your keys?" They sure were, and I was so elated and relieved. I think I felt like Leonard and Plump did when they made those last-second shots. I wanted to kiss the bartender, but all that hair was a turn-off. I settled for a hug by a blonde sitting with friends at the bar who seemed as happy as I was at the discovery of my car keys. "I'm so happy for you," she said. "I know what that can be like."

The bartender told me the keys had been sitting on the top of a game in the next room. I had put them there when I stopped to take a picture of a picture showing Bobby Plump with Oscar Robertson, two Indiana basketball legends. I knew that Robertson had been a star at Crispus Attucks High School in Indianapolis. The school had been named after an African-American and Native American man thought to be the first man killed in the American Revolution in 1770. Crispus Attucks had an all-black student body. The street that runs past the school is now named Dr. Martin Luther King Street.

Bobby Plump had sold insurance and been a financial counselor in addition to running a restaurant and bar. He might've gotten in the door of a lot of homes because he'd been a high school hero, and one of the most recognized names in the state of Indiana. "You can't believe how big high school basketball was in this state," said Plump when we talked. "Hinkle Field House was filled to the rafters for those playoff games. They said there were 30,000 people lined up in the streets to greet us when we turned home after winning the state title. We came back riding in Cadillacs. Some local dealer lent them to us for the ride. Hey, we were treated like kings."

As a schoolboy, Bobby Plump, the pride of Milan High's 1953 Indiana state championship basketball team, met Oscar Robertson. These two photos at left, can be found on the walls at "The Last Shot."

Bob Netolicky
He was a fine forward
for the ABA's best team

B ob Netolicky gave himself away when he told me he was a good friend of Art Heyman. "We hit it off when we first met," said Netolicky. "It's a shame he's not around anymore."

Netolicky, a 6–9, 225-pound all-star forward for the Indiana Pacers when they had the best team in the ABA, was a charter member of the league's all-flake team. In fact, you could call him the team's captain, or perhaps co-captain, when Heyman comes to mind. Let's just say they were both different and saw the world through dark-tinted sunglasses. Like Heyman, the No. 1 draft choice of the Knicks out of Duke in 1963, he believes people had him pegged wrong.

Neto played nine years as a pro, mostly with the Pacers except for a two-year stretch somewhere in there when he played for the Dallas Chaparrals and San Antonio Spurs, before returning to the Pacers. He averaged 16 points and nearly nine rebounds per game.

He was one of the reasons the ABA was fun to cover. We are both the same age, 77, as this book goes to press, and he is 18 days older than I am. So, we grew up together in the ABA. I didn't have nearly as much fun as Netolicky. We had not seen each other in 20 years, or since the 30th year reunion of the ABA, but we didn't miss a beat. It was always easy for us to talk.

There was a book and movie I liked as a schoolboy (in 1952) called "Scaramouche," by Rafael Sabatini. It had a great opening line and it could sum up Bob Netolicky: "He was born with a gift of laughter and a sense that the world was mad."

Bob Netolicky works in pivot for Indiana Pacers.

He was a child of privilege, born into a wealthy family, so he may have been spoiled. "If you're single," said Netolicky, "and you don't wear a gray flannel suit they say you're different. I wear mod clothes, enjoy good times and I like to party. If that's a flake, then I'm a flake."

Netolicky and Heyman had other things in common. Heyman owned a restaurant-saloon on the East Side of New York called Gobbler's Knob, which I visited while doing a story on Heyman for *Sport* magazine. Netolicky operated what was called "a New York-style nightclub and bar," according to the Pacers' press guide, in Indianapolis called Neto's.

Netolicky liked it when one writer described him as "The Broadway Joe of the ABA." Heyman would have liked to have been called that, and worked hard at trying to emulate his more famous and celebrated Manhattan buddy. Netolicky liked exotic pets and exotic women. He kept a lion and an ocelot in his pad at different times. He was a favorite of the female fans of the Pacers.

I had an opportunity to spend time with Neto in Indianapolis in the summer of 2018. He also helped me make contact with Bob Leonard and with Bobby Plump, two Hoosier heroes forever. When I met Neto at Plump's bar/restaurant called The Last Shot—what else?—two women fans who hadn't forgotten Neto stopped by to say hello.

Neto gave me a "I have no idea who these women are" look, but embraced them when they posed for pictures. Neto is responsible for organizing reunions and he is still leading the battle to get the NBA to offer pensions for the ABA alumni, as once promised when the leagues merged.

He told me that when Paul George was playing for the Pacers a few years back that Neto did the math and found that George made enough in one game to pay everyone employed by the Pacers when Neto was on the team, and that included the team's trainer and the office secretaries, for a full year.

George is now in the midst of a four-year contract that pays him an average of $35 million per year. He's one of the best paid players in the NBA.

*　*　*

In the first year of the ABA, I suggested to Pittsburgh Pipers' coach Vince Cazzetta that he trade for Netolicky. "Are you kidding me?" cried Cazzetta. "Every time he comes to town he gets together with Heyman. All those nuts stick together."

Netolicky, for sure, was not your ordinary pro ballplayer. Good for him. He was big and strong and had tons of potential. But he was an easy rider. Concentration and dedication were his weaknesses. Oh well, it's hard to be perfect, reasoned Netolicky.

In 2020, he moved with his wife to Austin where their daughter and grandchildren resided. I can't imagine Indy without Neto.

Despite his shortcomings, Netolicky was good enough to merit inclusion in the first four ABA All-Star Games, and in three of those games he scored about a dozen points. He averaged better than 18 points a game during the regular season, and 22 in the play-offs. He was a good swingman between forward and center. He might have been the league's best offensive center when he played the pivot. He was agile for a big man and had good speed. He was a solid offensive rebounder, unstoppable and extremely accurate with his sweeping hook shot. He had a good touch from 15 feet out, and always finished among the league's top percentage shooters. He rebounded in double figures for most of his career.

Quite a ballplayer? You bet! If he could only sharpen his competitive instincts and gotten more serious. Coach Bobby Leonard could have slept better at nights. He played the same way when he was a star at Drake University.

He has the distinction of having played for both sides in an ABA game in 1973. He was playing for the San Antonio Spurs in a game against the Pacers. The Spurs protested the outcome because of something that occurred in the last 30 seconds. The protest was upheld and the last 30 seconds had to be replayed in the next Pacers at Spurs contest on December 2, 1973. Netolicky had been traded to the Pacers in the interim. He played the last 30 seconds and the overtime for the Pacers. I don't know how that game ended.

"Individuals don't win championships," said Netolicky the year the Pacers won the ABA title. "Spencer Haywood won the scoring and rebounding titles in our league, but I'd rather have it this way. We won the championship."

Off the court, however, Neto was an individual, and then some. Now he had a Labrador Retriever as a pet. He drove a blue dune buggy about town. He may, in fact, be the only person ever pulled over in Indianapolis for driving a dune buggy without proper registration.

There's more. His signing with the Pacers is quite a story in itself. Mike Storen, who was later the front office boss of the Kentucky Colonels, was the first GM of the Indiana team. Netolicky was one of the few high NBA draft choices signed by the ABA in its first season. Netolicky was the No. 2 selection of the San Diego Rockets. So Storen drove his five-year-old Falcon station wagon out to the airport in Indianapolis to pick up the new recruit, who showed up flying his own airplane.

Bob Netolicky unleashes jump-shot over Dan Issel of Kentucky Colonels.

The week before we went to press, we learned that Mike Gale had died on July 31, 2020 at age 70. This was a shocker. Gale grew up in Philadelphia and graduated from Overbrook H.S., Wilt Chamberlain's alma mater. Mike was twice named to ABA's All-ABA Defensive First Five. He played for Colonels, Nets and Spurs. He was a real gentleman and a great guy.

MIKE GALE

When Storen made his first offer, Netolicky, the son of a well-to-do Iowa surgeon, replied, "I get more than that for an allowance."

Netolicky didn't hold up the Pacers too much, however. He was in too much of a hurry to haggle over contract terms. "I'm a beach nut," he explained. "I was drafted in the second round by San Diego, too, but I was on my way to Hawaii for the summer and I figured I might as well sign and get it over with."

Read that paragraph again. I would think if you were a self-proclaimed beach nut you might want to sign with the San Diego team. Maybe Neto didn't know there were no beaches in Indianapolis. Geography was never a strength in school.

Despite his average of more than 20 points and 10 rebounds, Indiana fans found fault with Neto. He was an easy target. First, he was so damn big. Then, too, he had to be the best-looking guy on the club, though Roger Brown and Freddie Lewis might not have agreed. As a result, Netolicky was often booed at home, and no one else on the team could say that. The fans felt that Neto was not sufficiently competitive. He often seemed lost on the floor, in a daze.

"It has been suggested," Pete Carry once wrote in a *Sports Illustrated* piece, "that he rests up during games for his late-night stands at his bar, Neto's."

One lady fan said of him, for whatever it's worth, "Neto's got the sexiest teeth in the ABA."

"They called me a screwed-up tavern owner," Neto said. "I patterned it after a New York-type singles bar. Indianapolis didn't have anything like it. I may as well cash in on my name. If we could win a few championships, I'd make a fortune."

Neto liked to tell a story of how two years earlier his manager had questioned Spencer Haywood at the door, when Haywood was only 20, and turned him away.

Neto said he had a nice pad in town, but that there wasn't any llama rug on the floor or a bottle of Scotch in the glove compartment of his car. "I am," he said proudly, "strictly a beer drinker."

"I didn't know that much about the two leagues," he said in an interview with Sam Ballantini that is in the *Remember the ABA* website. "I think we played a more wide-open game. In time, we got the players and there was parity that led to the merger. I think the NBA made a mistake by not using the red, white and blue ball.

"The fans loved it. You could see it. You could shoot better. It's perfect for a game in America...hey, red, white and blue."

George McGinnis and Bob Netolicky were All-Star forwards for the Indiana Pacers.

Best friends for life

Bob Netolicky and Mel Daniels knew each other for 50 years and they became the best of friends. Netolicky was born to rich parents in San Francisco and Daniels was born in a depressed section of Detroit. They had little in common except for basketball. They first met when Netolicky was playing basketball at Drake University in Des Moines, Iowa and Daniels was at Burlington (Iowa) Junior College. They played with and against each other in summer basketball games.

"It was much better to play with him rather than against him," acknowledged Netolicky.

They teamed up on the frontline of the Indiana Pacers in the second season of the ABA (1968–69) and the Pacers became the dominant team in the young league. Roger Brown was the other forward, and Freddie Lewis and Billy Keller, or Tom Thacker and John Barnhill were the guards. Mike Storen was the general manager, Bob Leonard was the coach and it was the best franchise in the league, along with the Kentucky Colonels.

I learned from a story that appeared by Nate Taylor in the archived *Indianapolis Star* about their special relationship until Mel Daniels died at age 71 on October 30, 2015.

Netolicky and Daniels had spoken on the telephone twice the night before, and had agreed to have lunch together at 1 p.m. on a Friday at Lincoln Square Pancake House in Westfield, a suburb of Indianapolis.

When Daniels didn't show up, and when no one picked up the telephone at his residence, Netolicky decided to drive out to the farm Daniels owned in Sheridan, a half-hour drive just north of Indianapolis. When he got there, he found Daniels' pick-up truck idling in the driveway. It was a truck the Pacers had given to Daniels that same year to recognize his contribution to the franchise. Daniels was slumped over the wheel.

Netolicky checked for a pulse and there was none. He called 911. Daniels had died of a heart attack. He had quadruple heart bypass surgery only two weeks earlier. "Thank God that I was the one who found him," said Netolicky. He called Cece, Mel's wife, who was out shopping, and former Pacers' coach Bob Leonard and GM Donny Walsh, and former teammate Darnell Hillman and others in the Pacers' family and told them to meet him at the hospital.

"My heart kind of hit the floor," said Netolicky. "It was like a surreal experience. I couldn't believe what was really happening. I am glad I was there. We were so close. If anybody had to find him I thank God it was me. It could have been worse if he had been driving when he had the heart attack. I guess it was just his time. I was the luckiest guy in the world to play with him," said Netolicky. "We'd have been friends forever."

Mel Daniels and Bob Netolicky

From We Changed the Game

Spencer Haywood
Still shining, after all these years

Spencer Haywood wasn't hard to find at a cocktail party on a Friday evening at the ABA's 50th anniversary reunion in the lobby of the Emmis Communications Building in downtown Indianapolis on April 6, 2018. It was as if a spotlight was shining on his handsome face.

It's always that way. His face is lit up and glowing, like one of those Thomas Kinkade bucolic scenes. According to Kinkade's company, the work of "the painter of light" appears in one of every 20 homes across America. But there is only one Spencer Haywood, always a 6–9 power forward.

When I flip through all the photographs I have of Haywood, his face is always glowing, his eyes are always bright, there's something going on upstairs. There was a light in the attic. Spencer is a smart man, in his own world.

He appeared to glow even more as I neared him, going by Billy Melchionni and Mack Calvin to get closer. I didn't plan on interviewing anyone at this gathering. I'd wait my turn, as always. I knew these players were there for a reunion, to see old friends and foes, to re-connect, to share stories. Just let it play, Jim. I'd get phone numbers and call them later, then it would be just the two of us sharing a line. I had imposed that no-interview rule on myself, but Haywood had a well-earned reputation for not adhering to anyone's rules, real or imagined.

Haywood would have none of that. Haywood wanted to talk, to share his stories. I didn't have to prod him. I got out my camera and my reporter's notebook, happy to oblige the big guy, and tried to keep up

Jim O'Brien

Spencer Haywood flashes signature smile and championship ring.

with him. It would have been even more of a test if he had a basketball in one of those so-large hands and he was dribbling down a basketball court, whether with an orange-brown ball, or a red, white and blue ball.

He wore a brilliant blue suit, custom-made, of course, and a matching tie, blue and pale gold pattern. His teeth were as white and perfect as his well-starched dress shirt, and the diamond cluster on the ring he was wearing. I should have asked him about the ring's significance. It looked like a championship ring of some sort.

* * *

Spencer Haywood was an important figure in the growth of pro basketball. He sued the NBA in an anti-trust action that negated the league's so called "four-year" rule. It gave way, at first, to a so-called "hardship rule," requiring players to prove they had a financial need to turn pro early. Who couldn't meet that requirement?

Spencer Haywood towers over his boss, Sam Schulman of Seattle SuperSonics. Seattle owner Sam Schulman sued NBA to keep Haywood on his team.

Haywood single-handedly freed players to get a job. I remember once having a conversation with Lou Carnesecca, when he was coaching the Nets, and Looie thought it was wrong to sign college players early. I said that Ralph Simpson said he had friends who came out of high school or left college early to get a job, any kind of job, and he wondered why he couldn't do the same.

To me, it was as simple as that. Carnesecca could have had Julius Erving on his Nets team, but refused to sign Dr. J after his junior year at the University of Massachusetts. Of course, Carnesecca also stayed at St. John's one more year to fulfill his contract before joining the Nets as their coach for two years. He then returned to St. John's because he was more comfortable with the college scene. What other coach did that?

I've read stories where Spencer Haywood was thought to be the first player drafted before he was eligible for the draft, but that isn't true. Not by an NBA team, and not by an ABA team. Haywood wasn't even the first from his high school, Pershing High in Detroit, to be selected before completing four years of college eligibility.

That honor goes to Ralph Simpson, who was signed by the Denver Rockets a year earlier. They were both coached by Wil Robinson, who was the first black head basketball coach at a traditionally white school, Illinois State University where his star player was Doug Collins. I will always remember it was Wil Robinson who shared this bit of wisdom with me: "Show me a man who drives a Cadillac and doesn't have a garage and I will show you a damn fool."

I think that's true if the Cadillac owner lives in the suburbs or in the city. Then, too, why does anyone buy a vehicle that doesn't fit in their garage?

One of Spencer Haywood's brothers directed him toward Robinson, sending him from Chicago to Detroit because he had heard about Wil Robinson, and knew he would be a good influence on his kid brother.

Haywood had nine siblings, and as a child in Silver City, Mississippi, Spencer joined them in picking cotton in the family's fields. Wendell Ladner, who grew up in Necaise Crossing, Mississippi, also picked cotton as a kid with the rest of the Ladners. Both had the muscles to show for it.

"The rules were different for people like us in a place like that," Haywood would write of his upbringing in one of his books. "We just lived. You had babies, and you worked and you tried to survive."

Haywood was five when he joined his family in the fields to pick cotton. There were no child labor laws in Silver City, Mississippi. It was in the Mississippi Delta, 30 miles from Yazoo City.

I recall reading about Yazoo City in *New Yorker* magazine in the '70s, stories by Willie Morris, a self-proclaimed "Good Ol' Boy" writer about the Southern experience. Morris made Yazoo City famous in books such as *North to Home* and *My Dog Skip,* a wonderful book turned into a real tear-jerker of a movie.

North to Home could have been a title for a book about Spencer Haywood.

Haywood went from picking cotton to picking the pockets of rich men who owned pro basketball teams, hiring out his services, some times at the same time, to the Denver Rockets of the ABA, then NBA teams such as the Seattle SuperSonics, New York Knicks, New Orleans Jazz, Los Angeles Lakers, Reyer Valenzia of Italy, and Washington Bullets.

One of the first things Haywood did when he got some big money to play pro ball was to buy a customized Cadillac. Marvin "Bad News" Barnes bought a silver Rolls-Royce. "It's a normal reaction, what I did, a kid out of the ghetto," said Haywood. "I had to show my wealth, but I found it's not necessary. I don't need a flashy car." I wonder whether Haywood had a garage to store his Cadillac. Wil Robinson is smiling somewhere.

That Cadillac, by the way, which Haywood liked to drive around the streets of Seattle, ended up in Silver City, Mississippi. "My goal was to put my mother in a new house, and I've done that," Haywood told Gil Lyons in the January 27, 1973 issue of *The Sporting News*. "And I put a big car in her garage." Haywood must have heard what Wil Robinson had to say about Cadillacs and garages. The car was a $13,000 custom Cadillac. You can't get a Cadillac or any other luxury car for $13,000 these days.

Lyons also alluded to Haywood having a "Bill Cosby smile," and no one would use that description these days. Oh, how some of the greatest have fallen.

* * *

Haywood resides in Las Vegas, lots of bright lights there along "the Neon Strip," as Cosby could tell you on his more lucid days. Haywood lives there with his wife, Linda. They have three daughters. He was originally married to a super model, Iman, when he was in New York with the Knicks from 1975 to 1979.

From "The Liberation of Spencer Haywood" by Arnold Hano for Sport Special:

He has come a long, long way. It is easy to remember. All he has to do is take off his shoes and socks, and look at his feet. Each toe balls under, like the claw end of a hammer. "Salvation Army shoes did that," he says.

Spencer Haywood was all-ABA as a rookie with Denver Rockets.

I worked in New York for three of those years, and spoke to Spencer a few times whenever I'd get assigned to the Knicks' beat from time to time. He was always a willing interview. He never met a microphone or notepad he didn't like.

Ralph Simpson and Spencer Haywood changed the game, and the way business has been conducted for the last 50 years. Today's players should all leave some chips in Haywood's name when they leave a Las Vegas hotel or casino. They did the same for basketball as what Curt Flood did for baseball, getting rid of the option clause that bound a player to one team forever.

When Haywood jumped leagues in 1970, leaving the ABA's Denver Rockets in favor of the NBA's Seattle Supersonics, the NBA front office tried to block the deal because Haywood's college class had not yet graduated. There was a rule in the league's constitution that forbade anyone playing unless their class had completed its four years of college eligibility. That's the reason Wilt Chamberlain played for the Harlem Globetrotters for a year before signing with the Philadelphia Warriors. They had actually drafted him as a "territorial pick" when he was still a senior at Philadelphia's Overbrook High School. He stayed three years at the University of Kansas.

Like Wilt—"Nobody loves Goliath"—Spencer saw himself as a mostly misunderstood pro athlete, thought to be making too much money, and flashing it as so many kids from the ghettos often did when they could afford to buy a gaudy set of wheels, gaudy clothes and, just maybe, a nice home for their mom.

> *"Charlie 'Helicopter' Hentz of the Pittsburgh Condors tore down two backboards in Raleigh, N.C. when he was playing against the Carolina Cougars. But this seldom is mentioned the way Jerome Lane is for breaking one backboard at the Pitt Field House. Hentz did his damage on Nov. 6, 1970. They didn't have a replacement for the banking board at the other end of the floor so they had to call the game with North Carolina ahead 122–107."*
> —**Sam Sciullo, Pittsburgh sports historian**

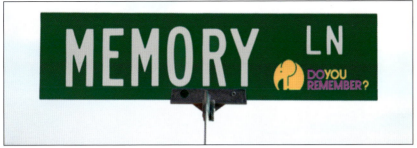

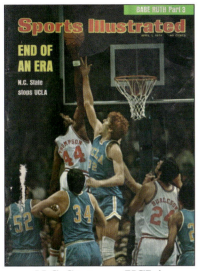

**N.C. State vs. UCLA
(Thompson vs. Walton)**

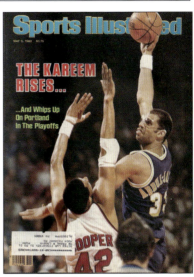

The Kareem Rises

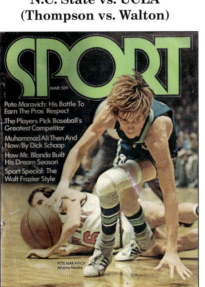

Pete Maravich

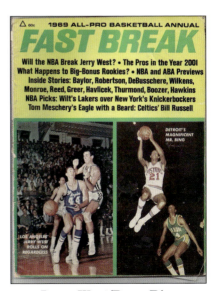

Jerry West/Dave Bing

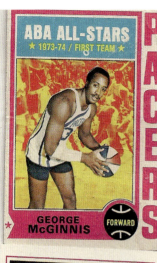

ABA ALL-STARS
★ 1973-74 / FIRST TEAM ★

GEORGE McGINNIS
FORWARD

PACERS

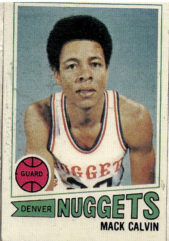

GUARD

DENVER NUGGETS

MACK CALVIN

KNICKS

NEW YORK EARL MONROE

FORWARD

PHILADELPHIA 76ERS

STEVE MIX

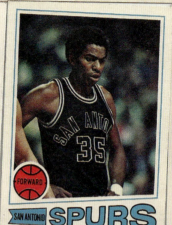

FORWARD

SAN ANTONIO SPURS

LARRY KENON

FORWARD

GOLDEN STATE WARRIORS

RICK BARR

FORWARD

PACERS

DARNELL HILLMAN

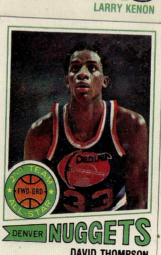

2ND TEAM
FWD-GRD
ALL-STAR

DENVER NUGGETS

DAVID THOMPSON

GRD-FWD

SAN ANTONIO SPURS

GEORGE GERVI

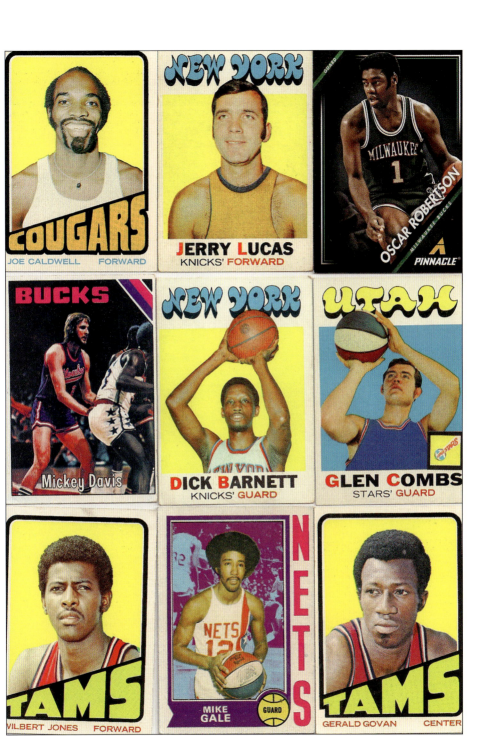

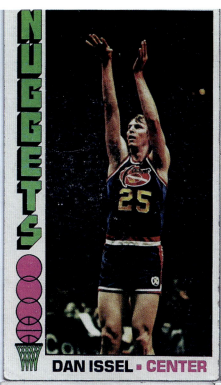

NUGGETS

DAN ISSEL ■ CENTER

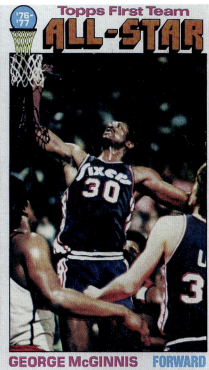

'76-'77 Topps First Team ALL-STAR

GEORGE McGINNIS FORWARD

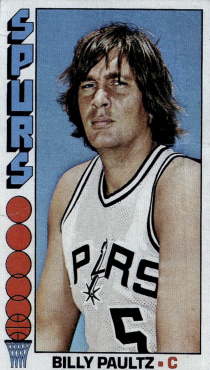

SPURS

BILLY PAULTZ ■ C

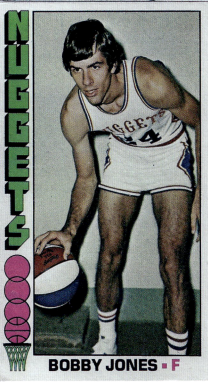

NUGGETS

BOBBY JONES ■ F

KNICKS

BILL BRADLEY ▪ **F**

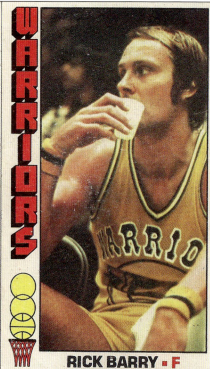

WARRIORS

RICK BARRY ▪ **F**

PACERS

BILLY KNIGHT ▪ **F**

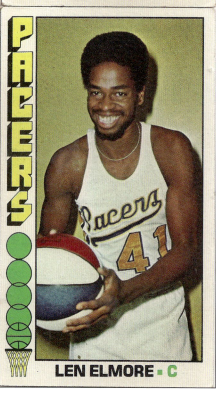

PACERS

LEN ELMORE ▪ **C**

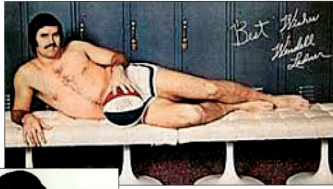

"Wondrous Wendell" Ladner, or "Mr. Excitement," posed for this picture at the height of his popularity with the Kentucky Colonels in 1972-73 season. A poster sold for $1.50 and many of the Colonels' female fans still treasure a copy.

Jim O'Brien

From ABA's 30th annual reunion in 1998 in Indianapolis,from left to right, Cincy Powell, Louie Dampier, radio voice Van Vance and Jim "Goose" Ligon of Kentucky Colonels.

Charles Barkley at Mario Lemieux's Celebrity Golf Outing at The Club at Nevillewood.

Photos by Jim O'Brien. All jerseys from personal collection of Calgary, Canada businessman Frank Mafrica.

HOOSIERS

Actor Gene Hackman as Coach Norman Dale in iconic motion picture "Hoosiers" (1986). Barbara Hershey was co-star along with Dennis Hopper, so good as "Shooter," the town drunk and father of one of the basketball team's star players. It's worth watching again. Also check out Ben Affleck's fine flick, "The Way Back," (March 2020) with a similar inspirational story line.

Denver Nuggets coach Larry Brown beseeches players and referees alike at Nassau Coliseum. Writers on press row include, left to right, Gerald Eskenazi of The New York Times, Jim O'Brien of the New York Post, Doug Smith of Newsday and Bernie Beglane of Long Island Press.

Miami Floridians owner Ned Doyle was in ABA heaven with the iconic Floridian ballgirls surrounding him. Doyle was a Madison Avenue ad executive, one of the co-founders and managing partners for Doyle, Dane & Bernbach, believed to be the most influential agency in advertising business back in the '60s and '70s.

Jim O'Brien

AMONG ABA'S BEST GUARDS are, left to right, Donnie Freeman, Maurice McHartley and Brian Taylor, as seen at league's 50th anniversary reunion in Indianapolis in April of 2018. This trio was also among the ABA's best dressers.

Two of Pittsburgh's finest basketball players: Mickey Davis of Monaca and Duquesne University while playing for Milwaukee Bucks against Billy Knight of Braddock and Pitt while playing for Indiana Pacers. That's Indiana's coach Bob Leonard and Len Elmore in background.

Western Kentucky publicity

BATTLE OF THE GIANTS—Jacksonville U.'s 7–2 Artis Gilmore challenges Western Kentucky's 6–11 Jim McDaniels for opening tip-off in NCAA Eastern Regional game at Joyce Center, Notre Dame, Indiana on March 13, 1971. Western Kentucky won 74–72, even though the Hilltoppers converted only 35 of 96 field goal attempts and four of 13 free throws. Gilmore had 12 points and 22 rebounds and McDaniels had 23 points and 13 rebounds. while leading his team to Final Four.

Remember the ABA/
Arthur Hundhausen

Jim McDaniels signed
with ABA's Carolina
Cougars before he
completed his senior
season at Western
Kentucky.

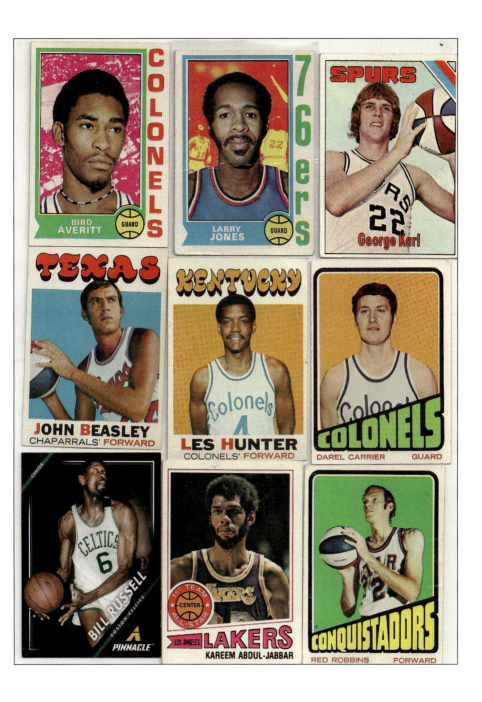

Courtesy of NBA Photos

James Harden of Houston,
LeBron James of Lakers,
Kevin Durant of Brooklyn Nets,
Jim Tucker of Syracuse Nats
and Harlem Globetrotters,
Rick Barry of Warriors.

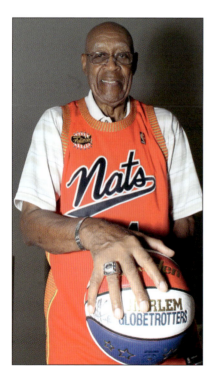

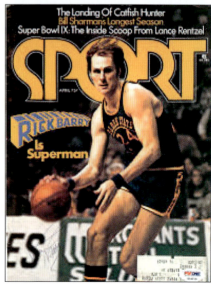

Spencer Haywood came into the ABA with the Denver Rockets in 1969–70 and had a phenomenal first season. He was the league's Rookie of the Year and and Most Valuable Player. He won the ABA scoring title with an average of 30.0 ppg and led the league in rebounding with a remarkable 19.5 rpg to set the ABA's all-time record.

Spencer Haywood's father was a carpenter and he died while his wife was eight months pregnant with Spencer. "My mother had to raise six sons and four daughters in a six-room frame house on $10 a week for scrubbing floors and $10 a month relief," said Haywood. There was no plumbing and no electricity in what Haywood would call a humble shack.

"We all worked from the time we could stand," he said in an interview for SPORT magazine early in his pro career. "I caddied, mowed lawns, barbered hair, picked cotton. I had to pick 300 pounds of cotton to get $6. As soon as any of us got old enough we left home and headed north to find some better life. And landed in lousy ghettos.

"At 13, I spent a summer in Chicago living with a married brother and married sister. The next summer, I went back to stay with an older brother, Andy, who wasn't married. Andy saw me turning bad and he also saw me turning into a tall cat who could really play basketball on the playgrounds, so he shipped me to my brother Leroy, who was playing for Bowling Green, and living summers in Detroit. Leroy fixed me up with Wil Robinson, a hot high school basketball coach there, who fixed me up with Ida and James Bell, who took me into their home. The three became my joint guardians and tried to straighten me out."

Basketball saved Spencer Haywood. "Basketball saved me from becoming an alky or an addict or a hood," said Haywood. "If you can't sing a song, or stuff some basketball into a hoop or something like that, you got to find some other way to make it."

Too often, it's a lame excuse to get into drugs and crime. Haywood had to hear stories about Reggie Harding, a Detroit schoolboy legend, who ended up dead at 30 because he couldn't find a way to make it. Harding, who was 7-feet tall and had played for the

Spencer Haywood was outstanding All-Star for West team in 1970 game in Indianapolis.

Pistons and Pacers, was shot dead on a street corner on "the mean streets of Detroit" after an argument with a friend.

Haywood was a star for Robinson's Pershing High that won the state title in Spencer's senior year. Wil wanted Spencer to go the University of Detroit. School officials told Robinson and Haywood that they were going to hire Robinson as their basketball coach to replace the retiring Bob Calihan, a local coaching legend. So, Spencer signed on to go to the University of Detroit, just as another local stud, Dave DeBusschere, once did.

Who knew back then that DeBusschere and Haywood would both end up as power forwards for the NBA's New York Knicks during the 70s, but never as teammates?

Haywood didn't care for Jim Harding, who got the job instead of Robinson, and felt that he and Robinson were both lied to and betrayed by school officials. That's the same Jim Harding who got into a fist-fight with Minnesota Pipers' owner Gabe Rubin when Harding was employed by the Pipers. So, Haywood turned pro early.

At 19, Haywood was the youngest player on the U.S. Olympic basketball team, the team's star in Mexico City. At 20, he was the youngest player in pro basketball.

He took the league by storm. He was named the MVP for both the season and the playoffs. He led the league in scoring (30 points per game) and rebounding (19.5 per game). In the ABA All-Star Game, he scored 23 points, grabbed 19 rebounds and blocked seven shots for the West team. His Denver teammate Larry Jones pumped in a game-high 30 points and had six assists in a 128–98 West victory.

Spencer Haywood of Seattle SuperSonics calls for ball with Knicks' Dave DeBusschere behind him. Both played high school and college ball in Detroit.

DeBusschere was one of his biggest boosters during Spencer's Seattle SuperSonics days. "He's so fluid," DeBusschere told Milton Gross, columnist for *The New York Post*. "And he does everything so very well. He glides and physically he's so very strong. He's good. No doubt about it."

Haywood came to the Knicks in the mid-70s when Willis Reed, the former captain of its two championship teams, had replaced Red Holzman as the coach. He was replacing DeBusschere on the team's front line.

Before long, Haywood was hooked on cocaine, something he once wrote that basketball saved him from. That helps explain how he ended up playing pro ball in Italy. He was cut from the Los Angeles Lakers during championship playoffs because he had fallen asleep during a practice session.

Haywood would later tell everyone how much he matured, how he had straightened out his priorities. "I put much emphasis on respect," he said to Lyons. "I don't give a damn if people really like me. But I want them to respect me."

He did his best to win the respect of kids at community centers wherever he played pro ball. He remembered vividly his early days as a street thug in Chicago and Detroit.

"I feel that I escaped hell and I want to reach down and help someone else out," he said. "I've stopped off at the playgrounds and played basketball and talked with a lot of kids. I wanted to get closer to them. Some are on the border-line, like I was. Maybe I can help straighten them out."

His net worth today is reportedly $3 million, a lot less than it should be. Early in his career in Seattle, an upstart sneaker company named Nike, led by Phil Knight, approached him to endorse their product. He had a choice between $100,000 (now equal to $500,000) and a 10% equity stake in the company. That would be worth over $10 billion today, give or take a few million lost to the drop in the stock market because of the coronavirus pandemic.

Spencer took the money and ran. He was street smart, but not Wall Street smart.

Ike Gellis
My boss was a beauty

I think Ike Gellis thought for a while that I was making up the stories I wrote about Julius Erving, George McGinnis, Bobby Jones and Marvin Barnes. He could not believe they were as good at playing basketball as I wrote about their heroics.

Ike Gellis was the sports editor of *The New York Post* and thus my boss during the decade of the '70s. He's the one who hired me and he gave me some great assignments during my nine years (1970–1979) on the staff. For that, I remain grateful.

He hired me on the spot one night at Madison Square Garden at the recommendation of Larry Merchant.

If their friend Budd Shulberg wrote a movie script about boxing, as he did with *The Harder They Fall*, he would have had Gellis in mind when he wrote about a big city sports editor. Or a corner man in the ring.

Gellis had a mug that brought the tough-guy movie actor Edward G. Robinson to mind, as well as the burnt end of one of the cigars favored by Steelers' owner Art Rooney Sr., a frequent visitor to the race tracks in the Gotham. The Chief would have loved Ike Gellis, his kind of guy.

When I reported for work in the spring of 1970, I asked Gellis if I had to do any editing or desk work, he said, "You don't even have a desk. Bite your tongue, young man; you're here to write."

While I was writing this book, I happened to read *Tabloid City* by Pete Hamill, one of the star writers on the staff of *The New York Post,* in the '60s and early '70s. Hamill was writing like Hemingway with one- and two-word paragraphs. I found the story confusing, but it made me realize I never really worked for a New York newspaper.

Ike Gellis look-alike Edward G. Robinson

Budd Schulberg. He wrote *The Harder They Fall* and *What Makes Sammy Run?*

Pete Hamill and Jimmy Breslin were star writers for *New York Post*. They both wrote best-selling books.

"When you're young you have no fear. You're ready to take on the world."
—Dave Anderson
Pulitzer Prize-winning columnist
The New York Times

I was never invited to join Hamill and Merchant or Vic Ziegel at Lion's Head Tavern for drinks and writing discussions in Greenwich Village. My loss. I was not a native New Yorker. I didn't reside in the city. I didn't speak the same language. Hamill died at 85 in August, 2020.

I was hardly ever in the office—none of us writers had a desk, that was true—and I seldom visited the office. Jimmy Cannon, the great sports columnist, once told me that the desk guys, the editors, are envious of those who get to cover games and travel the country on an expense account.

"They hate you to begin with," Cannon told me over dinner one night in Houston. "When you go to the office it only reminds them of how much they hate you!" He didn't mean just me, or that they hated me more than the other beat writers.

Within a month, however, Ike Gellis gave me a gift assignment, as the fourth writer covering the New York Knicks in their playoff pursuit of the first NBA championship in franchise history. I covered the playoff games against the Milwaukee Bucks, the Baltimore Bullets and the Los Angeles Lakers as the Knicks won their first NBA championship in history.

A year later, in the fall of 1970, he put me on the beat for the first year of Monday Night Football, which was the best football beat of all. No one had any idea of how big Monday Night Football would become.

One morning after I had covered a football game in Minneapolis, Gellis called me on the telephone and asked how the weather was when I arrived. "What was it doing?" he wanted to know.

"It was raining," I said.

"You didn't mention that in your advance story," growled Gellis. "A lot of our readers like to bet and they would want to know that." None more, I may add, than Ike Gellis.

"Remember to get the weather in your book," advised the great author Ernest Hemingway, who started out as a newspaper guy. Roger Kahn, one of the best writers in the sports-writing ranks, had a book with a collection of his stories called *How the Weather Was.*

A year later, Gellis sent me to spring training with the New York Mets—where I kept company as much as possible with Jimmy Cannon, while more established writers ducked him because he gave up drinking and was a royal pain in the ass as a result, sermonizing about his tee-totaling ways. I split the baseball beat with Maury Allen that spring and summer, covering the Mets to the mid-season All-Star break and then the Yankees the rest of the season. No one had a greater passion for the game of baseball than Maury Allen. He grew up on the Brooklyn Dodgers.

Jimmy Cannon and Milt Gross could be gruff with waitresses, just like Jack Nicholson in the movie *As Good As It Gets.* One night in Houston where Muhammad Ali would fight Buster Mathis, Cannon ordered a prime rib dinner. When Cannon went to the men's room, I called our waitress back to the table. "Please get his order right," I advised her. "He can get easily annoyed and you won't like that he has to say!"

Cannon came back to our table. So did the waitress. "How do you want your steak done?" she inquired.

Cannon exploded. "Prime rib is not a steak, Honey!" he hollered. Note the exclamation point in that last sentence. Then he gave her a lesson in steaks. I felt sorry for her.

Milton Gross would order coffee and finish by saying, "I want it hot-hot." He did the same with soup. Now, long into my 70s, I find myself giving the same instructions. I'll say I want it black, and the waitress wants to know if I want cream with it.

Milton Gross comes to mind...

San Diego's El Cortez Hotel where New York Mets stayed

"Ike Gellis was the world's shortest Jew" —Pete Hamill, Author, Tabloid City

Chairman of the Board: Ike Gellis, executive sports editor of *The New York Post*, props himself up in the middle, and his boss, executive editor Paul Sann is seen at far right.

*   *   *

I didn't realize at the time what a handicap I was working under. I didn't know baseball or most of the players and didn't have the connections of Dick Young, Jack Lang, Joe Trimble, Steve Jacobsen, Joe Gergen, Joe O'Day, Joe Durso and Joe Donnelley. Many of them also shared information—a peace pact so they wouldn't get scooped by the so-called competition. I never bought into that. I worked hard to get my own stories.

After I had left *The Post* and returned home to Pittsburgh in 1979, I was talking on the telephone with Dave Anderson, the Pulitzer Prize-winning sports columnist of *The New York Times*. I had just finished reading a book by St. Louis Cardinals manager Tony LaRussa, with Buzz Bissinger, called 3 *Nights in August*.

I told him how I'd been reading some good books about baseball. "I realize now that the established guys had an advantage on me, but how I never thought about that or worried about that when I was in the press box at Yankee Stadium or Shea Stadium, or covering a basketball game or hockey game at Madison Square Garden. I didn't know, for instance, what baseball players should be hitting their peak in June."

"When you're young," Anderson said, "you have no fear. You're ready to take on the world."

When I heard that Dave Anderson had died at age 87 in October of 2018, as I was researching and writing this book, I remembered what a nice man he had been, how he always wrote the right story, and how generous he was with his time and help with a young writer.

I listened and learned a lot from all the best writers. Gross often offered advice. "If it don't write easy," he liked to say, "it don't read easy."

Young said "the locker room is your office. Dress for the office. Look at how well the ballplayers dress. If you dress like the clubhouse guy they'll treat you like a clubhouse guy. When you're on the team bus or airplane you are their guest. Don't be spying on them or writing whatever off-color comments they might make. Use some journalistic judgment. If you write a critical story, show up in the locker room the next day to take the heat, even if it's your day off. Let them know you're not a hit-and-run guy."

Young and I were once the only writers who stayed in the same old hotel in San Diego as the Mets ballplayers because the other guys on the beat chose to stay at a nicer hotel on the outskirts of San Diego. We were both in bathing trunks at the hotel poolside one day, both typing stories in a pleasant surrounding when Young told me, "We're not out here on vacation. You have to stay with the team. You never know what'll happen next."

Ike Gellis seldom gave me direction or input like that and didn't mentor me about anything. He called me once in a while on the telephone and I remember every conversation.

The *New York* magazine had done an expose on how the New York Knicks gave out free tickets in the stands to some of the sports editors and writers in Manhattan. They even ran a seating chart showing which seats were allocated like that.

Suddenly, *The Post* got religion and we were not allowed to accept any freebies. The pro teams were all paying for us to travel with them—a practice that doesn't happen these days—and paying for hotels and even gave us the same "meal money" they gave their players. How about that arrangement?

Among other perks we lost at the same time was the ability to take our families to Kutsher's Country Club, a resort in New York's Catskill Mountains. That was always a great get-away and the rooms and meals were on owner Milt Kutsher.

Fellow newspapermen who enjoyed the Ike Gellis Dinner were clockwise from bottom left, Maury Allen, Stan Isaacs, Vic Ziegel, Leonard Cohen, Sid Friedlander, Jim O'Brien, Sy Horowitz. Comedian Phil Foster must have been on stage at the time. The author is the only one who's not Jewish at the round table, and the only one who's still alive.

I forget where I was, somewhere in the Midwest, when I got a call from Gellis. "Listen," he said in that raspy voice of his, "I know where Marvin Barnes is."

"Bad News" Barnes, as he was known, was a former All-America at Providence College, who wanted more money and went AWOL on the ABA's Spirits of St. Louis. No one knew where he had disappeared, except my intrepid boss.

"I'm up at Kutsher's," said Gellis, "and Marvin Barnes is here. You can't tell anyone you got that from me. I don't want anyone at the paper knowing I'm here."

Another exchange was a classic. Payola was frowned upon for disk jockeys and politicians but somehow okay for sports editors. The operators of the race tracks in New York—Belmont, Aqueduct and Yonkers Raceway in Westbury—underwrote a testimonial dinner in honor of Ike Gellis. I was among about six writers from the staff who were invited to sit at a complimentary table at a midtown hotel. Phil Foster, the comedian, was the emcee. I sat with Maury Allen, Vic Ziegel, Sid Friedlander, Stan Issacs and Sy Horowitz. Friedlander was the assistant sports editor at *The Post* and he was my main contact at the desk. He called me with assignments and to check on my whereabouts.

Ike Gellis was given a brand-new Mercedes-Benz by the track operators that night to show their gratitude for what he did on their behalf. A *Mercedes-Benz*! Talk about payola.

I came into the office a month or so later, and asked Gellis, "So how do you like your Mercedes?"

He gave me a look and said, "I wish the hell they'd throw me another dinner to pay for the upkeep on that car. Everything—like an oil and lube—costs a fortune."

* * *

A year later, he had me cover boxing, starting with the comeback fights of Muhammad Ali, and "The Fight of the Century" with Joe Frazier at Madison Square Garden. Ike Gellis was so good to me, which I am not sure I recognized at the time. Leonard Koppett called Gellis the best boss he ever had.

We had four ringside seats, first row just below the ropes. Milt Gross, our main columnist, and I occupied those seats. Gross was to my far right, and between us sat Paul Sann, our executive editor, and Ike Gellis. Nat Fleischer of *Ring* magazine was on my left. Scattered in seats about the Garden were Pete Hamill, Larry Merchant, Jose Torres, Gene Roswell and Paul Zimmerman, who all contributed stories to the March 9, 1971 issue. They were sitting 30 or more rows from ringside. Vic Ziegel, one of the best writers on the paper who previously was the boxing beat man, was working the desk that night. He was preparing for life as an editor, a position he later held at *The New York Daily News*. I recall that John Condon, the p.a. announcer for Knicks' games at Madison Square Garden and the boxing publicist, surreptitiously handed Sann a pair of leg pads for a goalie, courtesy of the New York Rangers.

Sann and Gellis both loved to bet on all sports events, and Sann had a lot to say about how things operated in the sports section.

I covered the Knicks and then the Nets, first of Rick Barry, and then of Julius "Dr. J" Erving, and then the start-up NHL franchise of the New York Islanders and a week or so here and then with the New York Rangers. I covered the New York Jets on Paul Zimmerman's day off, and did a Joe Namath story each time because Joe did not care for Coach Z. I covered the New York Giants with their own great quarterback, Fran Tarkenton.

I recall scolding Mike Lupica, a talented but fresh newcomer to the staff, when he said something critical about Gellis. "He brought you here from Boston," I said. "So don't be sniping at him."

Gellis always liked to tell me that his wife Kelly was Irish. Ike was Jewish. Just about everyone at *The Post* was Jewish, starting with the owner, Dorothy Schiff.

I loved Larry Merchant, Milt Gross, Stan Isaacs, Steve Jacobson, Joe Gergen, Vic Ziegel, Doug Smith, Dave Anderson, Gerry Ezkenazi. The Chipmunks reported diligently, wrote funny, and stood for righteousness.

Dorothy Schiff

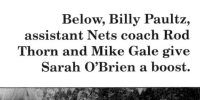

Below, Billy Paultz, assistant Nets coach Rod Thorn and Mike Gale give Sarah O'Brien a boost.

6-10 Billy Paultz carries umbrella to work.

Mike Gale

Those were the days...several members of the New York Nets, at the author's behest, conducted a basketball clinic on the cul-de-sac where he lived in Long Island's Baldwin community. They and the New York Islanders also conducted clinics in the parking lot of the nearby Baldwin Tennis Club. Jim O'Brien's 11-month-old daughter Sarah did not sharpen her basketball skills on August 7, 1974, but she was smart enough to pass on an athletic career in favor of becoming a pediatric hematologist/oncologist at Nationwide Children's Hospital in Columbus, and an associate professor in the Medical School at The Ohio State University. And now Mike Gale is gone, dead at age 70.

Milton Gross
No one worked harder than he did to get the right story

The Kansas City Chiefs were playing the San Francisco 49ers in Super Bowl LIV (54) in 2020, and I was watching the game on television with my wife Kathie in the comfort of our family room.

Milton Gross

I was thinking about Lenny Dawson and Milton Gross. Dawson, the quarterback of the Chiefs, was the hero and MVP of Super Bowl IV, played 50 years earlier at Tulane Stadium in New Orleans. Patrick Mahomes, the third-year quarterback of the Chiefs, would be the hero and MVP this time.

Surely, he knows about Lenny Dawson, but I doubt Mahomes has ever heard of Milton Gross. He was a sports columnist and nationally-syndicated writer for *The New York Post*, beginning in 1949.

I covered Super Bowl IV for *The Miami News* and moved that same year to *The New York Post* where I became a colleague of Milton Gross. He was great with newcomers and became a mentor.

I can still see him looking over his glasses with his dark eyes. They were often perched at the end of his nose. I could still envision Gross taking up a position at Dawson's dressing stall in a locker room after the game. Dawson wasn't evident yet, but Gross was going to gain and hold his spot for the post-game interview. Occasionally, he would grip the red-painted steel side of the stall. No one was going to move Milton Gross out of there. He was like Willis Reed posting up against Wilt Chamberlain, though Gross was a little guy and didn't have Reed's muscular thighs to strengthen his position.

Gross was about 5–6, the same size as Myron Cope, and just as feisty and sure of himself. Cope liked to tell everyone he had boxed in his youth. Gross grew up in Brooklyn and was proud of it. He often had a cigarette dangling from his lips, like one of the tough guys in the movie "On the Waterfront."

The media was able to go into the actual locker rooms after such big games back then; it was the start of 1970. You could describe the scene; something was always going on, hugs and hollering in the winning dressing room, heads down and disappointment in the eyes of the disenchanted losers. Scars still bloody red.

I recall Art Rooney Sr., the Steelers owner, telling me once that he'd like to have been a sportswriter if he weren't an owner. "I'd go to the losing locker room first," said Rooney. "That's where the action is."

Gross had a good idea of where the action was and he usually sought out the hero, though some of his best columns were about the defeated.

*　*　*

Joe Gergen of *Newsday*, a friendly and talented writer who I'd see at sports events in New York in the '70s, captured the spirit of Milton Gross as well as anyone in a reflection he wrote in 1990 about the sports staff of *The New York Post*. We thought we had the best sports staff of any paper in America.

"To this day, I don't know how Milton Gross did it," wrote Gergen. "As he'd find himself in a cramped room among reporters jostling for position, each eager to talk to the subject.

"Invariably this pursuit led him to hunch down close to the subject, whether it was a World Series game, the center who scored the winning basket or the heavyweight champion of the world, whisper to the athlete, and the athlete perhaps thinking himself stranded in a library would respond in hushed tones while rival newsmen (there were scant newswomen in those days), saw lips move and overheard nothing.

"After a pantomime conversation," Gergen goes on, "Gross would rise with a satisfied look on his face and depart, the recipient of a private interview in the most public of settings." I recall there was another sportswriter on *The Post* staff named Lester Bromberg, a crusty old colleague who covered boxing and would whisper in the same way to boxers he was interviewing after a fight. With Latino fighters, Bromberg would whisper in Spanish. I'm not making this up.

"If you run with the pack," Gross often said, "you'll write like the pack. I run alone."

Because I wrote for an afternoon newspaper in Miami, New York and Pittsburgh, I had later deadlines for filing stories. I would outwait the competition. I wanted to go one-on-one and was patient, if sometimes petulant with other writers.

Dick Macino, the late marketing representative at *The Pittsburgh Press*, told me once that when he was a sportswriter with another suburban newspaper, I gave him a glare when he stuck his nose and notepad into an interview session I was conducting with a ballplayer in the locker room. "There was no doubt you were pissed I dare enter the mix," Macino said. I smiled and offered a delinquent apology for my stance.

I didn't mean it.

Today, there are too many people in the clubhouse during the week and few ask questions. They are parasites. They simply stick their microphone in the face of the athlete being interviewed. They contribute nothing.

I had a good relationship with Joe Namath, owing to our similar Western Pennsylvania roots and knowing some of the same sports people. One day during practice, I was about to interview Namath in the dugout at Shea Stadium. A *New York Times* writer named Michael Strauss asked me if he could listen in on the interview. Strauss normally covered yachting or some such sophisticated sporting stuff.

"Absolutely not," I said. "Your paper comes out before mine and I don't want you beating me to the punch. I'll let you go first."

* * *

I learned a lot from Milton Gross during the three years I worked with him. Knowing I was going to cover the Nets, and then the Islanders, he suggested I buy a home near Nassau Coliseum in Uniondale, New York. So, I bought a home in Baldwin, about five miles from Nassau Coliseum. It was just as close to the only 24-hour Western Union office on Long Island. Gross lived in Rockville Centre, which abutted Baldwin at the eastern end.

I lived less than a mile from the Long Island Rail Road station in Baldwin. Rockville Centre was the next stop en route to Manhattan. It took about 45 minutes to get to Penn Station, below Madison Square Garden.

I lived just beyond the circulation coverage of *The New York Post,* so I was able to do publicity work for the Baldwin Tennis Club without having a conflict of interest. I could drive on highways to Yankee Stadium, Shea Stadium and the West Side Tennis Club, and Jones Beach.

I served as the sports editor of *The Post* Long Island edition for a year before moving back home to Pittsburgh.

One incident shows what a professional journalist Milton Gross was, right to the end. We were both present for a noon weigh-in of Muhammad Ali and

Joe Frazier at Madison Square Garden, the day before what was billed as "The Fight of the Century," set for March 8, 1971.

We had a late edition, the one most commuters would pick up on the way home from work, and I was under the gun to get the weights and what went on at the weigh-in—there was always something said when Ali was at any event. Even lunch.

I typed out my report in the office of boxing publicist John Condon—also the p.a. announcer at Knicks' games at the Garden—and Gross stood by me and read my report—as I was writing it—over the telephone back to our office on South Street in Lower Manhattan. A writer at the office would type out what Gross was giving him.

These days, of course, I could "text" the office with my report and it would take a few minutes to do so.

Gross wasn't too big to handle such a pedestrian task. He had started out as a copyboy for a Brooklyn newspaper so he knew the routine. He was looking out for the best interest of *The New York Post* and his younger colleague. "I want to write the kind of column that they (the editors) will want to play on the back page of the paper," said Gross.

The back page of the newspaper was, of course, the front page of the sports section. It is still like that. Dorothy Schiff, the owner of *The Post*, once considered dropping the entire sports section. Then she conducted a survey and learned that most readers bought the paper to read the sports section.

Milton Gross was the consummate pro. I remember him telling me how it was better in the old days when you traveled by train with the teams for games in Philadelphia, Pittsburgh, Baltimore and D.C. "You got to spend more time up close with the ballplayers," he said. "You got to know them better." Even when teams weren't traveling by train, Gross would regularly join athletes for breakfast and lunch and get them to tell stories about their formative years, some learning situation or experience from the past. He filled his notebook with such reflections.

Because he wrote for an afternoon newspaper, he had to have a different story than the morning newspapers. He had a formula that served him well and would work even today. It is more challenging today because few reporters get to travel on the airplane or chartered buses with the ballclub.

His columns were divided into three parts. He would start his column with a story that the athlete had shared with him earlier, then the second part of the column would be about what the athlete accomplished that day or night, and the bottom third would be what the athlete and his coach said after the event.

He wrote a wonderful column about Cazzie Russell after Russell had led the Knicks to victory in a playoff. He started off by telling you that Russell had returned during the off-season to his boyhood home of Chicago. While there, Russell re-visited a shoe shine stand where he had worked as a kid. The man he worked for was still there, and Cazzie asked him if he could shine shoes for him for awhile and did so. The point Gross made with the story that Russell, even though he was making a lot of money playing for the Knicks, had not forgotten his roots.

Then Coach Red Holzman and Russell offered their post-game reflections.

I wish I had fallen back on the Milton Gross formula when I blew the only magazine deadline in my life. I had just gotten out of a 21-month tour in the U.S. Army, the last ten months in Alaska, and I was assigned by *Sport* magazine to do a story in 1967 on Lem Barney, an outstanding cornerback for the Detroit Lions. I had traveled to Detroit and interviewed Barney, Mel Farr his teammate, Joe Schmidt, the coach, and Bill Ford, the owner, son of Edsel Ford and grandson of the great Henry Ford, and GM Russ Thomas. For whatever reason, I was unable to write the story. Gross was a regular contributor to *Sport* and other magazines. I still feel badly about that failure on my part. I should have fallen back on how Gross would have done it.

*   *   *

Most teams back then had former newspapermen as their publicists and those men understood and appreciated the needs of the newspaper reporters. This was especially true in New York where many newspapers had gone out of business, leaving many sportswriters without jobs. They'd pass along story ideas, set up exclusive interviews. Nowadays, their job is to keep you at a distance, mostly to keep the head coach and stars protected and happy.

Gross gained respect for his strong work ethics through the years. "He got off his duff and went to work," said Red Smith, a sports columnist for *The New York Times*. "He was always hustling. It wasn't by luck that he was always there for the big story."

Gross was one of the first sports writers to champion Black athletes, such as Jackie Robinson, Willie Mays, Don Newcombe, Joe Black and, especially, Floyd Patterson. He wrote about the special challenges they faced as Blacks and Latinos. He wrote with empathy and got them to share their innermost feelings.

In his obituary, Sam Goldaper wrote in *The New York Times* that Gross "was one of the first to portray the human aspect of athletes."

Gross died of heart failure at age 65 at Mercy Hospital in Rockville Centre. I remember going to his funeral service on a Friday afternoon at a synagogue in that community. His viewing was at the Gutterman's Funeral Home there. Most of our staff was present and so were sports writers and sports officials. Monte Irvin, a Hall of Fame baseball player for the New York Giants, came as a representative of Major League Baseball. But where were the athletes Gross had written about favorably all those years?

I believe that Vic Ziegel offered a kind and humorous eulogy, and some others such as Stan Isaacs of *Newsday* offered their thoughts. I'd never been to a service like this where those in attendance were encouraged to come up and speak.

I recall talking to Jane Gross, the daughter of Milton Gross. She was with *Sports Illustrated* but would later cover the Nets for *Newsday*. She is still recognized as the first female reporter to enter a men's basketball locker room after a game. That was the Knicks' dressing room, but I would see her later in the Nets' locker room after most games. She was little, like her dad, but never got lost in the crowd.

Milt was also survived by a son, Michael, a distinguished author these days. Milt's wife Estelle survived him as well.

At her dad's funeral service, I remember Jane telling me it didn't seem right for *The New York Post* to publish that day when Milton Gross's column was no longer in the paper. I know she wasn't serious, but I understood her feelings.

I recall another time when she was in a van or bus, traveling from an airport to the Nets' hotel on the road, and she was swearing to pepper her conversation. I scolded her gently afterward. "You don't have to swear to be accepted as one of the guys," I told her. "Have you heard any of them swearing when you're around?"

I cared about her and talked to her often. I think that's all she was seeking. Hey, she was the daughter of Milton Gross. She'd gone with her family to spring training, and that's how she got interested in being a sportswriter. Robin Herman was a female sportswriter for *The New York Times* then, and she covered hockey when I was also covering hockey. Herman won the right to enter the locker room after a game, and several of the players, especially Phil Esposito, started wearing robes and white towels around their midsections. I did my best to respect and assist Robin Herman and Jane Gross. They earned their spurs.

Yes, I learned a lot from Milton Gross and remain grateful to this day for his guidance.

Milton Gross with his daughter Jane.

New York Post delivery truck promoting Milton Gross, its lead sports columnist.

Michael Jordan
MJ put on quite a show
for my friend Adam Ference

My young friend Adam Ference told me he wanted to get in touch with Arizona Congresswoman Gabrielle Giffords.

When Adam asked me how he could do this, at first, I failed to make the connection. I thought it might be a nice gesture, but after a few seconds I realized why Adam had some special insights to offer Giffords about what had happened to her.

On January 8, 2011, Giffords was one of 18 people shot at a constituents' meeting at a supermarket parking lot in Casas Adobes, outside of Tucson. She was shot in the head in an assassination attempt and mass shooting. The shooter was a 22-year-old man named Jared Lee Loughner who had been fixated on Senator Giffords for some time, and had been stalking her.

Senator Giffords survived the shooting but six others died. Loughner was arrested and wounded by police on the scene. Loughner, who was deemed mentally incompetent, was convicted of murder and sentenced to life plus 140 years in federal prison.

I'd forgotten Adam's history, our history, and that he, too, was once shot in the head by a similarly-crazed young man. That happened 12 years earlier when Adam was a 16-year-old junior at Serra Catholic High School in McKeesport. He was shot in the back of his head while riding on a school bus from his home in Clairton. He can still hear the gunshot, feel the thud in his head, and wonder why or how he managed to live to tell his story. The bullet tore a hole in his skull and lodged in his brain. The young man who shot him then shot and killed himself.

"They had me walk off the bus," Adam recalled when we spoke on the telephone on Saturday, April 18, 2020. "They took me by ambulance to McKeesport Hospital, and then life-flighted me from there to Presbyterian Hospital in Oakland."

Adam at age 17

He was not out of danger. Besides his head wound, his right eye was swollen and covered by a large bandage. There's still a thin slice in his scalp where hair no longer grows. "They had to cut out a piece of my brain to remove the bullet," said Adam. We now have the kind of relationship where I could say, "That explains a lot about you."

I think I heard him laugh, or at least snicker.

That was sort of another bond we shared, besides our love for basketball and admiration for Michael Jordan. Just before my third birthday, I fell out of a fast-moving Iron City Cab when it swerved on wet railway tracks on the floor-board Glenwood Bridge and struck the top of my head on the top of the railing overlooking the Monongahela River. Doctors at Mercy Hospital feared for my life, and it required 48 stitches—one for each state in this country in 1945, I'd later tell people—to close the wounds. I had suffered a fractured skull, a setback I can now blame for my forgetfulness in my mid-70s.

I still have a coin-sized scar on my upper lip, hidden for the most part by a white mustache, and a bump on the backside of that lip where a plastic surgeon named Dr. John Gaisford did some handiwork a few years after the accident. I was reunited with Dr. Gaisford when I visited him at the West Penn Hospital where he was the director of the burn unit. I took my daughter Sarah, then a high school student who was working on a paper about "living skin" developed in a petri dish at Harvard to patch burn wounds.

"I was just training back then," said Dr. Gaisford of his handiwork with my lip. "You were one of my guinea pigs." How comforting to know.

Adam's father, Mike Ference, who was a regional sales representative for Sysco, called the Pittsburgh Steelers' office and asked if any of the players might stop by Presbyterian University Hospital to cheer up his son. Mike also mentioned that his son was a big fan of Michael Jordan.

Pat Hanlon, more recently the vice-president for communications with the New York Giants, was an assistant to Dan Edwards in the Steelers' publicity office at the time. Pat was one of my proteges, my first hire when I was the assistant athletic director for public relations, at Pitt in the mid-80s. I recommended Hanlon to Joe Gordon, the former publicist of the Steelers who was serving as an administrative assistant to team president Dan Rooney.

Hanlon knew I was also the editor of *Street and Smith's Basketball*, the No. 1-selling annual of its kind in the country. He had accompanied me to NBA All-Star Games in Charlotte and Chicago, sleeping on the floor or couch in the room we shared. He knew I had connections in the NBA. I told Pat I'd see what I could do regarding Michael Jordan, but I wasn't promising I could deliver on this request.

After all, Michael Jordan knew me, but we weren't exactly close pals or confidants. "First, I will do what I can do," I told Hanlon. Michael Jordan liked to remind me that he was not on the *Street and Smith's* High School All-America team going into his senior season in Wilmington, North Carolina. After all, Jordan had been the star that summer of the Five Star Basketball Camp at Robert Morris in Pittsburgh, my hometown.

Our magazine had gone to press prior to Jordan jumping off the schoolboy basketball charts with his outstanding play. His daily performances on the Moon Township campus were out of this world, basketball buff Jack McKay told me. I blamed the oversight and snub on Dave Krider, an Indiana scholastic sportswriter who compiled the list for us. Michael told me he went with his mother to an Eckerd's Drug Store—next to a super market, he said—in Wilmington to get a copy of the new *Street and Smith's*, only to discover that his name was not on the pre-season All-America high school listing.

I visited Adam Ference at the hospital, which was just across the street from Pitt Stadium, where I had an office with a view of the top of the hospital and the façade of the Pitt Medical School. He was wearing a Chicago Bulls' ballcap perched atop his bandaged head, and he was wearing a Michael Jordan T-shirt. I don't know if he was wearing Nike AirJordans under the covers.

I took him some surplus photos I had in my files of Michael Jordan, and a book about the Chicago Bulls.

I gave him a copy of the 1989-90 *Street and Smith's Basketball* that had Michael Jordan on the cover. I was the first editor of any of the *Street and Smith's* sports annuals to put a black ballplayer on the cover to be distributed in the South.

I convinced the stuffy questioning powers-that-be at Conde Nast Publications on New York's Madison Avenue that Michael Jordan could and should be on the cover across the country. We had regional covers at the time. Conde Nast also publishes *Vogue, Glamour, GQ, Self* and other much more important publications and let me run my own show. Plus, they never questioned my expense accounts in over 30 years with the company.

I remember there were four cheerleader-type young women in Adam's hospital room, including Adam's attractive friend, Renee Lex. His dad was there, too. As I am writing this in the spring of 2020, Adam and Renee have been married for 25 years, have four adult children, and reside in Peters Township, a few miles from my home in Washington County. He never felt sorry for himself or wondered "Why me?" In fact, he prided himself on saying it was the launching pad for so many good things the rest of his life.

Jordan sent a pair of his University of North Carolina shorts that he wore under his Bulls' shorts in NBA games, and signed the shorts for Adam. He also sent a signed photograph, and a ballcap. Tim Hallam, still the senior public and media relations director of the Bulls, arranged all this and told me—but not Adam—that Michael would welcome him if we could get to a Bulls' game in Cleveland. Hallam was a blond bespectacled man, one of the best in the p.r. business. Steve Schanwald, then the Bulls' vice-president for marketing and broadcasting, helped Hallam in the effort to get Michael Jordan to reach out to Adam.

Hallam told me that Jordan saw a needy child in every city the Bulls visited. It was the same way, Fudge Brown of the Miami Dolphins' public relations office told me, for Danny Marino, the Dolphins' Hall of Fame quarterback. "There's a Make-A-Wish Kid in every city who wants to meet Danny Marino," Ms. Brown said.

As I was saying goodbye to Adam, he put his arm around my shoulders and gave me a hug and thanked me for everything. It was an early Christmas gift.

* * *

I called Adam a few times after he returned home from the hospital, and one day he was so excited when he picked up the phone. "Mr. O'Brien! Mr. O'Brien! I'm

Mike Ference

Adam Ference got an autograph from Bulls' coach Phil Jackson.

Red Holzman once told me that the true measure of a star was the ability to make the people around him look good. Michael Jordan still needs to learn that lesson." —Phil Jackson
From his book *Sacred Hoops*
with Hugh Delehanty

Photo courtesy of Michael Jordan

Michael Jordan stands tall at extreme right, with Adam Ference directly below in team photo at Jordan's summer basketball camp.

hyper-ventilating today!" he began. "You won't believe what came in the mail today! Michael Jordan sent me his game shorts! He signed his name on the front of them. Oh, man, I'm going to wear them to gym class tomorrow!"

Adam and his family attended a Pitt vs. Arizona basketball game at the Civic Arena as my guests. Lute Olson, the classy head coach of the Wildcats, was told about Adam in advance. Olson came out of the visitors' locker room after a disappointing loss, carrying a manila envelope under his arm. As he approached Adam, he pulled several photographs of him and his team he had autographed for Adam and gave them to him, and talked to him before he did his post-game radio show back to Tucson.

Jordan also offered Adam a scholarship to his summer basketball camp in Chicago, if his parents could get him there. I recall Adam telling me that Jordan said you should never practice a shot you aren't going to attempt in a game. I think about that every time I see a Pitt basketball player attempting a dunk in the pre-game warmup.

Whenever Adam was advancing on me in a pickup game—we were the same size so we were often matched—I waited until he made this little swing move to his right, a maneuver he picked up a MJ's camp—to release a jumper.

The best player in our game was Myron Brown, whose jersey is retired at Slippery Rock University, and who had a brief stay with the Minnesota Timberwolves and with some foreign fives all over the world. He had been the second-round draft pick of the Wolves in 1991, the 34th player to be picked. Brown is a big fan of Adam Ference. I once told a fiend of Brown that I had guarded Myron once or twice in our games. "You *didn't guard* Myron Brown," the man assured me. "He could have had you for lunch."

Former Pirates' pitchers Bob Friend and Nellie Briles, sit with Adam and Mike Ference at the annual gathering at the wall that remains from Forbes Field

I admit that's the gospel truth.

Adam and his dad attended an annual gathering at the wall that remains of Forbes Field to celebrate the anniversary of the 7th game of the 1960 World Series. Seated left to right in accompanying photo are Bob Friend, Adam Ference, Nellie Briles and Mike Ference. Friend and Briles, both now deceased, were Pirates pitchers of note.

> **To Pat Hanlon, senior vice-president for communications of New York Giants, and Jim O'Brien, sports author:**
>
> *"I remain grateful for what you guys did for me way back then. You didn't know me from Adam—forgive me for that one—yet you reached out to help a kid who was hurting badly. Next thing I know, some Steelers are visiting me in the hospital. Then Michael Jordan is smiling at me, and putting his arm around my shoulder. That's pretty good for a kid from Clairton."*
> —Adam Ference
> April 12, 2020

*   *   *

In checking my files when I was writing this story, I found out that Pat Hanlon of the Steelers' public relations department had visited Adam the day after his dad had requested such a visit. Hanlon brought Louis Lipps and Warren Williams to visit Adam. "He cheered us up," said Hanlon. "He's quite a kid and he's got great spirit."

When I was checking facts with him for this story, Adam repeated his "thank you" to me and Pat Hanlon about how we came through for him after he was wounded.

Adam and I remain connected. We often guarded one another when we played basketball with our over-the-hill gang on Saturday and Sunday mornings. Adam is now nearing 50 and I am 78, and no one in our game is more aggressive about his game than Adam, and no one is more over the hill than me. I gave up the ghost at age 70 and no one tried to get me to change my mind about retirement from the courts. I now play pickle-ball, a game for the ages. And the aged.

Often, when Adam would attack me—trash-talking all the way like a kid from the Clairton outdoor courts—I wished I had never arranged for him to attend Michael Jordan's basketball camp. "I'm going to light you up!" Adam would warn me.

Adam gets his hair cut close to his skull, just a dark shadow, and you can still see a jagged scar on the back of his head where a .38-millimeter bullet penetrated his skull. He even sent me a copy of an x-ray of his head taken after his surgery. There is a circular line where his skull was cut and laid back like a flap so the surgeon could get to the bullet in his brain. The hole where the bullet penetrated the skull was still evident.

I had arranged, without telling Adam, for him to meet Michael Jordan in the visitors' locker room before the game. Tim Hallam of the Bulls and Bob Price, the public relations director of the Cavs, had made all the arrangements for us.

Jordan seldom went out for the pre-game shoot-around, preferring not to cause courtside commotion. Mike Ference missed a few turns on the road and I feared we were going to be late and miss seeing Michael Jordan. We made it in time, and Jordan was expecting us. He could not have been more cordial or generous with his time.

"Michael's very good about these things," said Hallam. "On this road trip, it's been a 'Disaster of the Week' tour for him. He has seen some child in every city who's had some sort of setback or illness."

En route to Richfield, I asked Adam why he liked Michael Jordan so much. "When I think of Michael Jordan," he said, "what I like about him is he goes beyond the court."

Adam's father was trying to take a photo of Adam and MJ, but fumbling with the camera, like he didn't know what he was doing. He was understandably nervous. Jordan asked Adam's father to hand him the camera and he showed him how to work it.

"I still have that photo somewhere," Adam admitted to me when we shared coffee and bagels at Panera's in McMurray, Pennsylvania in the summer of 2018. "Our heads are chopped off. It's terrible, but it's still a keepsake."

Adam didn't have a clue about what was going on when we entered the Coliseum about two hours before tip-off. I said I had to go to the visitors' clubhouse for a while and asked Adam and his dad to wait for me in the nearby corridor.

The Bulls' locker room is always an interesting scene before a game because Jordan is always the last one to dress. He does not go out early for the shoot-around. He says it always causes too much commotion and it makes it difficult for his teammates to get ready.

So all the Bulls were in their red, white and black uniforms and warm-up suits, about to go out on the court. Jordan had Walkman gear strapped on his glistening shaved head, listening to music, and was watching a scouting tape of the Cavaliers on a nearby monitor. He was in his own world.

He stopped what he was doing to come out and say hello to Adam Ference. Jordan looked great, wearing a black/brown designer jersey—it had an expensive look about it—and black slacks, and shoes that shone as brightly as his bald head and dark eyes. He moved easily and eagerly, through the hallways to where Adam and his dad were waiting. The vision in Adam's right eye was still blurred and limited—it frustrated him at times when he was reading or playing basketball—and sometimes the eye looked dull and lazy. But both of his eyes lit up like a Christmas tree as he recognized Michael Jordan coming toward him. He couldn't believe his eyes.

"Mr. Jordan, I just want to thank you for all the things you've done for me," said Adam excitedly, "and all the things you've sent me. I want you to know how much this means to me."

Jordan just smiled in response, then said, "Hey, I'm just happy you've recovered, that you're going to be okay, and I hear you're playing basketball. That's great! Howya feeling?"

Adam told him how things were going, and then posed for pictures with his hero. His father, understandably nervous, was having some problems with the settings on his camera. "You need to advance it again," said Jordan, helpfully. "You've got to double-pump it. I know about these things."

Of course, who knows more about double-pumping than Michael Jordan, or more about nervous fans with cameras? He signed a Bulls' pennant Adam had brought with him.

"You take care of yourself now," Jordan said as a parting shot. As Michael Jordan was about to return to the clubhouse, we all thanked him for what he had done.

"I just want to thank you," Jordan responded, "for giving me the opportunity to meet this young man."

We thought to ourselves, "is he for real? Does he ever not say the right thing?"

Phil Jackson, the coach of the Chicago Bulls and an old friend from his playing days with the New York Knicks, came over and talked to Adam, and signed an autograph and posed for a photo. "Michael is amazing," Jackson said, "but he is for real."

We had time to grab some dinner at a place in the rarified heights of Richfield Coliseum, and as we were standing in line to be seated, Michael Ference thought aloud, "I just remembered when Adam was in the hospital and asked me if Michael Jordan might call him. And now this!"

*   *   *

Our seats were high in the end zone, but in the middle, so the view wasn't bad. An what a performance Jordan put on. We may have witnessed the greatest game in Michael Jordan's career, though he certainly had more memorable games because of what was at stake.

The Bulls beat the Cavs 117–113 in overtime. Jordan had a career high of 69 points, a career high of

18 rebounds, plus six assists, four steals, one blocked shot. He hit 62% of his shots from the field, 91 per cent of his free throws (21 of 23) and he played 50 minutes. It was an ever longer night for the Cavs' Craig Ehlo, who was guarding Jordan most of the game. There were over 22,000 at Richfield Coliseum that night.

"I didn't think about being tired," Jordan said after the game, "because I wanted to win the game. I've been in that situation where I've scored a lot of points and we lost and I didn't want that to happen. So I kept pushing and telling myself, 'Don't stop. Don't stop. Keep going.' You feel better when you win."

It was one of Michael Jordan's greatest games. "He should adopt me and take me with him to all his games," said Adam Ference.

It was the best performance I had witnessed since I had a courtside seat along the press row at Atlanta's Superdome (Feb. 25, 1977) when "Pistol Pete" Maravich scored 68 points for the New Orleans Jazz against the New York Knicks, as Walt Frazier and Earl Monroe did their best to stop him. It was an NBA scoring record for a guard at the time. Until Jordan did his thing in Richfield for us. There are some great highlights of Maravich's game on YouTube that you can still view on your computer.

That afternoon at the hotel next to the Superdome, I told Knicks' coach Red Holzman what a great day I had, eating a shrimp cocktail and cheeseburger in my hotel room, and watching "One Flew Over the Cuckoo's Nest" with Jack Nicholson, on the television.

Red replied, "Yeah, this would be a great life if it weren't for the damn games!"

His father, Mike, had invited me to accompany him and his son to visit the Rock & Roll Hall of Fame in Cleveland, and then the NBA's 50th anniversary All-Star Game in Cleveland on February 9, 1997. We could walk from the Hall of Fame to the Cavaliers' home arena. All but three of the NBA's 50 greatest players were present that day. Jerry West was not allowed to fly by airplane at the time, Shaquille O'Neal did not come and Pete Maravich had died.

Photos by Jim O'Brien

Adam Ference at Panera's Restaurant in McMurray, Pa.

Mike Ference makes a point with John Garry and Larry O'Brien of WTAE Radio's "O'Brien and Garry Show."

Ron Harper had a different story

Adam Ference told me in April of 2020 that he had become a friend of Ron Harper, a former standout in the NBA, and how they played golf on occasion at Firestone Country Club in Akron and once at Oakmont County Club, two internationally famed courses. Harper had played with five teams in 15 seasons in the NBA and was on five championship teams during that time.

Harper, who was from Dayton, was the No. 1 draft choice of the Cleveland Cavaliers in 1986. He played for the Cavs for three seasons, then the Los Angeles Clippers, the Chicago Bulls and the Los Angeles Lakers until 2001.

"I told Ron about my experience with Michael Jordan," said Ference, "and Ron told me he attended that game when Jordan scored 69 points.

"Ron said he spoke to Jordan at court-side before the game began, and he told him he didn't care for the Cavs' Craig Ehlo. 'Light up Ehlo!' Harper said. So Harper said, 'It was me—not you—who was the main reason Jordan scored 69 points that night!' "

Jeff Carlick

Magic Johnson and Ron Harper maneuver for position under the hoop.

Freddie Lewis was a floor leader
for the Pacers, Pros and
Spirits of St. Louis

Freddie Lewis had a frightened look the last time I saw him, a worried look in his dark eyes. The skin on his face was as taut as onionskin paper. He did not look like the Freddie Lewis I knew better than most ABA players in his prime. There were deep wrinkles forming hoods over his eyebrows. Something was amiss.

Lewis had been a classmate of my wife Kathie Churchman at McKeesport High School, Class of '61, just east of Pittsburgh, and she had told me that everyone in her class liked Lewis. He was one of the most popular people in her school. I played off that relationship when I first met Freddie Lewis of the Indiana Pacers.

I handed her the phone to say hello during one of my conversations with her former classmate.

Lewis had told his teammates they could trust me, that I was okay, and that was particularly important in the case of Roger Brown, who trusted few individuals.

Julius Erving was regarded as the face of the ABA for his engaging manner, well-spoken way, and, most of all, his high-flying heroics, but, for me anyway, Freddie Lewis was the face of the ABA. He was the only one to start out in the NBA, play all nine years of the ABA's existence and finish up in the NBA. No one else can make such a claim. It was a handsome face, easy to break into a smile, a smile still full of bright white teeth.

He was an MVP in an ABA All-Star Game and in the ABA playoffs. He played in four All-Star Games and quarterbacked the Pacers to three ABA championships.

Frederick Lewis could play and he liked me. He was my key to the clubhouse of the Indiana Pacers, no matter where they might be playing. Who could ask for more?

He had a smile for everyone in those days. This time, as he stood just in front of a raised platform stage at Bankers Life Fieldhouse on June 25, 2018, he forced a smile. He steadied himself by holding onto the back of a chair that his friend Julius Erving had been sitting in moments before Freddie appeared, in the company of his last employer in the ABA, Dan Silna of the Spirits of St. Louis.

A man, all six feet of him, who was always in command of every basketball floor he ever moved on, looked lost.

"Freddie was always one of my favorites," said Silna, who made more money than anybody in the ABA, and used some of it to buy anniversary rings for all the players in attendance. Dr. J.'s chair was Freddie's anchor.

Freddie Lewis and Dan Silna, the floor leader and owner of the Spirits of St. Louis.

Lewis looked like a spirit of himself. He was bent over. He told me he was suffering from spinal stenosis, a curvature of the spine that sometimes accompanies advanced age. In fact, Freddie Lewis was in a wheelchair when they had a parade of over 140 former ABA players across the floor of the Fieldhouse to begin the program of the 50th anniversary of the founding of the ABA for the 1967–68 season.

I'd been reading books and viewing documentaries about the Civil War, and the parade of ABA players reminded me of images of the soldiers returning home after too many battles.

"I have arthritis in my lower back," he continued, "and I am in pain a great deal of the time. It's still a problem for me." Among the many images that remain in my mind from that dinner and program that night in Indianapolis are the sight of William "Bird" Averitt dragging the left side of his body as he boldly and proudly marched at his own pace in that parade of ABA alumni, the sight of "Big George" McGinnis getting help to ascend the stairs to that stage, and the sight of an old friend, Freddie Lewis, in that wheelchair and holding onto Dr. J's chair as we were reunited for the first time in over 10 years. We also saw each other at the ABA's 30th anniversary reunion, also in Indianapolis.

"I didn't recognize many of the people," said Lewis. "Just about everybody had changed. Seeing all the guys meant a lot to me. And now more of them are gone. I've lost too many teammates. That hurts, too."

I was sitting at a front row table hosted by Dick Tinkham, a well-known and respected attorney in Indianapolis, who was one of the owners of the Pacers in their ABA glory days. He, too, was bent over, suffering from multiple sclerosis, his chin hovering over the china on the table. His wife was looking after him. Tinkham died at age 86 of MS on October 14, 2018.

When I mentioned Bird Averitt and all the bad stuff that had happened to him since his playing days, Freddie said, "I feel for him. That Bird could fly."

When I told him I had seen and talked to Charlie Williams at a reunion of the Pittsburgh Pipers 1968 ABA championship team, Freddie said, "Sweet Charlie! He was a cool operator and a good guy. He was quick and you had to be careful with the ball whenever he guarded you. He'd steal you blind. He was a good guy. We were teammates in Memphis. I'm glad to hear he's doing well."

I asked him if it had been difficult for him to come back home to play against the Pipers and Condors with such small crowds at the Civic Arena.

"I always thought more people should have come out to support the team." Freddie must have forgotten about those sparse crowds because in 2006 he came back home and was an owner and general manager for the Pittsburgh Xplosion in a league that operated under the name of the American Basketball Association, but it was a poor imitation of the ABA, and then the Continental Basketball Association before the franchise folded in 2008. Armon Gilliam of Bethel Park, one of the coaches, died at age 47 in 2011 after playing in a pickup basketball game at LA Fitness in Bridgeville.

I recall having lunch with Lewis and another Pittsburgh basketball sensation, Kenny Durrett in 1999 at Atria's Restaurant & Tavern in Mt. Lebanon. Durrett died two years later, at age 52 of a heart attack.

Old friends Freddie Lewis and Kenny Durrett get together with author for lunch at Atria's Restaurant & Tavern in Mt. Lebanon.

Jim O'Brien

I didn't know it at the time, but I later learned from Lewis that he and Dr. J were good friends, and had remained in touch through the years. "I went to his mom's funeral in Roosevelt, New York," Lewis told me when we spoke at mid-afternoon, June 19, 2020, over two years later.

"Al and I were the only players there," allowed Lewis. Like me, Freddie had gotten forgetful. He was having a tough time coming up with Al's last name.

"Was it Al Skinner?" I asked him.

"Yes, Al Skinner," he said.

I knew that Al Skinner had followed Julius Erving at Roosevelt High School and at the University of Massachusetts, and had been a teammate on the New York Nets' championship team of 1976, a team I covered for *The New York Post*. Al Skinner was the kind of man who would show up at the funeral of a friend's mom. He was later the head coach at Boston College where he brought class to the Chestnut Hill, Massachusetts campus. His No. 30 is retired at UMass, where another of his teammates was a guard named Rick Pitino.

Skinner also played for the New Jersey Nets, the Detroit Pistons and the Philadelphia 76ers. An odd footnote to Skinner's career is that he is the only player to be listed DNP (Did Not Play) for both teams in one game in NBA history.

"I know Dr. J appreciated us being there," said Lewis. "I love The Doctor. He's always been good and kind to me and my family."

Freddie has two sons, Benjamin, and Ramsey, yeah Ramsey Lewis, same name as the great jazz musician. Now 56 and 54 respectively, Freddie said they had been treated well when they met Dr. J.

Lewis laughed when I asked him if any of his children were living with him. He told me their ages. He'd been divorced from his wife and their mother for quite some time. Her name is Inez Lewis and they were married for 13 years. "We're okay with each other now," said Freddie. "We talk about once a week."

*   *   *

The ABA had a lot of questionable characters in its ranks, but it also had some of the classiest competitors you would ever want to meet. I was listening to my favorite country singer Garth Brooks singing "The Dance" and "If Tomorrow Never Comes," and I was thinking about Freddie Lewis.

FREDDIE LEWIS

INDIANA PACERS

AMERICAN BASKETBALL ASSOCIATION

"You have to compete and compete and compete, and then you have to compete some more."
—Garth Brooks On making his way in the music world

*　*　*

I had talked to him on the telephone earlier that day, for the second time in three weeks, and said I would be calling him once again to tie up any loose ends. He said that would be fine.

I talked to him four times altogether.

The first time I called him, he didn't seem like or sound like Freddie Lewis. He'd always been upbeat, cheerful, eager to talk, and he just wasn't into it this time. I felt like a stranger calling out of the blue, and he seemed like a stranger singing the blues. There was ennui on his part, disinterest. I had to stoke some of the old fire.

He told me about some of his disappointments with the Pacers, the new management that could care less about Freddie Lewis, their refusal to retire his jersey number (14) to go up in the rafters of the Bankers Life Fieldhouse along with his former teammates, Mel Daniels, Roger Brown and George McGinnis, as well as a Pacer of a different generation, Reggie Miller. Bob "Slick" Leonard, his coach, has also been inducted into the Basketball Hall of Fame.

"They said something about wanting to just have Hall of Famers up there," said Freddie.

Reflecting on the glory days of the Indiana Pacers, Bob Leonard said, "Freddie was our steadiest performer and leader in the playoffs."

On another occasion, Leonard reflected: "Beer was a quarter, and the fans came early to get themselves ready for the action." On occasion, they booed Lewis whenever they thought he was being played ahead of Indiana favorite Rick Mount, a streak-shooting guard who had starred at Purdue. What were they thinking? But it still hurts.

Freddie had something to say about Slick Leonard. "When he dies, they should donate his body to science so they could find out how he managed to live so long."

Another great ABA point guard and coach, Larry Brown smiles when he reflects on those ABA days. "If you didn't have a fight in an ABA game, you weren't competing," said Brown.

Freddie Lewis was always competing. He was drafted and signed by the NBA Cincinnati Royals after an All-WAC first-team career at Arizona State University, and he played behind Oscar Robertson, "the Big O," and learned how to lead a pro team from the best in the business.

"Oscar took me under his wings and he taught me a lot," said Lewis. "He taught me how to handle situations instead of running all over the court helter-skelter."

He mentioned that it had bothered him to hear of the deaths, way too young of Moses Malone (age 60) and Maurice Lucas (58), and in the past year of Ron Thomas (67) and Les "Big Game" Hunter (77), and especially the more recent passing of Mike Storen (84).

"Storen and I started out together with the Cincinnati Royals," said Freddie. "Mike was in sales and marketing with the Royals. I was the first player he signed when he became the general manager of the Indiana Pacers.

"Oscar told him to sign Roger Brown as well, and we became the foundation for those great Pacers' teams. We both signed two-year no-cut contracts. Mike was my man. He picked up Mel Daniels for our second season. When he became one of the owners of the Memphis franchise, he made deals to get me and Mel and Roger Brown. None of us were happy about how the Pacers got rid of us. Then Mel got hurt, and Memphis needed a center and they traded me early in the season (after six games) to the Spirits of St. Louis in exchange for a center, Tom Owens. "I was so happy when I moved on to the Spirits of St. Louis. I was asked to make sure Marvin Barnes stayed out of trouble. I was told to monitor his movements. I was like a brother to Moses Malone and Maurice Lucas.

"Mike Storen was the best at what he did."

Leonard and Lewis both remember the first training camp for the Pacers. Over 160 candidates showed up, but most of them weren't good enough to play pro basketball on any level. Only seven survived the tryout, not enough to hold a scrimmage at the end of the camp.

"I often run into guys who ask me if I remember them," said Leonard. "I tell them I don't remember them. Then they tell me they were at that first training camp or tryout. They tell me they were the last player cut. It's always the last player cut. There was no last player cut. They cut themselves."

* * *

There was a headline in a 1975 issue of *The Sporting News* that read: **Script Set for Spirits and Lewis**, with the subhead **Fabulous Freddie.**

Against the New York Nets, a team that had won 12 straight games from the Spirits during the 1974–75 season, Lewis directed his team to four straight victories in the playoffs—the first time all season the Spirits had won that many games in succession.

Lewis averaged 25 points in the five games against the Nets, and in the fifth game, he scored the Spirits' last 10 points in a span of 1:51, including the game-winning jump shot with three seconds showing on the scoreboard clock.

Lewis scored the game-winning points in many games for the Pacers, especially in the playoffs.

FREDDIE LEWIS OF MCKEESPORT, PA.

* * *

The second telephone conversation with Freddie Lewis went much better. It started like the first, with stretches of uneasy silence, false starts, almost stutters-steps. I couldn't make out what he was saying to his mother, but I knew she was replying. Then Lewis lightened up and told me about the highlights of his pro career.

They were many. He was the captain of the Pacers when they won three ABA championships, in 1970, 1972 and 1973. He was the MVP in the 1972 ABA playoffs and he was the MVP in the 1975 ABA All-Star Game in San Antonio.

Lewis' line for that All-Star Game included 26 points, 10 assists, two steals, five rebounds in 33 minutes of a 151–124 victory for the East.

"I was playing with some of the greats in that game," said Lewis. "Guys like Gilmore, McGinnis, Issel, Gervin, Moses, Louie Dampier, James Silas, Marvin Barnes, Ralph Simpson, Mack Calvin. Check the roster and see who was in that game."

I did as Lewis suggested, and saw that Stew Johnson of Clairton was in that All-Star Game. "Stew and I played against each other in high school," said Lewis, "and we played in some summer games together. I liked Stew.

"I also look back and remember when we beat the New York Nets in four straight games in the ABA playoffs in 1975. We dropped the first game and then won the next four. We won a close one (108–107) and I scored the game-winning basket in the fifth and final game of the series."

His teammates on that St. Louis unit included Maurice Lucas, Marvin Barnes, Gus Gerard, Steve Jones and Mike Barr. It had a Pittsburgh flavor because

Mike Storen

Oscar Robertson

Albert Hall

Former Pitt star Melvin Bennett gets into scuffle with Maurice Lucas and Marvin Barnes of Spirits of St. Louis.

Lucas was from Schenley High School, Gerard from Laurel Highlands and Barr had played at Duquesne University. It included Barry Parkhill, whom I would later meet during a visit to the University of Virginia campus with my friend Ken Codeluppi, when his son Danny was checking out the UVA campus. It was familiar to me because our daughter, Sarah, was a Phi Beta Kappa graduate. Parkhill, who had played basketball there, was now into fund-raising for the Charlottesville school.

The Nets, who won the first game of the series before dropping four straight games, had a powerful lineup led by Julius Erving, Billy Paultz, Larry Kenon, John Williamson, Brian Taylor and Bill Melchionni.

"The ABA was a great experience for me," said Lewis. "I loved every minute of it."

*   *   *

How do you describe a scene when you can't see the scene?

Freddie Lewis was living with his 92-year-old mother, Thelma Lewis, in a home in the northwest end of Washington, D.C., in the same neighborhood as Howard University, one of the most esteemed traditionally black colleges in America.

"There have been protest marches and gatherings all month long," Lewis reported. "They've come close to where we are, but we're safe here. I hope things get better."

In my imagination, I could see Freddie Lewis in a dimly-lit living room, his mother in a bed or lying on the couch, Freddie looking after her. "No, she can get around," allowed Lewis when I asked questions about his mother. "She can get around with her walker, or with a cane. She likes to watch TV. She's very, very sharp. My mom is as sharp as a tack. She was a nurse for 35 years at Georgetown University Hospital."

Freddie Lewis was looking after his mother full-time. It was a 24–7 task or missionary effort. "I get her up in the morning, bathe her, get her dressed, and prepare meals and make sure she gets fed. I get her ready for bed at night. That's our daily schedule."

I had a friend and fellow sports author named Sam Sciullo who did that for his mother for about two or three years until she died in 2019, and I can't imagine filling that role. I think it's commendable, but it has to be awkward, stressful, so demanding. "There's no greater love a man can show for his mother," another friend said to me when I told him about Freddie Lewis and what he was doing these days.

"No one loved their mother more than I did," I told Lewis, "but I couldn't do what you're doing."

My mother lived for just over four years at a senior residence, Asbury Heights, four miles from our former home. My wife's parents were in the same senior care facility for short stays before they died. My mother died when she was 96. I didn't get cheated or short-changed. She was a great mother and I had her for a long time. I visited them often with my wife, and we thanked the caregivers every time we saw them. They loved my mother because she never forgot to say "Thank you."

"I'm doing what I need to be doing," said Lewis. "This is what she did for me when I was a baby. I just wish I had some help. I'm an only child, so I don't have a brother or a sister who could share some of this responsibility."

So Freddie Lewis, who played basketball with "The Big O," and was the floor leader for every basketball team he ever played for, from McKeesport High School to Arizona State University, to the NBA and the ABA and back to the NBA, is now assisting his mother rather than Mel Daniels, George McGinnis, Bob Netolicky and Roger Brown. Lewis is a care-giver 24/7.

There should be a Hall of Fame for Freddie Lewis and men and women, sons and daughters, like him. He once asked me to help him get inducted into the Western Pennsylvania Sports Hall of Fame.

I did, I knew he deserved it, and the officials of that Hall of Fame felt my word was good enough, even though Lewis didn't draw the needed number of votes for induction. Most of the voters didn't know anything about Freddie Lewis or his marvelous basketball career.

He had followed another McKeesport High grad Bobby Mulgado to Arizona State. Mulgado had been a great running back for the Wildcats and later with the Pittsburgh Valley Ironmen minor league football team. He then served his hometown for over 20 years as a police officer. Mulgado's name, and that of Danny White and Reggie Jackson are displayed on the wall as you enter Sun Devil Stadium at ASU. His No. 27 was retired soon after he finished his college career.

Lewis never attended the Western Pennsylvania Sports Hall of Fame and so he was never honored. You have to attend the dinner. "They wanted me to sell tickets, get at least two tables," he said. "So I passed."

I told him that there was no Dan Silna, or rich man, to underwrite the induction dinner, that it was organized and directed by some well-meaning sports enthusiasts, and they needed support from the honorees to fill the room and pay for the dinner and hotel room. I was hoping he could come someday. I promised to be there.

When Freddie was a senior at McKeesport High School, his parents moved to Washington D.C. where his father began working for Giant Food, which has seven locations in D.C. and over 160 sites altogether, mostly in Maryland and Virginia. It's not to be confused with Giant Eagle, Pittsburgh's most popular food market chain. Freddie stayed behind until he graduated.

"I graduated on June 11th and moved to D.C. on June 13th," he said. "My folks have been in this house ever since.

"I'm glad I'm where I'm needed. I've led a full and rich life. I've been in some special places with some special people."

His father's name was James. Freddie benefited from having two parents who loved him and raised him right.

It explains why he does what he does.

A friend of mine, Jack Sega of Oxnard, California came out of the same Steel Valley as Lewis so he could relate to his story. "I admire a man like Freddie Lewis who is still looking after his mother," Sega said to me. "It's a true love story."

**Freddie Lewis drives on John Roche in
ABA action.**

Doug Smith

A rival writer helped me
to cover more of the court and the Nets

When I traveled with the New York Nets in the early '70s, I had my own room at the hotels where we were staying except on two occasions.

Once I shared a room with twin beds with Barney Kremenko, a former New York sportswriter who'd given Willie Mays his nickname of the "Say Hey Kid," and served as the publicist for the Nets. He was a delightful fellow, older and wiser than me. His Jewish parents had emigrated to this country to escape oppression in Russia.

He was walking by the foot of the bed one morning in his T-shirt and undershorts and they were as wrinkled as his expansive brow. "Barney, how come your shorts are so wrinkled?" I called out to him.

He didn't have his glasses on yet and he fixed me with his protuberant eyes and said, "What the hell are you talking about?"

I told him my wife Kathie always ironed my underwear. "So, put her in the Wives' Hall of Fame," he said on his way to brush his teeth in the bathroom.

The other occasion where I shared a room with someone while traveling with the Nets was in Memphis and my roommate was my friend and beat rival, Doug Smith of Long Island's *Newsday*.

Smith happens to be a man of color. He is too light to refer to as black. The hotel didn't have enough rooms to accommodate the Nets. Plus, the players all had roommates in those days. I recall traveling with the Knicks and knowing that Bill Bradley and Dave DeBusschere were roommates on the road. With the

Mets, Tom Seaver shared a room with Bud Harrelson. Today, ballplayers have their own suites, and sometimes their own limousines to get to the sports venue, rather than take the team's chartered bus.

We were staying at the Hotel Peabody, just a block or half-mile from the Lorraine Hotel. That is where Dr. Martin Luther King Jr. had been assassinated two years earlier, while speaking on a balcony outside his room. I looked over at Smith in his bed, and said, "Once upon a time, we wouldn't have been permitted to share a hotel room in this town. I'm not so sure it's a good idea these days, either."

Smith had to smile, even though it also brought back bad memories.

Newspapers were hiring black sportswriters back then and assigning them to cover basketball because the majority of players were black, and editors thought they'd be able to communicate better with the players, that the players would be more comfortable in their company. It didn't always work. *The New York Times* had a black sportswriter covering the Nets. One day, I was interviewing Gus Johnson of the Indiana Pacers, whom I had covered when he was playing for the Baltimore Bullets against the New York Knicks in the 1970 NBA playoffs. The *Times* writer thought we were interviewing George McGinnis. When he realized his mistake— Johnson told him his name was not George—he left to find McGinnis. No advantage there, I thought at the time.

Smith and I became friends, but there was always an edge to our relationship because Smith would say things about race to stir the pot, or to test me on occasion. Once, when my wife and I visited him and his wife Shirley, at their home on Long Island, he played a tape of a diatribe by Malcolm X who preached a violent protest to White America. Malcolm X wanted to

267

kill white men. It was unsettling to say the least. I don't think Smith realized that it was so unsettling and upsetting. He later apologized.

Another time, when the Smiths came to our home in Baldwin, Long Island, he stopped before entering our home and pointed out a statue in the yard across the cul-de-sac. It was one of those little black lawn jockeys. This one held a horse reign in his right hand. "That's nice," said Smith, sarcastically.

Smith was an outstanding reporter and a fine competitor in all respects, but the real edge I thought he enjoyed on me in covering the Nets was that he was a good tennis player and often played on the road with the Nets' coaches, Kevin Loughery and Rod Thorn, with a coach or official from the team the Nets were playing that night.

They'd have a few beers and snacks afterward and talk about basketball. Smith was privy to these observations, and I was not. He had access to the coaches for more time than I did. In order to play on an even field, so to speak, I asked Smith if he would teach me how to play tennis. I had a tennis racquet at home, but didn't play the game. In Hazelwood, where I grew up, there was a tennis court at the local playground, but there was never a net stretched across the black poles on each side of the court. So no one ever played tennis there.

Smith was a fine tennis player and had competed for the team at Hampton (Virginia) Institute and had met the great Arthur Ashe at tennis competitions in Virginia. I have never played the game as well as Smith. We were going to Greensboro, North Carolina, for a game with the Cougars. Team president Carl Scheer had arranged for the Nets' coaches and Smith to play on clay courts at a country club in Greensboro. Smith had instructed me to bring my tennis racquet with me on this trip.

Doug Miller

NETS Doug Smith of *Newsday* **showed Jim O'Brien how to play tennis and how to spend more time with basketball coaches on a different court.**

When we arrived in Greensboro, Smith inquired, "Do you have your tennis racquet with you?"

I said I did and showed him my wooden-framed racquet, a real relic. "Good," he said, "I've got a match lined up for us today."

If I felt more tension I think the strings on my racquet would have broken. "A match?" I said, incredulously.

Yes, a match. Smith and I were paired to play Loughery and Thorn, two former first-rate NBA guards. I was 30 at the time and had played guard on our CYO basketball team in Pittsburgh. I was All-CYO, but that hardly measures up to their experience and athletic skills. The only sport I played in college was as a goalie for the freshmen soccer team at Pitt. I had never played soccer prior to going to Pitt, but it was one of the sport rotations we had in physical education classes.

Loughery was 32 and 6–3 and had played ten years in the NBA, mostly with the Bullets. Thorn was 31 and 6–4 and had played nine years in the NBA, mostly with the Seattle Supersonics. But they had started out as teammates for one season in Baltimore.

Somehow, I survived that day. I learned under fire. Playing tennis with Loughery, Thorn and Smith definitely helped me to get better in a hurry. It led to good things.

I recalled playing tennis with Loughery and Red Auerbach of the Boston Celtics at Kutsher's Hotel & Country Club in the Catskills, and with Rick Barry, Billy Knight and Connie Hawkins later on. Basketball players are naturals at playing tennis.

I started writing about the tennis scene in New York. I started covering the U.S. Open Tennis Championships at the West Side Tennis Club where they had grass courts. I saw John McEnroe, a local favorite from Douglaston, New York, make his pro debut against the once-great Pancho Gonzales at the West Side Tennis Club.

Julius Erving playing tennis

We lived in Baldwin, Long Island, next to Rockville Centre, and my wife Kathie and I started playing at the Baldwin Tennis Club. It was located outside the circulation area of *The New York Post,* so I didn't think there was any conflict of interest. I started doing some public relations work for Fred and Lucille Hansen at the Baldwin Tennis Club in exchange for free tennis time. My neighbor and good buddy, Bill Hodges, a highly-respected attorney in Baldwin, often joined me for tennis after work at the Baldwin Tennis Club.

That developed into something much bigger and I started getting paid $100 a week and then $200 a week for my efforts. I lined up World Team Tennis teams to practice there before their matches at Nassau Coliseum, just five miles away.

Among those who practiced at the Baldwin Tennis Club were Billie Jean King, Virginia Wade, the Amitraj Brothers, Bobby Riggs, Cat Stevens, Chris Evert and Fred Stolle and I would take photographs of club members with these tennis greats and put them on walls throughout the club. The idea was to make it their club. The members loved bringing friends to play and pointing out their own photographs on the walls, posing with such great players.

Vitas Gerulaitis, who grew up in Sands Point on Long Island, came to Long Island a day early for a match with the New York Sets, and did a free clinic for club members on my behalf. Bobby Riggs did the same.

Jim O'Brien, the founding editor of Street and Smith's Basketball Yearbook shows Julius Erving his likeness on the cover. Jim and Dr. J both had blacker hair in those days.

I had players from the New York Islanders, such as Bert Marshall, Bobby Nystrom, Lorne Henning and Garry Howatt, play tennis there as my guests. I had Julius Erving and Earl "The Pearl' Monroe come there and play as my guests. More photos with smiling club members.

I managed to get a tennis pro who had a big junior program at a club in mid-Long Island to come to work at the Baldwin Tennis Club. Two weeks on the job, he told the owner he could handle publicity, and there went my free-lance job.

I shed no tears when the tennis club closed a year later.

There was a tennis tournament for members of the media that preceded the U.S. Open at the West Side Tennis Club. I managed to get scolded by a member for wearing blue shorts onto its hallowed grounds. I had to go back into the clubhouse and buy a pair of white shorts so I could play there. The rule was "all-white" outfits in those days.

I recall that the famous photographer, Gordon Parks, was among those who played in our tournament. Doug Smith was one of the best players of the newspapermen. Will Grimsley of the Associated Press, I was told, usually won the tournament and he did that year.

When I was 32, I was part of a winning team and we beat a former Wimbledon champion named Sarah Palfrey Danzig. Her husband, Allison Danzig, was one of the snooty sportswriters with *The New York Times* and he covered the tennis beat. I called Kathie on the phone in the clubhouse—there were no cell phones then—and told her I'd beaten a woman who was a Wimbledon champion.

"How old is she?" Kathie wanted to know.

Kathie believes she was born to keep me humble.

The woman was 62 then, 30 years my senior. When she died at age 83, her obituary described Sarah Palfrey Danzig as "one of the most elegant tennis players ever to grace a grass court" in the 1930s.

The U.S. Open moved to the new National Tennis Center at Flushing Meadows in 1978, close to Shea Stadium where the Mets played.

Doug Smith was standing on the sideline for the media final doubles match, shaking his head in disbelief. I was out there on the court with a writer from *The Wall Street Journal*. I didn't really know him and I can't recall his name. He was a good player.

We beat a doubles duo that included famous tennis commentator Bud Collins of Boston, who is now in the Tennis Hall of Fame for his contributions as a writer, commentator and ambassador for the sport. This was in the semi-finals. Collins wanted to entertain the crowd. I wanted to win. I wanted to beat Collins. And we did. We advanced to the finals and, sure enough, Will Grimsley, the AP's top sportswriter, was out there in his all-white gear, with a partner whose name I don't recall. We won.

I wish John McEnroe would mention some day during a telecast of the U.S. Open the little-known fact of who was on the winning doubles team in the first tournament ever held at what is now known as the Billy Jean King Tennis Center.

On March 24, 1982, while covering the Steelers for *The Pittsburgh Press*, I teamed with Ray Evans to win the men's tournament among the owners, coaches, front-office executives and writers at the NFL Owners Meeting in Rancho Mirage, California. My wife Kathie, who is 5-8, won the Class B Women's title with Mary Jack Stephens, the diminutive wife of the Buffalo Bills' head coach Kay Stephens at the time. They were the female version of Mutt and Jeff in tennis outfits.

I recall that most of the owners' wives were outfitted in the latest tennis attire from boutiques, but Pat Rooney, normally a sharp dresser, showed up wearing one of her husband Dan's white T-shirts. Pat came to play, not to model anything.

Kathie and I have continued to play tennis, then platform tennis and now, more often, a game called pickleball that is popular in senior communities in Florida and Arizona, and also with school kids as part of their gym classes.

I have Doug Smith to thank for a lifetime of fun and games. We visited Smith and his current wife, Anne, in Washington, D.C. about ten years ago, and stayed in their home in downtown D.C. We spent two days visiting the Newseum, which is a great venue underwritten by major media in the United States.

Smith went from *Newsday* to become the tennis writer for *USA Today*, and covered all the major tournaments in the world. It had to be a great beat. He is now retired in South Florida. I still hear from him from time to time.

Photos by Clifford Low

Kevin Loughery, Willis Reed, Earl "The Pearl" Monroe and Jim O'Brien enjoyed racquet sports.

George Tinsley
One of ABA's best success stories

I am grateful that George Tinsley took his cream-colored suit with him and thus was a standout at two ABA reunions we both attended in April and May of 2018.

The first took place with a league-wide gathering of over 140 former ABA players in Indianapolis, and the second of about 40 former Kentucky Colonels in Tinsley's hometown of Louisville.

Tinsley, to be honest, was not on my checklist of players I wanted to be sure to see and get pictures and contact information for use in my sequel to my basketball memoir *Looking Up.* He was one of my finds, like a long shot in the Kentucky Derby. A good story, in so many ways, that I had missed in earlier years.

I exchanged greetings and a few words with Tinsley in Indianapolis and sat next to him in a corporate suite high overlooking the home stretch at Churchill Downs a few days before the 144th running of the Kentucky Derby. We enjoyed a buffet lunch by the window. I'm sure we both thought that was pretty good. Tinsley and Artis Gilmore both wore straw hats with black bands, and they were there with Dan Issel, Louie Dampier and Darel Carrier among other former Colonels. Louisville businessman Steve Higdon orchestrated this reunion and it was a well-organized three-day event for all who joined in the fun. Tinsley is all of 6-5, so I was looking up at him most of the time we stood around, soaking up the glorious layout that is the iconic Churchill Downs. With so many tall men on the grounds there were more than the usual two steeples that are an instant identifier of the internationally famous race track.

It was wonderful to spend time with Bobby Rascoe, Joe Hamilton, Cincy Powell, Les "Big Game" Hunter, Randy Mahaffey, Mike Gale—Gale was particularly great with us—Darel Carrier, Chuck Williams and Lloyd "Pink" Gardner, the team's trainer. Hunter was wearing a Loyola of Chicago ballcap and was eager to talk about how well his alma mater had done in the NCAA Basketball Tournament. Hunter looked tired and sedate otherwise and Ron Thomas had a wild and scared look in his eyes after he was escorted by Hamilton to the team's hotel from a nursing home nearby. William "Bird" Averitt looked like he had returned wounded from the Civil War, but he showed great courage in just showing up. He and his wife both suffered a broken neck in an auto accident 20 years earlier. He looked like someone who had suffered a stroke, with one arm virtually useless—I later learned his left side was paralyzed—and was worse for the wear as was his shiny olive green suit, but he had a permanent smile on his face, and told everyone he was enjoying the time of his life, only topped by being a member of the Colonels' ABA title team in 1975.

He shared a room at the hotel with host Steve Higdon and they talked the nights away. "Bird told me it was the best time of his life except for the night the Colonels won the title," said Higdon, who helped open a lot of doors for me at tourist spots around Louisville and Lexington.

The Colonels were then owned by John Y. Brown and Ellie Brown, since divorced and married to others, and it was good to see them together again. The team's coach, Hubie Brown, was not in attendance as he was doing color commentary for a televised NBA game.

We were able to get a close-up look at the favorite Justify in the stable area at Churchill Downs on a Wednesday morning and that beautiful chestnut-colored thoroughbred went on to win the Triple Crown.

ABA players from the past get together at 30th anniversary reunion in Indianapolis, from left to right, Cincy Powell, James Jones, Willie Wise, Zelmo Beaty and Art Becker. These were classy guys and, boy, they could play basketball with the best of them.

Joe Hamilton, left, brought his former Colonels' teammate Ron Thomas to the team's 50th anniversary reunion to receive his ABA anniversary ring Dan Silna had bought for all the ABA alumni in attendance. Thomas was residing at a senior rehab facility and he died two months later.

I was there when Joe Hamilton brought former teammate Ron Thomas into the hotel in a wheelchair. Thomas was quite ill. He was presented with a 50th anniversary ABA ring, which were given at the behest of Dan Silna, former owner of the Spirits of St. Louis. Silna picked up the tab for over a hundred rings for the ABA alumni in attendance at a reunion in Indianapolis earlier in the year. I learned that Silna was helping out my old friend Freddie Lewis, a classmate of my wife Kathie at McKeesport (Pa.) High School. I believe Silna provided the financial backing when Lewis brought a revived ABA team (2006–2008) to Pittsburgh called the Pittsburgh Xplosion.

Thomas died at age 67 on July 14, 2018. He had been a high school star and a University of Louisville star (a Final Four team) and was a member of the Colonels' ABA title team in 1975. "We called him 'The Plumber' because he had the shooting touch of a plumber," said teammate Dan Issel.

The Dropping Dimes Foundation, formed in Indianapolis to aid needy ABA players, picked up the tab for his funeral expenses.

* * *

Some bad things struck like a bolt of lightning in the life of the Tinsley Family. It could be a chapter in the inspirational book by Rabbi Harold Schiller—*When Bad Things Happen to Good People.*

Tinsley's daughter, Penni Danielle Tinsley, a smart, multi-talented and beautiful young woman died after a difficult illness at age 43. She passed away at home with her mother, Seretha, and her father, George, and her brother, George II, at her bedside.

I have two daughters, Sarah and Rebecca, who are in their mid-40s, Rebecca is 43, and I can't imagine what this challenge was like for the Tinsley family. (See a Memorial to Penni Danielle Tinsley elsewhere in this chapter.) How do you deal with the death of such a promising child, or any child for that matter?

Up till then, George Tinsley had enjoyed an enviable life, and he is far better off than the majority of retired pro basketball players. Life, for the most part, has been good to him and his family. Yet he was never the favorite, not as an infant, abandoned by his birth mother and left with a neighbor who looked after such children—her last name was Tinsley—not as a college student, not as an adult. He was always an underdog. His is definitely a rags-to-riches story.

So many of the players he played with and against didn't know how to cope with the real world, after their ball-playing days were over. There are so many stories of how their lives spiraled downward. His ABA alumni friends have been waiting for a league pension—for 44 now 45 years—like the steelworkers of Pittsburgh and the Ohio Valley—and it's still just a pipe dream. Tinsley was the exception. His game—the restaurant business—just got better.

He won several minority entrepreneur-of-the-year awards. He had to dig deep into his personal mantra for survival and success in dealing with the death of his daughter, and the pain it caused his daughter, his son and their mother.

As I write this tribute to the Tinsleys, I can see a color photo of George and Kentucky Colonels' teammate Wayne Chapman that I took at the 50th anniversary reunion of the Colonels at Churchill Downs in Louisville in May of 2018. George is in a white suit, of course, with a black-and-white checkered dress shirt with a white collar, and a dark hat. He's holding a take-out cup of coffee and the brightest smile this side of heaven.

Former Colonels' teammates and friends Wayne Chapman and George Tinsley are reunited in Louisville. Chapman played at Western Kentucky and Tinsley at Kentucky Wesleyan.

He started out in "Smoketown," a mostly black community on the edge of downtown Louisville that traces its roots to the Civil War. Smoketown alumni include Cassius Clay, renamed Muhammad Ali, and former ABA teammate Joe Hamilton. At Christmas time, they ought to call the community "Tinsley Town."

He's gone from being abandoned by his mother when he was seven months old to flying around the southeastern region of the United States in a corporate jet to check out his holdings.

His greatest success, he says, is his family. He has been married to his wife, Seretha, for 45 years at this writing.

They have been living in Winter Haven, Florida, and I recall visiting that community when I was covering the New York Yankees and the New York Mets and it was the winter base for the Boston Red Sox. I remember thinking it would be a great place to live.

And I would never have found his fabled story if he hadn't been wearing that cream-colored suit. I'm not sure the slacks and jacket were the same cream color. Even in a white suit, George Tinsley would never be mistaken for one of his mentors in the fast-food business, the iconic Colonel Sanders.

"I checked out the difference in the color of the top and bottom—cream and white—but it's hard to break away from old habits when you grow up poor," said Joe Hamilton when I spoke to him at a later date. Tinsley and Maurice "Toothpick" McHartley were the only ABA alumni to strut their stuff in cream-colored or white suits. I am drawn to people who dare to be different. My wife Kathie accuses me of attracting "crazies," but George Tinsley is not crazy, though there were times some of his best friends thought he might be because of the business risks he was willing to take.

Tinsley was never a star or a starter in the ABA, playing for the Washington Caps, the Miami Floridians and the Kentucky Colonels. I never stopped and talked to him at his locker after a game. He was just a journeyman ballplayer in the ABA. He was never the story at any game I covered. I never needed him. My loss. But he's a better story today than he was then.

He is an entrepreneur now, a franchising success, starting out with Kentucky Fried Chicken, and moving through TGI Fridays, Starbucks and some other business ventures. At 72 in September of 2018, he was still going strong. His company owned and operated five different restaurants at the Tampa International Airport, including Shula's Bar & Grill, TGI Fridays, and Starbucks, but lost some spaces when the airport reopened after renovations.

So many of the former ABA players are still hoping and praying for a pension from the NBA to save the day. Most are in their late 60s and 70s now. They remind me of the steelworkers in Pittsburgh who sat around on park benches, idling, believing the mills would re-open and they'd draw a paycheck again. George Tinsley went to work and created his own destiny.

*   *   *

That's the scary part of being a sportswriter. When I was writing one of my books on the Steelers I had not planned on interviewing J.T. Thomas, a defensive back from Macon, Georgia, and Thomas turned out to be the best story in the book.

When I was doing a book on the 1960 Pirates I had not thought about interviewing Sam Narron. After all, he was the bullpen catcher. But I found myself in North Carolina on a Thanksgiving holiday and had to interview someone while I was there. I tried to get hold of Wilmer "Vinegar Bend" Mizell, but he was back home for the holidays in Vinegar Bend, Alabama.

I didn't know that Narron had been the bullpen catcher for the "Boys of Summer" Brooklyn Dodgers, that he had been a member of the St. Louis Cardinals' famed "Gas House Gang," and that he had broken in as a pinch-hitter for Dizzy Dean against Carl Hubbell at Sportsmens Park in St. Louis. Dean and Hubbell are both in the Baseball Hall of Fame.

I didn't know Sam Narron was a natural story-teller, and such a nice man. His wife Virginia filled in the spaces when Narron drew a blank on somebody's name. His home was like a baseball museum and he even had an old-time steel barber chair in the center of the kitchen area. EMIL J. PAIDAR was engraved in the foot rest, a name I recognized from my childhood at my next-door neighbor's barber shop.

One of the best basketball stories would be Dr. Fletcher Johnson, a heart surgeon who had been the "sixth man" on the great Duquesne University team of the '50s, whom I tabbed "The real Dr. J." He had quite a story, too. Educated in German-speaking Cologne to become a celebrated heart surgeon in New York City and nearby Nyack.

George T. Tinsley Sr. is also some story. He sent me a small book called *More Than Just French Fries* after we had talked on the telephone following our meeting in Louisville. The book is about 15 business leaders sharing insights on franchising success, and Tinsley is the first chapter in the book.

I want my first chapter to capture the reader's attention and I suspect that author Jania Bailey felt the same way when she assembled her how-to book for business people.

* * *

This is a summary of the accomplishments of George Tinsley:

George grew up in Smoketown, an inner-city neighborhood one mile southeast of downtown Louisville. Smoketown has been a historically black neighborhood since the Civil War, according to documents sent to me by George Tinsley, and it's the only neighborhood in the city that has had such a continuous presence.

Smoketown *is also the name of a book about the black renaissance in Pittsburgh by author Mark Whitaker, focusing on the black community of the city from the 1920s through the 1950s. It's the same Hill District from which Pulitzer Prize-winning author*

August Wilson drew his series of plays. I remember Wilson living in Hazelwood when we were teenagers. He was a frequent visitor to the Carnegie Library there. Wilson's father was German, his mother African-American and he had an odd cocoa-colored freckled face, as I recall. He lived at that time on Sylvan Avenue, between Gladstone Junior High School and the home at 160 Hazelwood Avenue of my friend Herb Douglas Jr., who had won a bronze medal in the long jump in the 1948 Olympic Games in London, England.

Tinsley was a gifted young athlete and he was offered a scholarship to Kentucky Wesleyan College in Owensboro in 1966. As a freshman, Tinsley, a 6–5 forward, led the Panthers to the first of three Division II NCAA championships over the next four years. He was heralded as a "defensive demon" when they won two national titles in 1968 and 1969 and was twice named All-America and was an alternate on the 1968 U.S. Olympic basketball team. Dallas Thornton was another Louisville product who played basketball at Kentucky Wesleyan and in the ABA and with the Harlem Globetrotters.

"UK wasn't in the picture for us back then," offered Joe Hamilton. "That's why so many small colleges in the South had such great football and basketball teams."

Tinsley was drafted by the NBA Chicago Bulls and the ABA Oakland Oaks but ended up with the Washington Caps before he became a Kentucky Colonel. He played three years until the ABA was absorbed by the NBA in 1972.

He was a Dean's List student when he graduated from Kentucky Wesleyan and was the first African-American to receive the prestigious Oak and Ivy Award for academic achievement.

One of his teammates with the Colonels, Walt Simon, an ABA charter member, was responsible

Tinsley's teammates at Colonels' 50th anniversary reunion included, left to right, Bird Averitt, Les Hunter (in his burgundy Loyola U. ballcap), Cincy Powell, with Tinsley and Artis Gilmore in background, and Wayne Chapman.

for hiring minorities for management training for Kentucky Fried Chicken, and he hired Tinsley. Tinsley accompanied Colonel Sanders on tours of the restaurants and said he learned a lot about marketing and sales from the Colonel, as well as how to cook "great chicken." He was with KFC for eight years and then bought some franchises and diversified with holdings in other restaurant chains. He had the distinction of being the first athlete and African-American to give the commencement speech in his school's history.

Tinsley told me he managed to attend the 30th year reunion of the ABA in Indianapolis, even though he wasn't really among the invited ABA alumni. Walt Simon encouraged him to attend.

"It was basically organized for the top 30 or so guys, former ABA all-stars and the Indiana Pacers," Tinsley told me.

"Walt was sick and fighting for his life at the time," he continued. "Goose Ligon went with us to Indianapolis. I knew some of the guys and I struck up a friendship with Dr. J, Julius Erving. He took a liking to me. I owned ten restaurants at the time. I took many of the fellows out to lunch on me at a TGI Fridays in downtown Indianapolis. Dr. J appointed me the secretary of the ABA alumni. The other guys figured if Dr. J thought I was worthy of such a position that was good enough for them. I ended up serving on the board of the players' association, and now I am involved with the NBA Retired Players Association. Rick Barry and I are still fighting for the ABA players, still trying to get the NBA to fund a pension for us. So many of our guys have died and it really wouldn't cost the league much money to fund such a pension. We were promised a pension when the leagues merged in the off-season in 1976. We managed to get money for some of our players, such as Bird Averitt and some others who were in bad financial and physical shape."

Simon was another ABA success story. He always struck me as a real gentleman in his eight years in the ABA. Simon enjoyed a 22-year career with Kentucky Fried Chicken, and was a manager in charge of equal employment when he approached Tinsley about joining his new team. Simon, a graduate of little Benedict College, was later promoted to vice president for franchising, believed to be the first African-American to be a vice-president with a Fortune 500 company. He, too, was an ABA success story, a star on and off the court.

Simon died in 1997 at age 56 of brain cancer.

Tinsley still is thankful to Walt Simon for selling him on a career opportunity with Kentucky Fried Chicken. What could be better than working with the Colonel himself?

"I've been blessed," said Tinsley. "When I was seven months old, my mother dropped me off at the home of woman named Willie Tinsley who looked after such kids. I lived with her until I was 13 and then she died, and I was taken in by her son. I lived with him till I went to college and I never came back home.

"My mother came back into the picture and I learned that I had actually played against my brother when we played the University of Hawaii. His name was Johnny Penebacker. Our family name was actually Penebanker. With a c instead of an n."

I told Tinsley he was better served with the name Tinsley. "George Penebanker sounds like a character out of a Charles Dickens novel."

George grinned when I said that. "In truth, though, you are a character out of a Charles Dickens novel. Maybe Oliver Twist."

"You could say that," he said.

Steve Higdon successfully nominated Tinsley for the Kentucky Basketball Hall of Fame. "He may be the most successful basketball player in the history of Kentucky," Higdon told me in a phone conversation on the 4th of July 2018. "He was better known for his defensive play when he led Kentucky Wesleyan to three Division II championships in four years. He was hurt and didn't play in the post-season tournament in the only year they didn't win the title. He is a great man and a great friend."

Tinsley summed up his life this way back in 2016 and it proved more prophetic that he might have intended:

"Having played and coached team sports, I came to understand at a young age that you're going to win some games. When you lose, you learn how to improve for the next game so that you have a better chance at winning. When you win, you must understand that you could lose the next time, if you don't prepare yourself. My career in sports was fairly brief, but it was a great opportunity that prepared me for my next step in life."

Tinsley cited the fragility of going into business, how most new businesses fail within three to five years of opening their doors. The coronavirus of 2020 put an end to a lot of people's dreams.

"If you don't perform, you're not going to be around for long," Tinsley tells prospective hires. "You have to listen to others' opinions. You have to attract quality talent."

And, finally, "Smile every chance you get. Not because life has been easy, perfect, or exactly as you had anticipated, but because you choose to be happy and grateful for all the good things you do have and all the problems you know that you don't have."

"Good people are good because they've come to wisdom through failure. We get very little wisdom through success, you know."
—William Saroyan

"You can't hope it will happen; you have to make it happen."
—Herb Douglas, at 98, the oldest-living African-American Olympic medalist (1948, bronze medal in the long jump).

One of my proofreaders, Pat Santelli, ends all his e-mails with this message: "Make a great day!"

A Memorial to
Penni Danielle Tinsley

Dare to dream and keep the faith,
doing it right, whatever it takes*

To further extend the pain and gain of the Tinsley Story, I suggest you Google a YouTube offering, just four minutes and 31 seconds in length, a tribute to Penni Danielle Tinsley.

You will be struck by her beauty, her talent, her many accomplishments, her generous concern for inspiring and helping other people. It's worth your time. If you have a daughter, or two, it should bring tears to your eyes.

Penni graduated at the top of her class from the drama school at the University of North Carolina at Chapel Hill and spent 12 years in New York City, pursuing different dreams, dance, runway model, theater. Her message to all is "Keep Being Creative." She created a foundation to help fund others in their dream pursuits.

Penni had a passion for life and learning, which she inherited from her parents, and she made the most of her 43 years. She was diagnosed in 2009 with Parkinson's MSA and cervical dystonia. MSA means Multiple System Atrophy.

Its symptoms are light-headedness, dizziness and fainting spells, passing out, balance and mobility problems, bladder dysfunction, sleep disturbances, poor blood pressure

control. It's not a pretty picture even when you are so beautiful.

That's when she left New York City and moved in with her family back home in Winter Haven, Florida. With her health challenges, she had to go home. She was often seen at her father's side, helping him to oversee a chain of restaurants in the family business. Most didn't realize how perilous her condition was and what awaited her.

Everyone who worked with her and all of the family's friends in the pro basketball world were saddened by her tragic long suffering and death. Their hearts and condolence expressions went out to George, Seretha and George II, and friends and relatives of the Tinsley family.

This YouTube offering has been viewed by over 10,000 as of May 15, 2020. There are cameo appearances in it by the likes of Muhammad Ali, from Louisville's Smoketown section, just like her dad, and Charles Barkley, a member of the Basketball Hall of Fame and an ESPN analyst.

It's quite a tribute to a beautiful person.

* These are all titles in the Pittsburgh Proud series.

Maurice McHartley
The ABA's 50th year anniversary drew many still familiar faces to Indy

A well-tailored man came walking my way, moving to a Motown beat mostly out of habit. He was wearing a straw-colored hat with a black band around it, a cream-colored suit that made him a standout in the crowd at a cocktail party on the eve of the ABA's 50th anniversary reunion in Indianapolis the first weekend in April, 2018. I recognized him right away. He smiled when he saw that I was eyeing him.

He looked like a character in the all-black cast of "Guys and Dolls" that my wife Kathie and I had caught on Broadway back in 1976. The show was based on stories written by newspaper columnist Damon Runyon—famous for his dot-and-dash reports on the Manhattan celebrity scene—and included Runyonesque characters such as Sky Masterton, Benny Southstreet, Nicely-Nicely Johnson, Sarah Brown, Joey Biltmore, Rusty Charlie and, of course, General Cartwright, the leader of the Save-A-Soul Mission. There was also a nattily-dressed Nathan Detroit, who ran an illegal floating crap game. McHartley would have been well cast as Nathan Detroit.

He looked a little different, like we all did, but I knew it was Maurice "Mo" McHartley, also known as Maurice "Toothpick" McHartley. He smiled when I said, "You've got to be Maurice McHartley. Where's your toothpick?"

Now he smiled even more. "I must have forgotten to bring some," he said.

"I thought about bringing some, just in case I came across you here," I said.

Then I spotted an extra-long toothpick stuck in an olive in a cocktail glass someone had emptied, and I freed it and gave it to Maurice McHartley. "You've got to have your signature stick," I said.

He took it from me and slipped it behind his pocket square. Then he retrieved it and stuck it between his teeth and posed for a picture. He often played in games with a toothpick protruding from the corner of his mouth. Imagine that...as much a remembrance of the ABA scene as the tri-colored red, white and blue ball.

He shook my hand heartily, like he was holding onto his past, embracing someone who could certify he was a terrific basketball player once upon a time. When they get old, ballplayers appreciate sportswriters more. They weren't such a pain in the ass, after all.

Who else is going to tell the world he averaged 12.4 points in 189 ABA games with four different teams over three seasons? As Maurice likes to say of others, he could play.

This meeting took place in the lobby of the Emmis Communications Building in downtown Indianapolis. Jeff Smulyan, who also owned Major League Baseball's Seattle Mariners once upon a time, is the owner of the media company, a hometown boy makes good story.

Soon after I met McHartley, I got a great embrace from Donnie Freeman, one of my ABA favorites, then I was reacquainted with Spencer Haywood, Bill Melchionni and Brian Taylor and James T. Silas. I was in ABA heaven, or maybe just outside the pearly gates. Les "Big Game" Hunter was there, and at a similar celebration in Louisville a month later. And now he's gone, the number of ABA alumni dwindling.

The skin around McHartley's dark eyes was purple red, and he wasn't wearing any eye shadow, just an old man's sadness. He had been a journeyman ball-player, playing wherever he could get a paycheck, and he'd been down too many roads. He was living in East Point, Georgia at the time, but he would move with his wife to an apartment in Atlanta before we would talk again, twice, on May 1 and May 3, 2020.

I have a photo propped up on one of the speakers that flank my computer at my writing desk. It's one of the shots I took of him at the reunion, and I feel like he's talking to me as I write this chapter. You can't see the toothpick I presented him for the picture I took of him, but it's there, if you look closer, in the middle of his mouth.

*　*　*

Players such as Maurice "Toothpick" McHartley helped make up a colorful cast in the early days of the ABA. It was great to see these guys once again. He played pro ball, first with the Eastern Basketball League (EBL) and then with the Continental Basketball Association (CBA) and then with the American Basketball Association.

He was a charter member of the ABA, first with the New York Nets (1967-68) before I got to New York, and then with the Dallas Chaparrals (1968-69), and then the Miami Floridians (1969), the same year that I moved to Miami to write sports for *The Miami News*. That's when I started to write a column about the ABA in *The Sporting News*, a nationally-distributed sports tabloid best known for its extensive baseball coverage. I wrote for TSN about the ABA and then the NBA for nine years.

I don't think I ever interviewed Maurice McHartley, but I was always enchanted with his name and his game, on and off the court. I missed a good story by not talking to him then, my mistake, and I am glad our paths crossed once again.

Terry Stembridge, the classy radio voice of the Chaparrals, thought of Maurice as "Mr. Cool." He was one of Terry's favorite pirates, or Chaps, anyway. Stembridge told Terry Pluto, the author of the 1990 iconic book about the ABA—*Loose Balls*—about this.

Pluto beat me to the punch in that respect, and the Akron-based writer admitted he had never been to an ABA game. But he knew where to get the ABA stories.

"Maurice used to have a toothpick in the corner of his mouth, or he wouldn't play," said Stembridge. "He was way ahead of everybody when it came to fashion, because he was the first guy on the team to wear bell-bottoms and stuff like that. He worked hard at being Mr. Cool."

McHartley had to laugh when I told him what Stembridge had said about him. "Terry was cool, too," he said.

*   *   *

This was in a spacious ballroom with a rectangular bar in the center, free drinks and a popular gathering area near the Indianapolis Convention Center at the ABA's 50th year anniversary reunion on April 6, 2018.

When we met in Indianapolis in 2018, we were both 75 years old, Maurice Franklin McHartley having been born on August 1, 1942 in Detroit, 19 days before I was born at Mercy Hospital in Pittsburgh. Connie Hawkins, the ABA's all-time best player, had been born in Brooklyn as Cornelius Lance Hawkins a month earlier. The Hawk had died, at age 75, just before the reunion. He would have attracted a lot of attention.

I recognized Maurice McHartley right away. The same could not be said for many of the other ABA players who came to Indy to be with each other, maybe for the last time unless they had another reunion sooner

MAURICE McHARTLEY

DALLAS CHAPARRALS

AMERICAN BASKETBALL ASSOCIATION

MAURICE McHARTLEY
Dallas Chaparrals 6-3 185

Courtesy of Maurice McHartley

McHartley starred with Wilmington (Del.) Blue Bombers in Eastern Basketball League.

than later. There were some whose names I remembered well that I could not have picked out of a police lineup. And I pride myself on recognizing faces.

This reunion, like most reunions, was full of faces that had aged and not always well. There were wrinkles and scars where there used to be handsome faces, and some foggy mind sets. Lots of bad knees and not-so-steady strides. Canes and wheelchairs were modes of transportation rather than Cadillacs and Lincolns.

*   *   *

I talked briefly with McHartley and he told me about how he had played basketball on neighborhood playgrounds with some of Detroit's finest in his formative years, players such as Mel Daniels, John Brisker, Chet Walker, the legendary (for all the wrong reasons) Reggie Harding, Kevin Willis, and even a skinny young kid named George Gervin, later known as George "Ice Man" Gervin when he teamed up with Dr. J and the Virginia Squires, and later led the NBA in scoring three straight seasons with the San Antonio Spurs.

One of the few white players in those Detroit playgrounds was Dave DeBusschere. Bill Bridges, who played power forward in the ABL and the NBA, once said of DeBusschere, "He gives 100 per cent in every game, at both ends of the court." Bridges, a 6–6 forward for the Kansas City Steers, had led that league in rebounding for two seasons and set the single-game scoring record for the ABL with 55 points. Bridges later played for the St. Louis and Atlanta Hawks.

In those games in the playgrounds of Detroit, there was Spencer Haywood and Ralph Simpson, who starred at the University of Detroit and Michigan State University, respectively, before they changed the game by challenging the rules and leaving college early to play for pay in the ABA, which earned its name as an "outlaw league" in honest fashion.

There were more to come, such as Chris Webber and Jalen Rose and Dan Roundfield, and a precocious kid from nearby Pontiac known as Earvin "Magic" Johnson.

Sometimes Dave Bing, a star with the Detroit Pistons, would join in the fun, along with teammates Joe Strawder and Ray Scott. I had seen Dave Bing play as a sophomore at Syracuse University in 1964 at the Manheim Field House. Bing would become the mayor of Detroit long after his playing days with the Pistons, a real success story.

There were so many great basketball players in Detroit. They came along at the same time a man named Berry Gordy, who was once an auto maker in Motown when that acronym stood for the city's main industry—building cars, motor vehicles—emerged as man who created a new Motown, known internationally for its upbeat music and its singers and musicians.

Check out the list of the men and women who once ruled the music world: Marvin Gaye, The Temptations, Stevie Wonder, Diana Ross and The Supremes, Smokey Robinson, The Four Tops, Martha Reeves and the Vandellas, The Spinners, Contours, Little Willie John and Edwin Starr. All from Detroit.

There were so many stars that came out of Detroit, too many in some cases. McHartley went to North Carolina A&T and when he completed his career there he was not quite good enough to play in the NBA. Or, as was the case for many, maybe he just didn't get the right opportunity.

Like many of the original cast in the ABA, McHartley had starred in the Eastern Professional Basketball League, playing for the Wilmington (Del.) Blue Bombers. Whereas Bing went from Syracuse to play for the NBA Pistons in Detroit, his roommate as a freshman and the captain of the Syracuse team, Jim Boeheim, had to settle for playing for Scranton in the EBL. Boeheim would become the coach at Syracuse, succeeding Roy Danforth who followed Fred Lewis, and he would never leave his alma mater. It wasn't because of the wonderful weather in the winter in upstate New York, but because he had found a home for a lifetime. Other EBL alumni included Donnie Freeman, Bill Melchionni, Levern "Jelly" Tart, Wayne Hightower, Walt Simon, Willie Somerset, Hank Whitney and Willie Murrell.

There were only 12 teams in the NBA in 1967. There were 11 in the newly-formed ABA. That's a total of 23 teams. Today, at last glance, there are 30 teams in the NBA, and no one questions the players' abilities on any of those teams. But the ABA was branded as a minor league by naysayers of that era. Red Auerbach was among those who liked to put down the caliber of ballplayers in the upstart league.

There are now NBA teams in places where ABA teams once struggled to succeed at the box office, namely Charlotte, Minneapolis, San Antonio, Dallas, Miami and Long Island.

Detroit, like my hometown of Pittsburgh, lost most of its mills and industrial businesses, and has been seriously challenged to stay financially afloat. My friend Marvin Zelkowitz suggests that anyone who wants to read a good book about Detroit should check out *Broke* by Jodi Kirschener.

I'd also recommend A.J. Baime's fast-paced *The Arsenal of Democracy*, about how Henry and Edsel Ford and other auto builders in Detroit switched from assembling automobiles to B-24 bombers for our use in World War II and how this changed our country and Detroit forever.

I moved around the room and spotted some more familiar faces. Del Harris, who had coached in the league in several cities, was the easiest to identify. He still has a full head of silver hair, combed just so, and he was as friendly and affable as ever, the kind of coach that one found more often in the ABA than in the NBA. There were no Red Auerbachs or Greg Popoviches in the ABA, boorish types who thought they were above it all. Most of them were like Red Holzman and Bill Sharman, who always had time to talk and explain things to roving reporters.

I knew I had a picture at home showing Harris and Mel Daniels with me at The Pitt Field House in the mid-80s when I was the assistant athletic director for public relations at my alma mater, and when Pitt had the kind of players that drew pro scouts to courtside seats.

Michael Dradzinski/University of Pittsburgh

Professional basketball scouts Del Harris and Mel Daniels were hosted on press row at Pitt Field House in mid-80s by author Jim O'Brien, then the assistant athletic director for public relations at his alma mater.

I saw Walt Szczerbiak, who had grown up on the South Side of Pittsburgh, played at St. Casimir High School in the Catholic Class B League, then George Washington University, and after a brief fling in the ABA became a star at Real Madrid in Spain, one of the better teams in the European Pro Basketball League. He led his team to three European League championships.

His son, Wally Szczerbiak, was born in Madrid and grew up on Long Island after his dad retired from playing basketball. Wally went on to play ten seasons with four different teams in the NBA.

Walter Szczerbiak was quite the success story. His parents were both Ukrainians who met in a German refugee camp in the last days of World War II. He was born in Hamburg, in West Germany, a city I had visited on a Viking Cruise in the summer of 2016. His parents immigrated to the USA.

At age 27, he was getting paid $35,000 a year—big money in those days—and living in a free apartment in Madrid, overlooking a snow-capped mountain. He's still considered one of the most influential American basketball players in Europe.

His wife, Marilyn, is someone you like right away.

With his sweeping silver-gray hair, Walter still looks like someone who produces and directs movie films in Europe.

I saw Peter Vecsey, once a colleague at *The New York Post,* who became the dominant pro basketball writer in The Big Apple and was given the Curt Gowdy Award by the Basketball Hall of Fame for his work. "You should have stayed at *The Post*, and together we would have dominated the NBA coverage," Vecsey was kind enough to say.

Vecsey and Szczerbiak had a heated exchange, mostly because Vecsey, who had once coached

Szczerbiak in Harlem's Summer Rucker League, won't forgive Szczerbiak for once having the temerity to say that Nate "Tiny" Archibald," one of Vecsey's favorite New Yorkers, was "over-rated."

Szczerbiak wanted to kiss and make up, but Vecsey was having none of that. This sort of thing always happens at reunions. I failed in my peace-making efforts. I learned later on that they met at a coach's funeral in New York and made peace in honor of the coach.

I came across Henry Logan, who was also dressed for "Guys and Dolls," and his attorney "who has no money" who identified himself as Logan's agent. I doubt he is kept busy or well-employed as Henry Logan's agent. Logan had played for the Oakland Oaks in the second year of the ABA. "I never saw a better ballhandler; he was amazing with what he could do with a basketball," said Rick Barry who had signed with the Oakland Oaks but was not allowed to play the first year in the ABA because he was still under contract with the San Francisco Warriors.

Bill Melchionni, who led the league in assists four straight seasons with the New York Nets, feeding, first, Rick Barry and then Julius Erving, was talking to some old acquaintances.

When I first entered the JW Marriott Hotel the previous afternoon, I spotted Melchionni with two of his former Nets' teammates, Brian Taylor and Barry, and they were the first players I personally greeted. It felt good to be back in their company. I wasn't sure how Barry would receive me because he could be moody and difficult, but he was fine and gracious.

Then I came upon Spencer Haywood, gleaming from top to bottom in a sharp dark-blue suit, a well-pressed white dress shirt, and a coordinated blue and gold tie. He had a silver bar between his shirt collar tips. He was all smiles, gleaming teeth, gleaming coal-dark eyes, and eager to talk.

I knew Haywood from his days with the Denver Rockets, when he was the ABA's Rookie of the Year and its MVP, and better yet when he played for the New York Knicks. This was in the '70s. He was the star of the U.S.A. basketball team that won the gold medal in the 1968 Olympic Games in Mexico City. Those were the Olympic Games in which track men Tommie Smith and John Carlos thrust black-gloved hands to the sky when they stood on the medal-winners stand as a black protest of injustice in our country. Haywood was then a student at Trinidad Junior College.

"This is great, seeing all these guys," said Haywood.

I had not really been interviewing any of these players because I thought their time was better spent hugging each other, and reminiscing about their playing days, but Haywood would have none of that. He wanted to be interviewed. That always set the ABA players apart from most professional athletes—and I covered all sports in my days in Miami, New York and Pittsburgh. They were like professional boxers in that respect; they needed attention, they needed to sell tickets, they needed to talk to newsmen to get the word out about their worthiness.

He told me he left the University of Detroit because of a broken promise. He told me a story I had never heard before. He said that Wil Robinson, his coach at Pershing High School in Detroit, had been told he'd be hired as the basketball coach at the University of Detroit.

The school is now called University of Detroit Mercy. It's where Dave DeBusschere once starred in two sports, and at age 24, became the player-coach of the Detroit Pistons while also playing baseball as a pitcher for the Chicago White Sox. Ralph Simpson, who had also played for Robinson, as did Mel Daniels, at Pershing High was going to transfer from Michigan

State to be reunited with Haywood and their high school coach.

But the University of Detroit officials reneged on their offer and hired Jim Harding as the head basketball coach. He was a bit of a tyrant. He would later coach the Pittsburgh Condors and get into a celebrated scuffle with Gabe Rubin, the team's owner.

Haywood didn't like Harding, a stern sort, and he had signed on to play for Wil Robinson, so instead he signed with the Denver Rockets.

I got to know Wil Robinson. He was a fine man and a wise man. He would be the first black head coach at a mostly white college, Illinois State University, with Doug Collins as his star backcourt man.

I remember Robinson once telling me about his early days in the Detroit ghettos. "Show me a man who has a Cadillac who doesn't have a garage," he told me, "and I'll show you a damn fool."

McHartley admitted to me, in a later phone conversation, that he once owned a Cadillac but didn't have a garage. Spencer Haywood gave me his business card. "Call me anytime," he said. "We can talk."

I had picked up a phone number from Maurice McHartley at that cocktail party in Indianapolis.

I called him twice in early May 2020. At one point in our conversation, I told him he was only the third-best basketball player named Maurice.

I asked him if he remembered the other ones. He couldn't come up with the names. I told him it was Maurice Stokes, a former star at Westinghouse High School in Pittsburgh, and at little St. Francis of Loretto (Pa.) College, and with the NBA Royals in Rochester, New York and Cincinnati, Ohio, and the second best was another Pittsburgh high school (Schenley) product, Maurice Lucas, who starred at Marquette University and in the ABA and NBA.

At the mention of Maurice Stokes, McHartley said, "He was a big dude, strong, yeah, I remember him now. I can see him now. He could play."

McHartley was also called "Mo," same as Stokes, and "Reece."

I then told McHartley he was the second-best basketball player called "Reece."

"Who was better than me?" said McHartley, now playing my game. "Reece 'Goose' Tatum," I said, "the star of the Harlem Globetrotters in the '40s and '50s." Tatum was certainly the world-touring team's most entertaining player.

Tatum's first pro team was the Louisville Black Colonels and his final team was the Detroit Stars, and somewhere in between Tatum played for the Birmingham Black Barons before he played for the Harlem Globetrotters, and the Indianapolis Clowns. See a pattern to Reece's pro resume?

Bill Sharman
Notes and Letters from L.A.

B ill Sharman sent me letters, notes, photos and scouting reports regularly when he was coaching in the ABA and the NBA. He wrote lengthy reports on the strengths and weaknesses of teams in both leagues and was a great source, along with reports sent to me by Richie Guerin and Cotton Fitzsimmons and Larry Creger. They were the basis for my detailed evaluations of all pro teams in my annuals, *The Complete Handbook of Pro Basketball.*

We'd visit with each other in Los Angeles and in Pittsburgh, where his son Tom, a high school teacher, resides in the southern suburb of Peters Township. This meant a lot to me.

Back in the '50s, Sharman was paired with Bob Cousy in the backcourt of the Boston Celtics. I still have a coverless copy of a sports magazine published during that span, somewhere in the mid-50s when I was 12 or 13 years old, that I saved. Sharman was featured in the NBA section.

The magazine had a section on each of the major sports, with thumbnail head shots and brief bios of the best in each sport. Red Holzman was then a backcourt-man for the Rochester Royals. He was the coach of the NBA champion Knicks when I arrived in New York in 1970. I had a wonderful opportunity to be part of a four-man writing team for *The New York Post,* covering the Knicks when they won the first title in the team's history.

What were the odds that a kid who devoured sports magazines would someday meet and get to know Sharman and Holzman, and have them regard me as a friend in the business?

I found a type-written letter on Los Angeles Lakers stationery in my files when I got my house in order during the stay-at-home edict during the coronavirus pandemic. It was dated March 4, 1982.

Dear Jim:

Received your letter regarding the A.B.A. story. It was certainly nice hearing from you again. Sounds like you have really been busy since I've seen you last. Sorry we missed each other at the All-Star Game, for it would have been fun to reminisce back over a few years.

Jim, I'm not exactly sure what you want or need for this A.B.A. story so I thought I would just make a few notes, observations, memories, etc.

1. You asked me how I now regard the A.B.A. I guess the final word on the league was that it was a financial disaster. However, I do believe it was an artistic success. When they folded and the four teams merged with the N.B.A., they had just about reached parity. In fact, the last year the two leagues played against each other in exhibition games, the A.B.A. had a better record.

2. Although the N.B.A. seemed to sign and keep most of the good big centers, I felt the A.B.A. developed a great number of superstars and exciting players during their short period of existence. Such players as Julius "Dr. J" Erving, George Gervin, Rick Barry, George McGinnis, Maurice Lucas, David Thompson, Mark Olberding, Artis Gilmore, Spencer Haywood, Willie Wise, Dan Issel, Louie Dampier, James Silas; etc. Most of these are still playing and are great stars in the N.B.A. today.

3. I guess my fondest memory was winning the championship our first year in Utah in 1971. We beat Kentucky in seven games in the final championship series. However, we had to win the seventh game against the defending champion Indiana Pacers to qualify for the championship series. It was a very exciting and successful year, especially since it was the first major league sports team ever in the state of Utah.

4. I believe the most painful memory I have is when I was coaching the San Francisco Warriors and the Oakland Oaks A.B.A. club signed Rick Barry away from us. Rick had averaged 35 points a game the year before and we got all the way to the finals before Philadelphia beat us in six games. However, we had a young club with Nate Thurmond at center and, with Barry coming back, I felt we might have a good shot at winning the championship. With him gone – and he had to sit out the season because of his contract with us—plus a few key injuries, we had a fair but disappointing season.

5. Since I was one of the first coaches to suggest the three-point line and basket, I'm pleased to see it has been adopted and considered successful in the N.B.A. We had used it in the old Abe Saperstein A.B.L. league during the 1961–62 season. I had pushed for it way back then. Saperstein had me shoot to test the distance and I suggested it be 25 feet to the back of the basket rather than to the front of the hoop. I still think the line should be brought in another nine inches to a foot to allow teams and coaches to utilize the very exciting play a lot more.

6. The red, white and blue basketball never caught on, however, I do believe it at least brought attention to the old dull brown basketballs that were being used throughout the country. Now all schools and teams use a much brighter orange colored ball.

Hope this will help a little. Perhaps sometime soon we will have the opportunity to cross along the basketball trails.

Kindest regards,
Bill Sharman
General Manager
BS/mll

Sharman sent me a note card on Lakers' stationery in early August of 2009. It was hand-written but not dated.

Dear Jim,
Just a note to say hello, and to mention again how nice and enjoyable to see you again! Plus, my son and his wife certainly enjoyed the evening and hearing some of your very (many) wonderful stories!

Accordingly, I thought I would send

Author with Lakers general manager Bill Sharman.

Kathleen Churchman O'Brien

you a couple of my pictures and etc. And, if you don't like them they always make a good "target," for your dart board. Let me know if there is any way I can help you with your book. Best wishes, All my best, Bill

IV PHOENIX (SUNS)

(A) STRONG-POINTS —— Phoenix has one of the most physical and aggressive clubs in the league. Last year they were able to over-power many of the other teams with size and strength! They also had the shooting and ~~fitness~~ to wind up with one of the top records in the league. With the addition of Charlie Scott, who changed leagues, and was the leading scorer in the A.B.A. last year, they should be able to challenge any team for the title. They have moved over from the mid-west division to an even stronger Pacific-division which means ~~injuries will play a vital role in~~ the final standings.

(B) WEAK-POINTS ——— In acquiring the rights to sign Charlie Scott from the A.B.A., Phoenix ~~~~ will have to compensate the Boston Celtics with a top player. This could be a ~~~~ negative factor, as the suns starting line-up complemented each other extremely well last season, ~~and sometimes breaking~~ up a unit that works well together is hard to replace.

(C) GENERAL-COMMENTS ——— Corky Calhoun, the Phoenix number one draft pick could become a big help. Although his scouting reports were varied by the so called experts, many feel he is a real sleeper and an excellent type of player for pro-ball.

This is a sample of pro basketball scouting report from Coach Bill Sharman for use in *The Complete Handbook of Pro Basketball*.

Bill Russell
You don't have to be a shooter to be a force in this sport

Bill Russell was a student of the game, and he single-handedly revolutionized the sport. He wanted to know what his opponents liked to do—does he always drive left and which hand does he favor?—and he made sure no one got to do what they wanted to do near the hoop. That was his domain. He anticipated moves and shots and blocked shots like nobody before him, and few since.

In 1955 the NCAA coaches' rules committee introduced what became known as "Russell's Rules," by widening the free throw lane to 12 feet and making it illegal to touch the ball on its downward arc. It didn't restrict Russell because he was quicker than most big men and still beat them to the ball.

William Fenton Russell was born in Monroe, Louisiana on February 12, 1934 and his family moved to California during World War II when Russell was 9 years old. That's when he began playing basketball. Russell grew up like few kids in the modest projects of Oakland, California. As a skinny 6–2, 128-pounder, he failed to make any sports teams in junior high school and served as the mascot for the high school team. He made the basketball team in tenth grade and became a standout at McClymonds High School in Oakland. He was 6–7 by his senior year, and gained a scholarship to the University of San Francisco.

McClymonds High also produced two baseball greats, Frank Robinson, the only player to win MVP honors in both the National and American League, and Frank's teammate on the Cincinnati Reds, Vada Pinson.

Boston teammate Bailey Howell gets out of the way of high-kicking Bill Russell.

But Russell was the greatest graduate of the school. He could jump. At USF, he could touch a spot on the backboard that is 14 feet high, four feet above the rim. He high-jumped a near world-record six feet nine inches—almost his height—during his student days at the University of San Francisco.

At 6–9½, he was an intimidating defensive force and a great rebounder at both ends of the floor. As a sophomore, he became the team's starting center and led the Dons to 55 consecutive wins and back-to-back NCAA championships.

The team was coached by Phil Woolpert and included two other future NBA players, K.C. Jones and Mike Farmer. Russell and Jones led the Dons to a victory over LaSalle in 1955, when LaSalle's star player, Tom Gola, was regarded as the finest college basketball player in the country. Russell was better.

In 1955 and 1956, Russell was named to the All-America team. As a senior, he was named the National Player of the Year in 1956. He scored 1,636 points (20.7 average) and 1,606 rebounds (20.3 average) in 79 games. He didn't shoot much from outside, but his left-handed hook shot was lethal.

"Shooting is of relatively little importance in a player's overall game," he said at the time.

He averaged 19.2 points and 19.9 rebounds as a sophomore at USF, then 21.4 points and 20.3 rebounds as a junior, and 20.6 points and 21 rebounds as a senior. Read those statistics one more time. Nobody puts up double-doubles like that anymore. He set a long-standing record for rebounds in an NCAA Final Four game with 27 against Iowa in 1956. Russell scored 26 points in that same title-game victory.

That same year, Russell starred for the U.S. team that won all eight games by at least 30 or more points to win the gold medal in the 1956 Olympic Games in

Melbourne, Australia. This author was 14 at the time and became a big fan of the Olympic Games that year.

Russell and Jones would later team up to lead the Boston Celtics to eight straight NBA titles and 11 championships in 13 seasons. At the end of the 1965-66 season, Red Auerbach retired as coach and named Russell as his successor.

It was more difficult for a black man to be the leader of a college or pro basketball team in those days, but Russell never backed down from a challenge. Russell refused to attend ceremonies in Springfield, Massachusetts, when he was enshrined in the Basketball Hall of Fame in 1975. It was his "personal protest" to what he had endured in his playing days.

He helped clear the lane for many black ballplayers.

"I played because I enjoyed it," he said, "but there's more to it than that. I played because I was dedicated to being the best. I was part of a team, and I dedicated myself to making that team the best."

* * *

That was quite an accomplishment at the University of San Francisco. The Dons had no "home court" advantage because the school had no gymnasium on campus. The Dons played most home games at Kezar Pavilion a few blocks away from the school, and some games each season across town at the Cow Palace. They usually practiced at St. Ignatius High School or at Kezar when it was free between San Francisco high school games. Occasionally, when neither of these sites was available the Dons squeezed into the San Francisco Boys Club's Page Street Gym.

The Dons had one of the greatest football teams ever assembled at any school in the country during that same period. They had an undefeated team in

1951 and turned down a major bowl bid when they were asked to leave two black players at home. USF gave up football after that season, citing the high costs. An Orange Bowl paycheck could have saved the program.

The Dons gained a lot of respect for not going along with the bowl committee's request. Russell knew about that story only too well.

The 1950 USF football team was coached by Joe Kuharich and included the likes of future Pro Football Hall of Famers Ollie Matson, Gino Marchetti, Bill Stanfel and Bob St. Clair, the quarterback was future NFLer Ed Brown and the school's sports information director was a young man named Pete Rozelle, the future NFL commissioner.

* * *

John Wooden, the legendary coach at UCLA, had a great deal of respect for Russell. "Russell's the greatest defensive man I've ever seen," said Wooden.

In an era dominated by offensive tactics, Russell drew rave reviews for his defensive play. "I've never seen anybody like him," said Coach Frank McGuire of North Carolina. "When he sticks those long arms up in the air, you just can't get a shot off within 12 or 15 feet of the basket."

* * *

There was a story about Bill Russell by Charles Maher of the *Los Angeles Times* that reveals another side of this multi-dimensional man.

This was when Russell was about to take over as coach and general manager of the Seattle Supersonics. He was giving up a gig as an analyst of NBA games for ABC.

"I hate to think of myself, ten years from now, doing the color on basketball. It doesn't seem like a meaningful job to me," said Russell.

Instead of taking an airplane from Los Angeles to Seattle, Russell decided to travel to his new job on a motorcycle. It took him a few days to do this.

Asked why he didn't just fly up, Russell responded, "The West Coast is one of the most beautiful places in the world and if you fly you lose too much."

Bill Russell never liked to lose anything.

Bill Bradley summed up Bill Russell's career nicely in *Life on the Run*: "Most probably, he was overlooked because his greatest accomplishments were in the game's subtleties, and in seeking to guarantee team victory in a society that tends to focus attention on the individual achiever."

Bob Pettit
You can't keep a good man down too long

Bob Pettit was born and bred in Baton Rouge, Louisiana. He was 5–10 as a high school freshman, but awkward. He was cut when he tried out for the football, baseball and the basketball team.

"The basketball coach ran out of uniforms before he got to me," Pettit liked to tell people.

After Pettit was cut, his dad put up a basketball hoop in their backyard, and Bob put two reading lamps in a window of his home, pointing them toward that hoop. "I shot at that basket for hours on end," recalled Pettit, "sometimes until nine o'clock at night."

I did the same thing and I also kept statistics on our street games and wrote about it in a local weekly newspaper. What it did was lead me to a career as a writer and editor for basketball publications.

Bob's father would come out at night and shoot with his son. Sometimes his mother would come out. My mother always told me she played in bloomers on her St. Joseph's Academy basketball team in the Ohio Valley, but she resisted the temptation to show me how it was done.

As a junior, Pettit played and helped the Baton Rouge High School basketball team win a city title, and as a senior he scored enough points to help the team win the state championship. He had grown seven inches to 6-5 by that time. "That was so important back then to win a high school championship."

* * *

Fifteen colleges offered Pettit athletic scholarships, but he settled for the one from his hometown school, Louisiana State University. He only lived in a dormitory for one year, and stayed at home the other three years. He was a cheap date.

At LSU, Robert Lee Pettit Jr. developed into a fine 6–9 pivot. He was called "Big Blue." The nickname stemmed from him wearing a dark blue overcoat. Buddy Blattner, the LSU broadcaster, started calling him "Big Blue," and it stuck. Pettit was respected for his demeanor on and off the court. He always had class.

"And the worst nights I had, the harder I worked," recalled Pettit, who was still a sleek and handsome man at 71 years of age, when he attended the 2003 NCAA Final Four men's basketball championship and the announcement of the new Basketball Hall of Fame class in New Orleans.

My wife Kathie took a photo of Pettit and me at the Hyatt. We were there for my induction into the U.S. Basketball Writers Association Hall of Fame. I was the first Pittsburgher to be honored. Mike DeCourcy, who followed me at *The Pittsburgh Press* (1983–93) and as a basketball columnist for *The Sporting News,* was similarly honored in 2012. I was joined by Bill Jauss of the *Chicago Tribune* as an honoree in 2003.

Kathleen Churchman O'Brien

Bob Pettit and Jim O'Brien in New Orleans on April 7, 2003.

* * *

As a 6–9, 205-pound forward, Pettit was an 11-time
NBA All-Star, a three-time MVP in the league's All-
Star Game and one-time co-MVP, and he led the St.
Louis Hawks to the 1958 NBA championship over the
Boston Celtics. He was installed into the Basketball
Hall of Fame in 1970 in the same class as Bob Cousy.
Bill Russell, who didn't praise a lot of people, once said
of Pettit, "There's not a greater competitor in sports
today than Bob Pettit."

"If my shot was missing, I went to the boards like
a crazy man," said Pettit. "I think during my career I
averaged eight to ten points a game off the offensive

Hawks archives

**Bob Pettit and Cliff Hagan led St. Louis Hawks to NBA
championship in 1958.**

"I don't think any player had the desire to play and excel more than I did. To do that, you've got to play every night."
—Bob Pettit

boards. I had a great desire to play. I really did. I don't think many players had the desire to play and excel any stronger than I did. To do that, you've got to play every night."

One of the highlights of Pettit's pro career came in Game 6 of the NBA championship series in 1958. He scored 50 points, an NBA playoff record at the time, to lead the Hawks to a 110–109 victory over the celebrated Celtics. He scored 19 of the Hawks' final 21 points, including the game-winning basket in the last 15 seconds. He hit 19 of 34 field goal attempts, 12 of 15 free throws, and led the Hawks with 19 rebounds. Teammate Cliff Hagan was the only other Hawk to score in double figures with 15 points.

Alex Hannum had this to say in praise of Pettit: "I was an old-timer when he broke in and I saw him mature into a great player. Pettit played so well at LSU that his coach, Cliff Wells, said at the time, 'He's the best big man in college basketball today.'"

Pettit scored as many as 60 points in one outing at LSU and 50 in another. He was a consensus second-team All-America in 1953 and a first-team All-America in 1954. He averaged 27.8 points and 15.1 rebounds in his three-year collegiate career.

Pettit was a member of the last all-white NBA championship team. That was in 1958. Alex Hannum was the coach and some of Pettit's teammates included future Hall of Fame players Cliff Hagan, Ed Macauley and Slater Martin, as well as Jack McMahon, Chuck Share, Frank Selvy and Win Wilfong. I watched them on black-and-white television in those days.

"I had always looked at basketball as just a stepping stone in life," said Pettit, who entered the banking business after he retired from the NBA at age 32.

"Basketball has been a tremendous part of my life. No matter what I do, people always will remember my basketball career."

Mack Calvin
Overcame challenges all the way
and eyes the Basketball Hall of Fame

Mack Calvin was more than kind to me in his ABA heyday. He had an easy smile, an actual sparkle in his dark eyes, and Calvin passed the basketball and praise to teammates, opponents and even some sportswriters in his career. When he signed something it always included a warm note over his signature.

Nothing had changed when I met Mack Calvin as he came into the lobby of the JW Marriott Hotel in downtown Indianapolis late in the afternoon of April 6, 2018 to join old friends and foes alike for the 50th year anniversary of the American Basketball Association.

He passed by me in an electric-blue sport coat that was way too snug, just like mine, but snug-fitting suits—"skinny suits"—are now in fashion which is great for us guys who have put on weight since we met for the first time back in the 1969–70 season when Calvin was the lead guard for the Los Angeles Stars. I was writing sports for *The Miami News* that season. Calvin would come to the Floridians the following year, after I had moved on to New York, in a trade for another of my favorites, Donnie Freeman.

Calvin and Freeman were two of the friendliest fellows in the ABA ranks, and also two of the league's best backcourtmen.

Calvin had his eyes fixed on his family, so he didn't notice me. "Mack," I called out to Calvin as he stood with his wife and daughter and their bags, about five yards away.

He looked back in my direction. He came over right away and gave me a big hug. "I always liked interviewing you," I said, "because I could look you in the eyes."

It was the same way with Joe Hamilton, another small guard from those days, when he came by and hugged us both. Those guys didn't hug much back in their playing days, but they do now. "I'm just happy to be alive," said Brian Taylor. "It's a joy just to be here."

Taylor, Hamilton and Calvin were calling me "a legend," so, of course, I was happy to be in their company. "That just means we're getting old," I said.

Calvin was listed at 6-feet in his playing days, but I don't believe he was ever that tall, maybe a shade shorter, and closer to my 5–8½. Now he was another shade shorter. All the players at their gathering looked a little smaller, even Artis Gilmore, who was 7–2 when he played in the ABA and NBA. The body frame folds a bit after a while.

Calvin had played his college ball at USC, but I noticed his tie was light blue and yellow striped, UCLA colors. Calvin looked down when I called this color choice to his attention. "I was trying to coordinate it with my coat," he said.

"I want to talk to you later, if you've got some time," he told me. "I want to share some stuff with you. And I need your help to get into the Basketball Hall of Fame."

I had a quick comeback to that comment. "I can't help you anymore," I said. "I was on the nominating committee for the Hall of Fame for five years, and I later got Connie Hawkins into the Hall of Fame, but I'm out of the loop these days. I don't have any influence in that respect."

Then, too, to be honest, Calvin was a considerable talent, but he might have been just shy of the kind of career needed to get Hall of Fame consideration, especially if the ABA days are the best part of your resume. He was an outstanding guard for seven seasons in the ABA, but he was just a journeyman as a player and coach in the NBA, playing for nine teams altogether in his pro career, and putting in some coaching stints with the Milwaukee Bucks, San Antonio Spurs and LA Clippers.

He was one of the ABA's best players and personalities, but I don't think of him as a great player, someone such as The Hawk, Dr. J or The Iceman, or George McGinnis, Dan Issel, Spencer Haywood or Rick Barry.

I talked to some other ABA players at the reunion and they all agreed with my assessment, though they might have told Calvin he deserved such an honor. I hope he makes it. It would be a real overcoming-the-odds-to-become-successful story. If there was a Hall of Fame for good guys he and Donnie Freeman would be the ABA's best backcourt pairing.

It's harder now for an ABA player to make it. The Hall of Fame folded its ABA veterans committee in 2015, and it only permits—and this is ridiculous—only one former ABA player per HOF class. There are other ABA players who deserve to be inducted.

The year after the ABA was absorbed into the NBA, ten of the 20 players picked for the All-Star game had an ABA background, and five of the ten starters were ABA alumni. What about equal rights?

Maurice Lucas and Dave Twardzik from the ABA teamed up with Bill Walton to lead the Portland Trail Blazers to the NBA championship that first year after the NBA admitted four new teams, plus players in a dispersal draft that strengthened some of their existing franchises.

*   *   *

Calvin came back to the same spot where we had met the next morning—Saturday—and sat down next to me in the hotel lobby.

"I do a lot of motivational speaking for the LA School District and for the Fellowship of Christian Athletes," he began. "I try to inspire people. If I could succeed, they can succeed. It's a matter of making the right choices, being dedicated to doing good things, and treating people right. It's a matter of keeping good company."

Then Calvin came clean. "I want to write a book," he said, "and you can help me. I'll pay you for whatever advice or help you can give me. You will be paid for your efforts. I trust you with my story."

I thought I already knew Mack Calvin's story, but what I knew fell far short of his background story, his rise from poverty and a poor home environment and other school challenges that could have ended badly. But Mack Calvin was up to those challenges and then some. He got help from someone who cared, and now it's Mack's mission to provide that kind of mentoring and guidance to others similarly challenged. I listened with great attention to his story. Much of it was new to me. "We were poor," said Calvin in what sounded like a confession. "My father was an alcoholic. He had a fourth-grade education and my mother was a high school graduate."

I had to stop him there. My father got as far as fifth grade before he dropped out to take a job in the mechanics' shop of the Baltimore & Ohio Railroad about a block from our home in Glenwood. My grandfather, Richard Burns, was the yardmaster of the Glenwood Yard and got him the job, even though my dad was just 15 at the time and had to lie about his age. My mother graduated second in her class, or so she always told me, at St. Joseph's Academy in Bridgeport, Ohio.

"My father was abusive," said Calvin. "He was abusive with my mother and me and our family. It was a nightmare."

Mack Calvin

FLORIDIANS

AMERICAN BASKETBALL ASSOCIATION

Mack "The Knife" Calvin
with ABA's signature
basketball.

**Billy Keller of Indiana Pacers
and Mack Calvin, who played
with several ABA teams, liked
to kid about who was the taller
of the two terrific guards.**

Mine was not. My dad, Dan O'Brien, was what they called a pleasant drunk rather than a mean drunk like the fathers of some of my friends. He was never in my face and the older I get the more I appreciate that. From the age of ten I always thought I was looking out for my dad rather than the other way around.

"I started playing basketball when I was nine or ten at parks and recreation in South Central LA," continued Calvin. "We were poor so it was just basketball that I had to keep me busy and keep me out of trouble."

*   *   *

I could say the same. Except I was never good enough as a basketball player to make any meaningful teams. I did make the Pittsburgh CYO All-Star team. The Catholic Youth Organization provided a place to play for kids who weren't talented enough to play on their high school teams.

My parents never pushed me toward a college education. I was told to stay out of trouble, and be nice to my elders; that's it. There were rules that were expected to be honored. You could only go so far from the house, and you had to come home when the street lights came on. Trouble was easy to come by in our community, but I have often told people that when you grew up in Glenwood or neighboring Hazelwood, in the inner-city of Pittsburgh, you could also learn how not to get into trouble. You knew when it was best to stay home.

My 11th grade English teacher at Taylor Allderdice High School in the Squirrel Hill section of the city, Lois Josephs, told me, "Jimmy, people will always judge you by the way you speak and the company you keep."

When I am delivering a talk to some group I often finish with Mrs. Joseph's message and add that I think she would be proud of the way I speak and the company I keep.

"I came out of grade school with a third-grade reading level," said Calvin. "And I stuttered. So, I was ashamed to stand up and speak in class. The kids would make fun of me. Then I started cutting classes. I did the same thing in high school. I was reading at a 7th grade level as a senior in high school."

Wilt Chamberlain also stuttered in his Philadelphia school days, but he became a smooth speaker as an adult.

Calvin became a student at Long Beach Polytechnic High School, a school that produced such great athletes as baseball's Tony Gwynn, football's DeSean Jackson and tennis Hall of Fame member Billie Jean King, according to a research report done by Brian Rzeppa. It was a guest story in a Los Angeles Clippers' game program when Calvin was coaching the Clippers. Over 100 colleges came calling on Calvin to play basket-ball for them. Rzeppa's research provided some items I didn't have in my files. Calvin had covered much of that same ground when he spoke to me that Saturday in the hotel lobby, and added a few gems.

"I was unable to qualify for any of the scholarships I was offered," said Calvin. "I had a 1.9 GPA coming out of high school and if it weren't for an arts and crafts teacher changing my grade from a D to a C, I wouldn't have graduated from high school.

"I didn't really have anyone to push me to connect with education. So, I went to Long Beach City College and ran into difficulty right away. I was missing classes in the first few weeks. My coach told me, 'Mack, you're doing the same thing you did in high school. You're cutting classes. Why are you doing that?'

"I started crying. I told him I couldn't read like the other students, and I was ashamed of myself. He set me up with some tutors and got me into some classes that would benefit me. He told me if I continued to cut classes, he was done with me. He would cut me from the team and I would lose my scholarship. That did it. One man turned things around for me. I want to be that man in some other people's life.

"By the time I graduated from Long Beach Junior College, I had made the Dean's List and had a 3.5 GPA." His choice for a college came down to UCLA, coached by the great John Wooden, or USC, coached by Bob Boyd, another personable and greatly respected man.

"John Wooden came to my home to recruit me, and I was told he usually had his assistants make the home calls. I didn't feel good about having him in our home because it was not much to look at. We would later move out of the project to a better home.

"I got along well with Boyd. I thought he really liked me, so I went to USC. The choice wasn't really difficult for me."

UCLA publicity photo

UCLA Glory Days in 70s had, left to right, assistant coaches Gary Cunningham and Denny Crum, with head coach John Wooden. They wanted Mack Calvin, but he chose to go with Bob Boyd at Southern Cal. "John Wooden came to my home to recruit me," recalled Calvin, "and I was under the understanding that his assistants usually made the house calls in recruiting process."

That said, it would seem like UCLA would have been tough to turn down. Wooden had just won the first of seven consecutive national championships. Lew Alcindor—who changed his name to Kareem Abdul-Jabbar in the NBA—and Bill Walton were the leaders for the Bruins' basketball team from the late '60s into the early '70s.

Boyd was a booster of Calvin as well. "There is no limit to what Mack can do," said the USC coach. "He is a quick, strong little guy. He is a champion. His attitude and his manner are absorbed by the entire team."

* * *

The ABA had a lot of outstanding guards such as Steve Jones, James Jones and Larry Jones, and Louie Dampier and Darel Carrier, Charlie Williams and Chuck Williams, Billy Keller, Donnie Freeman, Mack Calvin, Joe Hamilton, Billy Melchionni, Brian Taylor, Glen Combs, Warren Armstrong, Ron Boone, Larry Brown, Al Smith, James T. Silas, George Karl, John Williamson, Charlie Scott, John Roche and Freddie Lewis.

When I attended the 50th anniversary of the ABA's beginning, back in April and May of 2018, in Indianapolis, Louisville and Pittsburgh, I had a chance to connect with these guys once again.

I didn't have to look up at Calvin and Hamilton and Keller, for instance, because, I swear, we were now the same size—about 5–9—and not the 6–0 that was next to their names in game programs back in the late '60s and early '70s. Calvin was an ABA All-Star four consecutive seasons.

By any measuring stick, Mack Calvin was outstanding. So was Carrier, and both mentioned that they had allies that were conducting campaigns to get them into the Basketball Hall of Fame. Once upon a time, I had the kind of connections to help them in that regard. But no longer. Yes, I'm out of the loop, as my wife Kathie keeps reminding me.

Here's a tale that goes back to December 13, 1970. I was then working at *The New York Post*, following a year of covering the Floridians now and then for *The Miami News*. My main beat back then were the Dolphins in their final season in the American Football League.

Calvin and Larry Jones were a formidable back-court combination for the Floridians. Calvin was all-ABA first team, averaging 27.2 points per game, and Larry Jones was averaging 24.3 points per game. The year before, when I first arrived in Miami, the Floridians' roster included guards Larry Cannon and Donnie Freeman, and forwards Simmie Hill and Art Heyman (talk about crazies), centers Skip Thoren and Al Cueto—who at 6–8 was billed as the "world's tallest Cuban."

Calvin kept insisting he was 70½ to 72½ inches, when Joe Donnelly of Long Island's *Newsday*, who was my size, challenged Calvin about his height. Calvin said he was six feet, ½ inch, but admitted under cross-examination that he donned shoes to measure himself. "They must have lifts," wrote a doubting Donnelley, who could offer a chin as formidable as Calvin's when confronted about anything.

But I can set the record straight with stories about these talented and resourceful men, and certify that they were the real deal.

Donnelley caught Calvin after an outstanding night during the 1970–71 season when he led the Floridians to a 100–97 victory over the Nets at Island Garden in West Hempstead.

Calvin came into the game as the scoring leader in the ABA, and was second only to the Nets' Billy Melchionni in assists. Calvin was the total offensive

New York Nets Publicity Photo

Tom "Trooper" Washington and Mack Calvin of Floridians put the squeeze on Nets' point guard Bill Melchionni.

Jim O'Brien

Three of ABA's best backcourtmen, Mack Calvin, Bill Melchionni and Larry Jones, were reunited at 30th year anniversary reunion in Indianapolis in summer of 1998.

leader, as Donnelly pointed out, directly or indirectly responsible for more than 45 points a game.

Calvin told Donnelly that when he'd go into drug stores, he'd check out newspapers and magazines, and basketball box scores to see how the guys his size were doing. "I'd look to see how Joe Hamilton, who is even smaller than me, to see how he was doing. I want to see how many minutes Calvin Murphy played, how many he scored," confessed Calvin. "The same with Nate 'Tiny' Archibald. I root for them because they're guys like me. I want to see what the small man is doing in the other league."

Calvin had come through in the clutch when the Floridians defeated the Nets, and the week before he scored 43 points in a win over Kentucky.

Melchionni, who had come to the ABA from the NBA's Philadelphia 76ers team of Wilt Chamberlain & Co., knew what was going on in both leagues. He continued to live in Philadelphia and commuted to Long Island to play for the Nets.

He recognized Calvin's cat-quick skills and toughness. "He runs so damn much," commented Melchionni, "and he's such a good opportunist. He makes the most of what he has."

In addition to scoring, Calvin passed the ball to Larry Jones that night at Island Garden and Jones, the Floridians' other guard, was hot with 33 points, including 12 in the last period. "They speak for themselves," winning coach Hal Blitman said of his backcourt combination.

Calvin had clicked with Larry Brown when he was his coach with the Carolina Cougars so he was happy when Brown became the coach of the Denver Nuggets, and Carl Scheer, who had been his boss as GM of the Cougars took a similar post in Denver, and claimed Calvin in a trade.

"It's one of the first things I did," said Scheer. "Every winning team needs a guy like Mack. We were fortunate to get him."

"I'm as happy as I ever thought I could be," the 26-year-old Calvin told Jim Bukata, the ABA's director of public relations. "Here, we have talent and togetherness—friendliness and togetherness."

In his second season in the ABA, Calvin averaged 27.2 points a game to rank fourth among ABA scorers for the 1970–71 season. He made a marvelous Madison Square Garden debut by scoring 41 points against the Utah Stars in a St. Patrick's Day doubleheader. No one was happier that night than Ned Doyle, the Madison Avenue ad executive who owned the Floridians. Always the imaginative one, Doyle had an O' on the jerseys of all his players. So it was Mack O'Calvin who scored 43 points on St. Patrick's Day.

Texas-born, but a Southern Californian since then, Calvin had come a long way since his first days in the ABA. Bob Boyd had to sell Bill Sharman on giving Calvin a chance with the LA Stars. Sharman had been a star at USC before joining Bob Cousy in the backcourt of the Boston Celtics, and that connection helped Calvin. In his den, the most dominant decoration is a photograph showing him driving around Lew Alcindor. Lew, of course, later known as Kareem Abdul-Jabbar, played for national championship teams at UCLA while Calvin worked cross-town for the second-best team in LA, the Southern Cal Trojans.

Calvin can recall beating UCLA and while he admits basketball is a big man's game, a little guy can give everyone fits from time to time. Calvin could, that's for sure.

*   *   *

USC Coach Bob Boyd used to have his players take a test administered by a team of psychologists at San Jose State University.

In 1968, when Calvin took the test, his score was the most nearly perfect of any of the 10,000 athletes who had been examined previously.

Boyd said, "The test tells you about a player's talent for winning, about how he will react under adverse circumstances. It tells you about how much of a player's physical ability he can give you when the situation is the toughest. The people who administered the test had no idea if Calvin was two feet tall or eight feet tall. They just said that the tougher the situation gets, the better this guy likes it."

In historian Ron Chernow's book about Ulysses S. Grant—called simply *Grant*—the one-time Union general turned president was thought to have the same quality, calm before the storm. At his best in battle, able to size up a situation and then act upon it. In short, Grant didn't panic. Neither did Mack Calvin.

Correspondence from Mack Calvin
I came across a letter in my files from Mack Calvin dated September 15, 1997:

Dear Jim: It was great to see you several weeks ago at the 30th ABA reunion. The league and former ABA players are indebted to you for your honest and candid comments about the players; you reported the facts. I am grateful to you for your many years of support.

Sincerely, Mack Calvin, Former ABA Player

Wondrous Wendell, Mr. Excitement
Ladner loved life, women and basketball

W ondrous Wendell. That's all it says at the upper-left-hand corner of a folded paper page full of type-written notes about Wendell Larry Ladner, the pride of Necaise Crossing, Mississippi, and what one of his favorite foes, Rick Barry, had to say about him.

It's one of the discoveries I came across in my files while working on this book. I never know what newspaper clippings, interview notes on yellow legal paper, little reporter's notebooks, letters from pro basketball executives, bubble gum cards and photos I am going to find in the storage room to the left of my writing desk.

Wendell Ladner was a legendary figure in the American Basketball Association and one of the reasons the ABA was so much fun to cover. Ladner played for five ABA teams in five seasons from 1970 to 1975. Ladner led the league with three mid-season trades on his resume.

Ladner crammed a lot of clutch play, craziness, lovely women and fun into an all-too-short life. He died at age 26 on June 24, 1975, when he was a passenger on Eastern Air Lines 66 that plummeted to earth in a severe thunderstorm near Kennedy Airport in Jamaica, Queens. If form held true, those two surviving flight attendants both had Wendell Ladner's contact information in their respective purses.

"I never saw anything like it," Van Vance, the radio voice of the Kentucky Colonels once said. "Whenever we'd fly somewhere, when we got off the plane, Wendell had the phone numbers of all the stewardesses."

It would have added to Ladner's legendary status had he lived to talk about it, but as we learned in the case of the Pirates' Roberto Clemente, death in an airplane crash can contribute to a saintly status.

Ladner was identified by the medical examiners at the crash site by the ABA championship ring the Nets were awarded after the 1973–74 season.

I was driving into the backyard of the home of my in-laws, Harvey and Barbara Churchman, when I learned of Ladner's death. A few years earlier, I learned of the death of Gil Hodges, the manager of the New York Mets, in the same manner. You need to keep in mind there were no cell phones in the '70s.

Ladner had just spent two weeks visiting his parents, Mr. and Mrs. Aaron Ladner, in Necaise Crossing, Mississippi, where they raised cotton. Ladner had boarded the flight in New Orleans that was headed for New York.

When I said goodbye to Ladner in the Nets' locker room at Nassau Memorial Coliseum at the conclusion of the 1974–75 season, I told him, "I'll see you here next year." To which Wendell replied, "You won't be seeing me here next year."

It also brought to mind a remark one of the ABA coaches, Tom Nissalke, once said of him. "He's *a vanishing breed*, a guy who comes out every game and gives his all. I'd love to have him. I don't know whether I'd want him as a ballplayer or as a bodyguard."

The Nets got Wendell Ladner and Mike Gale when they traded John Roche to the Colonels midway through the 1973–74 season. I still can't believe the Colonels traded such a fan favorite, but owner John Y. Brown fell in love with Roche, who'd had some high-scoring games against the Colonels and wanted the former University of South Carolina All-American badly.

Before that 1973–74 season, Ladner had teamed up with Colonels' co-owner Ellie Brown in hosting

Kentucky Colonels co-owners John Y. and Ellie Brown, with Dave Vance, their general manager/public relations director, one of the ABA's best in that department.

Pros' forward Wendell Ladner, here storming New York superstar Rick Barry, made the 1971 ABA All-Rookie Team.

coffee klatches around Louisville aimed at selling season tickets to women fans.

Ellie, a beautiful woman herself, was a big fan of Wendell Ladner. "The ladies all loved him," she said. "He was such a handsome rogue."

Ladner believed he was a cross between Mark Spitz, the Olympic swimming sensation, and Burt Reynolds, the movie actor. They all brandished dark eyes and dark mustaches.

Burt Reynolds   **Mark Spitz**   **Wendell Ladner**

"Wendell doesn't know the meaning of the word fear ... as well as a few other words." —Babe McCarthy, his coach at Memphis and Kentucky

Babe McCarthy coached the Kentucky Colonels.

George Gervin
What a showman

There was something distinguishable about the way he walked. The way he talked. You had to smile when George Gervin came your way. Just something about him.

He was something out of Motown as much as the Temptations, Diana Ross and the Supremes, and Marvin Gaye. He was something out of a Broadway musical like Nathan Detroit, a street hustler who runs an illegal floating craps game in the all-black cast of "Guys and Dolls." Now that Gervin's older and has whisker-like lines around his mouth and eyes, Mr. Mistoffelees from "Cats" comes to mind. Maybe that's a bit of a stretch.

Excerpt about Mister Mistoffelees:

He is quiet and small, he is black
From his ears to the tip of his tail.
He can creep through the tiniest
   crack.
He can walk on the narrowest rail.
He can pick any card from a pack.
He is equally cunning with dice.
He is always deceiving you into
   believing,

That he's only looking for mice.
He can play any trick with a cork
Or a spoon and a bit of fish-paste
If you look for a knife or a fork,
And you think it is merely
   misplaced
You have seen it one moment and
Then it is gawn! But you'll find it
Next week lying out on the lawn.
      —T.S. Eliot, *Old Possum's Book*
                  Of Practical Cats

From "Cats" publicity

Mister Mistoffelees

339

Like George Gervin when he left the floor farther from the basket than Wilt ever did in doing his signature finger-tip roll shot. He was a showman, for sure, second in aerial art only to Julius Erving. As good as Gervin was, and few were superior in pure athletic ability, he was always second to Dr. J.

He had the name and the game. His teammates dubbed him "Iceberg Slim," after a notorious pimp-turned-author who produced a best-selling book, and simply "Ice." He was slim and cool and, as Dr. J said with a wink of the eye, "George had a little gangsta in him."

He owed that to his boyhood on the playgrounds in Detroit that spawned so many great basketball players and boxers—Joe Louis, Sugar Ray Robinson and John Brisker come to mind —and his scrapes with the law right through his college days at Eastern Michigan University in Ypsilanti. He did his best to play the badass role.

He weighed only 178 pounds when he was dispatched to the Spurs. "I have a good appetite," he said, "but nothing sticks."

Dave Bing, a former Detroit Piston and later the mayor of Detroit, knew them all. He was one of their heroes.

Gervin had starred at Martin Luther King Jr. High School in Detroit, but struggled on and off the court. He had a growth spurt as a senior and led his team to the state quarterfinals. Gervin averaged 31 points and 20 rebounds that season. He was named to the all-state team by *The Detroit Free Press.*

I might have been working at the *Free Press* that year, 1970, but turned down a job offer from the Knight-Ridder owned newspaper to join *The New York Post* instead.

*   *   *

I had no idea, until I was researching his story for this book, that George Gervin got to Eastern Michigan by way of California State University, Long Beach where he was recruited by Jerry Tarkanian. Tark the Shark and Gervin—he wasn't yet nicknamed "Iceman" or "Ice"—seemed like a likely match. Long Beach was a long way from Detroit, however, and it didn't work out. The cultural shock was too much for Gervin, and he left Long Beach during his first term there and returned home.

Tark needed that towel he always held on the bench to wipe away the tears after Gervin had gone home. Had he stayed at Long Beach, Gervin would have been a teammate of "Easy Ed" Ratleff, a two-time first-team All-America player from Columbus, Ohio.

His career could have ended there, like it did for so many young men in the asphalt playgrounds of Detroit, Chicago, LA, Philadelphia, New York and Baltimore to name just a few of the breeding grounds for sports and crime. It was a different kind of "one and done" activity.

It happened in my hometown of Pittsburgh. Talented athletes would get scholarships to colleges and come home to stay in less than a year. They couldn't handle the academic demands or being so far from home.

As a sophomore during the 1971–72 season at Eastern Michigan, Gervin averaged 29.5 points as a forward.

At the end of that season, Gervin lost his cool in a post-season College Division II game against Roanoke (Va.) State, and pummeled an opponent unmercifully. His behavior scared people, even those who were promoting his place among the elite of college ball.

"I was playing a game," explained Gervin, "and I punched a guy. It just happened."

Gervin was apologetic about punching the player from Norfolk State. "I really wanted to win," he said. "We had won 18 in a row. I couldn't take it no more. I just exploded. It was the first and last fight I ever had in a basketball game, even on the playgrounds where tempers always flared up. It's not like me."

He got kicked off the team, was banned from further involvement with the program. Invitations to try out for the U.S.A. Pan American and Olympic basketball team were withdrawn. Ratleff, from Long Beach, played on those teams.

Those Long Beach State teams in the early '70s compiled a 75–9 record over a three-season period. It could have been better. "I went there for a couple of weeks," said Gervin, "but I couldn't adjust to the lifestyle and the climate. I was just a young guy from Michigan and it was too drastic a change for me. I missed my family and decided I'd be better off near home."

His Long Beach teammates, besides Ratleff, would have included five other players who went on to play in the NBA

* * *

No one back then could have seen what the future held in store for George Gervin or that in 1996 he would be named one of the 50 Greatest Players in NBA history. I was present for that 50th NBA anniversary ceremony, not far from the platform where the players were announced at the All-Star Game in Cleveland.

He would have a great 14-year career in the ABA and the NBA with a career scoring average of 26.2 points per game. For the sake of comparison, Michael

GEORGE 'ICE MAN' GERVIN
"George always had a little gangsta in him," said Julius
Erving at 50th year anniversary reunion of ABA.

Jordan averaged 27.9 points per game in his career, and Kobe Bryant 25 points per game.

Between the ages of 25 and 28, when Gervin was at the top of his game, he led the San Antonio Spurs and the NBA in scoring four out of five seasons. Jordan was the NBA scoring leader in ten of his 15 seasons, with time outs for brief fling at baseball and for premature retirement.

Back in 1991, a George Gervin Community Youth Center opened in San Antonio. Gervin showed up on occasion to check out the kids and put on a show for them. They reminded him of his troubled youth in Detroit. Gervin was a popular figure in San Antonio, as revered as Davy Crockett, Jim Bowie and the brave men who defended the Alamo against Santa Ana and his Mexican marauders.

Santa Ana

The Alamo, by the way, was within a short walk of the hotels where most of the visiting teams stayed, but few players ever took the time to check out this historical Texas landmark. To his credit, "Super John" Williamson of the New York Nets did visit The Alamo. I can verify it because I saw him there.

Williamson had come from a hardscrabble background in New Haven, Connecticut similar to Gervin's.

When Gervin was playing for the Pontiac Chaparrals in the CBA, he scored 50 points in a game. He was spotted that night by John Kerr, an assistant coach and scout for Al Bianchi and the Virginia Squires. Kerr reportedly signed Gervin to a $40,000 contract, but that sounds high to me.

His teammates included Julius Erving, Fatty Taylor, Jim Eakins, Ray Scott and Swen Nater and, as George recalled it, "We had so much talent. We thought we'd win an ABA championship."

In his second season, Gervin was teamed on the frontline of the Virginia Squires with Dr. J and Swen Nater. That was quite a frontline. The ABA-Star Game was played at the Norfolk (Va.) Scope that season and there were rumors that Gervin might be sold for cash. That occurred soon after, the Squires shipping him to the San Antonio Spurs for $225,000. What a steal! I was named the president of the ABA Writers' Association for no compensation. What a deal!

But the Squires had serious financial shortcomings, and soon Erving was dealt to the Nets, and Nater and Gervin to the San Antonio Spurs. "If they could trade The Doctor," said Gervin, "they could trade anyone."

I have the cover of the February 2, 1974 copy of *The Sporting News* on display in a room next to where I am writing this story. George Gervin is shown dunking the red, white and blue ball with Nets' guards Brian Taylor and John Williamson behind him. The headline reads:

Super Squire
George Gervin
RED HOT ICE-MAN

With the Spurs, Gervin averaged around 30 points per game when he was the NBA's scoring leader. That prompted him to shout out from the stage in the Bankers Life Field House, "I can still throw down 30 on all of you!"

He shared that stage with an assembly of some of the greatest players in ABA or NBA history such as Spencer Haywood, George McGinnis, Doug Moe, Rick Barry, Dan Issel and Julius Erving. It may have been the greatest assembly of basketball talent since the NBA's 50th anniversary celebration in Cleveland in 1996.

The first time I interviewed Gervin was at the 1974 ABA All-Star Game in Norfolk for that cover story of *The Sporting News.*

The city of Detroit produces some of the best pro basketball talent in assembly-line fashion like its automobile manufacturing plants.

Gervin said he first took notice of the ABA after Spencer Haywood and Ralph Simpson signed with the Denver Rockets.

"I knew them both well," said Gervin, "and I knew I could play with them and hold my own."

He was disillusioned to learn he had been sold by the Squires to the San Antonio Spurs during what should have been a big event for him, his first ABA All-Star Game appearance at age 21. His agent was New York-based Irwin Weiner, who also represented Dr. J and Walt Frazier.

"I don't think it has affected my playing," Gervin told Joe Gergen of *Newsday* when he played for the Spurs against the Nets in New York right after the All-Star break. "I've gone through quite a few changes. There's always rumors about trades but I never paid much attention. I know if I ever hear them again, I'll listen."

ABA Commissioner Mike Storen tried to stop that trade but a federal judge ruled that Storen could not stop the sale.

I was always impressed with Gervin as a player. He shot his long jump shot just like Jerry Lucas, who was playing for the Knicks at the time, with his feet forward and perpendicular to his hands at the instant of release, his body bent like a boomerang heading on a vertical slant away from the basket.

In their first meeting of the season, Gervin outscored Erving 43–9. "I don't compare myself with him," said Gervin. "He's one of the best, no doubt about that.

"I don't mind being compared with him. But I'm not trying to imitate him. I have my own foot to plant. I haven't put my whole game together yet."

Two of Michigan's all-time greatest players, George Gervin and Magic Johnson, size each other up for photographer.

Peter Vecsey
Another Hoop de Jour column from *New York Post* columnist exclusively for Looking Up Once Again

C ontrary to what you might've heard, Jim O'Brien and I were never rivals. I hardly qualified as a rival because, most days, I couldn't compete with his torrent of timely information and trustworthy sources he'd developed at the college and pro levels. Jim was entrenched in the ABA years before I arrived. Still, playing catch-up every day was a positive incentive. I knew what kind of homework had to be done. Understood the value of assembling a network of reliable sources. When Rupert Murdoch bought the *New York Post* in 1976, I left the *Daily News* and joined Jim on the pro basketball beat... at the same time four ABA teams each paid millions to enroll in the NBA fraternity. I was excited at the prospects of tag-teaming *The Times*, *News*, *Newsday* and the Jersey newspapers. Given that both Jim and I were both willing to put in the time on our dimes, we would've consistently broken stories. Unfortunately, after about three years, he decided to return to hometown Pittsburgh, where 40 years later, he's still manufacturing live copy in book form. I never stopped thinking about how we would've ruled roundball.

* * *

By far, George Thompson is the most overlooked player in Marquette (20.4) basketball history despite holding the school's scoring record for 40 years despite playing but three seasons. Teammate Dean "The

Dream" Meminger got all the headlines when Al McGuire's squads were contending for titles, but the smart money wanted the ball in Thompson's hands with court about to be adjourned. His five ABA seasons (15.6) went equally unnoticed, basically because he had the misfortune to play for losing outfits. Still, when the ABA All Stars evenly battled the NBA All Stars at Nassau Coliseum in 1972, coach Al Bianchi made sure Thompson was in uniform.

* * *

I first saw Lloyd "Sonny" Dove play junior varsity for St. Francis Prep. I was a sub on Archbishop Molloy's varsity waiting to play the feature game. Sonny stood out because of the way he pranced on the break and danced on defense. The 6–8 multipurpose forward was such a good scorer (No. 8 in St. John's history) and rebounder (No. 2) that the Pistons drafted him No. 4 overall. Sadly, his roommate was reprehensible

Lloyd "Sonny" Dove

Reggie Harding. Sonny told me Reggie shot heroin in the room, a habit he shared with Dove. Drugs (later a bicycle accident) were his downfall, though he enjoyed two productive years with the Nets. Tragically, after having cleaned up his act, Dove died when the cab he was driving skidded off a partially open Hamilton Avenue Bridge in Brooklyn. The safety gate was inoperative because of a power failure. Dove was 37, two years younger than me.

Had Roger Brown not been wrongly black-balled by the NBA, and wasted years being restricted to playing semi-pro, there's every reason to believe the 6–6 Man Of a Thousand Moves (but especially a pristine jumper from the International Dateline) would've been among the greatest of all time. Oscar Robertson recognized supreme skills when he chanced to see Rajah play, and recommended the Pacers sign him. Despite having lost a great deal of bounce, his knees held up long enough for him to become a vital contributor for three Indiana championships. No forward was harder to score on than Willie Wise, who repeatedly says Brown was tougher to defend than Julius Erving or Rick Barry.

* * *

Dave DeBusschere was one of a limited number of exceptional athletes to play professional basketball (Pistons & Knicks) and baseball (White Sox). After he retired, No. 22 would occasionally participate in evening pickup games at assorted city gyms.

One night, an elderly janitor was sweeping up on one side of the floor while six of us played at the other.

"I know who you are," the janitor said, pointing at DeBusschere. "I know who you are."

This went on for about ten minutes. Finally, DeBusschere turned toward the guy and said, "OK, who am I?"

"You pitched for the White Sox."

* * *

I laughed out loud when Phil Jackson referred to Dennis Rodman as a maverick in a segment of ESPN's *Last Dance*. Who else remembers that "Maverick" was the title of Jackson's first book of many authored by

Charley Rosen? Though I covered the Knicks for several seasons while Jackson was still active, my last name was butchered in the book. Not to mention my street cred was seriously questioned. Jackson accused me of thinking only black players could play.

* * *

When Willis Reed was Nets GM, I surprised him after a game with a framed photo of him sitting alongside Jackie Robinson. They had been judges at a beauty contest. Reed got emotional. He had never seen the photo. Naturally, I had a duplicate on hand and asked him to sign it. That photo is part of my photo shrine to Jackie, whose treasured autograph was placed in the frame along with two 1956 World Series tickets.

* * *

During Wendell Ladner's tour with the Kentucky Colonels, he dove for a loose woman, er, ball, and crashed into a glass water cooler on the sideline. It shattered into shards. Unruffled, Ladner brushed the glass off his body and got back on the court. "Wendell doesn't know the meaning of fear, and a lot of other words, too," wrote SI's Peter Carry of a quote from ABA coach Babe McCarthy.

* * *

When Larry Kenon turned pro after UCLA's Bill Walton destroyed Memphis State (44 points off 21–22 from the field, plus 13 rebounds) in the NCAA title game, he came to New York for the summer and played for my team at Rucker Park. We were walking in my downtown neighborhood one day when Kenon

Larry Kenon

stopped at a blacktopped playground to watch a softball game. He was both hypnotized and mystified. What's the matter, I asked. After a couple second pause, he replied, "How do they slide?"

* * *

If not for Super John Williamson's second half exploits in Game 6 of the Finals (16 of his 28 points were amassed in the fourth quadrant; Julius Erving did not score a field goal in the 12 minutes), the series would've shifted to Denver and the Nuggets very likely would've beaten the Nets.

John Williamson

As a rookie, the self-anointed "Super John" beat out George Bruns (based on a one-on-one match, arranged by Kevin Loughery) for the fourth guard spot on the roster. Following a 9-game losing streak, which followed four wins to start the season, Loughery replaced John Roche with Williamson in San Antonio against the Spurs. At some point during the first quarter, rough customer Rich Jones welcomed Super John to the league by 'bowing him in the back of the head. A few minutes later, the 6–9 forward got worse from the 6–4 Williamson. The losing streak ended. "What goes around, comes around," Super John said in the locker room. It was the first time I'd heard the biblical expression.

* * *

After Rod Thorn, a Nets assistant under Loughery, had been Bulls GM for a while, he hired his long time buddy (they'd also played together in the NBA) to coach. The previous season, Reggie Theus had averaged 23 points and made the All Star team. Chicago fans adored him. Loughery benched him, terminating his playing streak at 429, and keeping him in dry dock, except for a couple minutes here and there, until the trade deadline, at which time he was shipped to the Kings for Steve Johnson. To this day, nobody's quite sure why. Was it because Reggie held out for two weeks? Was Theus' defense deficient? Was it because ownership interfered by voicing disapproval? Were the fans responsible for constantly chanting, "We want Reggie"? "What a shame," Theus told me recently. "I was fifteen minutes away from playing with Michael Jordan the next season. Hey, I could've been John Paxson."

* * *

When Rick Barry played for the Warriors, his four sons often got to be ball boys. It was Brent's turn on this particular night when Rick became outraged about something or other and got ejected. As he was leaving the court he grabbed Brent around the waist and carried him toward the locker room. Brent, eight or nine, loudly protested. "Put me down! You got thrown out of the game, not me!"

Rick Barry shoots over Virginia's Neil Johnson.

* * *

Billy Paultz once told me that when Wes Unseld turned his back on him under the basket it was like playing against a handball court. In 1978, the Bullets beat the SuperSonics in seven games. It was the franchise's one and only championship. Unseld converted a crucial missed shot of his to take the lead and iced matters with two critical free throws after missing a pair shortly before. I was asked by PR person Brian McIntyre to vote with four other members of the media for the MVP award. Unseld and Elvin Hayes both had two votes when I cast mine for the handball court.

Years later, Unseld, one of two players ever to win the NBA's top rookie award and MVP in the same season (Chamberlain is the other) told me he didn't feel appreciated. "But I stopped trying to please people long ago. All I cared about was that I was making a living."

In that case, I informed the captain of the All Worst Interview Team, you owe me a few good quotes because my vote broke a 2–2 deadlock in *Sport Magazine*'s MVP balloting in the 1978 playoffs. Subsequently, "you got a car and a better contract."

"Owe you? I'm mad at you!" Unseld retorted. "Because of you, I'm in a higher tax bracket."

Peter Vecsey has authored a book on basketball due for publication this fall, 2020. Dr. J was best man at Pete's wedding.

George R. Thompson III
He always knew where he was going

I wish I could have you listen in on a telephone conversation I am having with George Thompson just to hear how he says, "The Hawk is coming! The Hawk is coming!"

Thompson says it in a theatrical stage whisper, the way those words once were relayed along the chain-link fence surrounding the Rucker Park basketball court in Harlem. Thompson has a bit of Broadway in him, as well as Brooklyn, where he was born and grew up. "The Hawk is coming! The Hawk is coming!"

They were mostly young black kids hanging onto the fence for dear life, to hold prized viewing positions for the basketball activity on summer days and nights. You had to get there early to claim your spot. It was worth the wait. Holcombe Rucker Park was named for a highly-respected local teacher and playground director for the New York City Department of Parks and Recreation who started a basketball tournament at another playground site in New York City and moved it later to its present location to get kids off the street and get them involved in basketball.

It was located at the corner of 155th Street and Frederick Douglass Boulevard, and you could get there by subway train or bus, or just walking if you lived in the neighborhood just below Coogan's Bluff, just east of where the Polo Grounds once stood.

Some of the stars who came out to play there included Wilt Chamberlain, Julius "Dr. J" Erving, Earl "The Pearl" Monroe, Dean Meminger, Kareem Abdul-Jabbar (when he was known as Lew Alcindor), Chris Mullin, Stephon Marbury, Jamal Mashburn, Rafer

"Skip to my Lou" Alston, Jumpin' Jackie Jackson, Nate "The Skate" Archibald, Kenny Anderson, Tom Henderson, Joe "The Destroyer" Hammond, World Metta Peace previously known as Lloyd Free, Walter Sczerbiak and Satch Sanders. And don't forget playground legend Earl "The Goat" Manigault. I once interviewed Tom Henderson in Hawaii, where he went to college, when I was there for MLB owners' meetings.

*　*　*

Connie "The Hawk" Hawkins was a New York City schoolboy legend and one of many local standouts who could wow those kids on the fences with his free-lance swoops to the hoops and one-handed dunks from every direction. His real name was Cornelius Lance Hawkins.

George Robert Thompson III said, "I grew up a block away from Connie Hawkins' home, and there was a basketball court near us where we played as youngsters. If you were going to stay you had to learn how to play. And I mean *play*. You could learn from the best. Connie had an older brother who was a good ballplayer, too."

George Thompson always wanted to learn how to play, how to learn, how to get out of the ghetto and make something of himself, and he's still at it. He's fun to talk with over the telephone and it's definitely a smart-phone when you're talking to George Thompson III. "Don't forget that third (III). My grandfather was George Thompson, my father was George Thompson Jr. and our son is George Thompson IV."

I reminded him that former boxing champion George Foreman felt so proud of his name that he named all five of his sons George. Fortunately, he also gave them nicknames such as "Red" and "Little Joey" and "Big Wheel" so people could tell them apart. "I called all my boys George Edward Foreman so we would all have something in common," he explained.

Thompson remembers that Sihugo Green, a great basketball player from Boys High School in Brooklyn's Bedford-Stuyvesant neighborhood, who starred at Duquesne University in Pittsburgh and in the NBA, had a storefront in the Brooklyn neighborhood after he retired from the NBA. "He had desks and chairs, and we could go there to study," said Thompson. "This was the mid-60s and the government was throwing money into poor communities to see if it would improve things, and all Si had to do was pick up the phone and he got the money for a safe haven for kids in our neighborhood. Everyone knew Si."

George Thompson

Lenny Wilkens, one of only four men to be named to the Basketball Hall of Fame as a coach and as a player, was also a Boys High student. The other three similarly honored are John Wooden, Bill Sharman and Tommy Heinsohn.

"Once when I was with the Bucks and we were playing the Boston Celtics," recalled Thompson at the mention of Tommy Heinsohn, "they sent him in to beat me up. He had a nickname I can't recall."

I looked it up and Heinsohn's teammates called him "Tommy Gun" because he liked to shoot the ball as much as George Thompson. Someone figured out that Tommy Heinsohn shot the ball twice for every three minutes he was in the game. Thompson had the same shoot-first reputation. Thompson went to Erasmus Hall High School on Flatbush Avenue that also turned out Doug Moe and Billy Cunningham, and great writers and sports authors such as Roger Kahn (*Boys of Summer*) and Bernard Malamud (*The Natural*), and more than 50 other famous alumni.*

*Erasmus Hall has
a distinguished alumni list

Singers Beverly Sills, Barbra Streisand, Neil Diamond, actresses Mae West, Susan Hayward, Barbara Stanwyck, White Sox and Bulls owner Jerry Reinsdorf, Oakland Raiders' owner Al Davis, Cleveland Browns coach Sam Rutigliano, Olympic swimmer Eleanor Holm, early dropout Moe Howard who became one of The Three Stooges, Waite Hoyt and Don McMahon, major league baseball pitchers, comedian Marty Ingels (husband of Shirley Jones), theatrical promoter and Jets' owner Sonny Werblin, Pro Football Hall of Famer Sid Luckman, syndicated newspaper columnist Dorothy Kilgallen, and Knicks founder and Madison Square Garden punjab Ned Irish, international chess champion Bobby Fischer, detective writer Mickey Spillane, Top Rank boxing promoter Bob Arum.

MAE WEST

BARBRA
STREISAND

Thompson and I bounced such names around like so many orange-brown or red, white and blue basketballs—Thompson scored in both pro leagues—and he had me in a game of his own. He spoke quietly in all our phone conversations, like a Brooklyn bookie writing numbers in a street corner phone booth when there were such things. "You've worked the waterfront, Jim, you know how it was." I wondered whether Thompson knew that *The New York Post* was located in a shabby six-story building at 210 South Street at the southern tip of Manhattan, right along the East River that separates Manhattan from Brooklyn. There's an 80-story luxury condo tower next door these days, "with spectacular views." Yes, I worked the waterfront.

There were no views of the river from the building because of highway ramps. I had previously enjoyed a great view from my desk at *The Miami News* where I could look out at Biscayne Bay. I didn't even have a desk at *The New York Post,* which was a blessing and I don't remember any windows.

He set me up, for starters, by saying, "I used to read your stories all the time in national sports publications and *The New York Post*. Yeah, I read you. You didn't write about me enough."

"We'll make that up to you with this story," I promised. "I was in Miami and New York when you were playing in Pittsburgh. Believe it not, during the four years (1979–1983) I wrote sports in Pittsburgh, I was never assigned to cover a basketball game."

"How'd that happen?" he said. I told him he should understand that better than anyone. Thompson understood. "Yeah, I could never convince Larry Costello I deserved to play more with Milwaukee."

He teased me about certain details of stories, reluctant to "out" former teammates and friends, even foes, and I knew how it felt to be set up for the kill on a basketball court by George Thompson. It was one-on-one, and I was always a step or so behind him. He'd feint one way and another, hollering to his teammates to clear this side of the court, and just when I thought he was revealing something special, he'd take a step back, as I could only imagine, and wait awhile. If I was patient, he'd be patient. Like the summer action at Rucker Park, it was worth the wait.

He said Connie Hawkins used to walk by his four-story apartment house in Brooklyn, on the way to the neighborhood courts, and George would be sitting out front. "He'd just say, 'Let's go,' and we'd be off to play. I was about 16 or 17 at the time. Roger Brown would be there some times. He was my man, too. Roger would tell me to control my competitiveness. He'd say, 'George, just take it out on them.' And that's pretty much what I did. I got thrown out of one game in college and one game in the pros. I was into quality and quantity; I saw the scoreboard.

"You can call me anytime," said George Thompson. "I'm like everybody else, cooped up safely at home. I'll answer your questions as best I can. You know how it goes with stories. They change and get better and better the older we get. I'm here in my pajamas and I'm at your beck and call, so don't be looking at your watch."

His home was now a Milwaukee suburb called Glendale, less than ten miles from downtown. Milwaukee was his adopted home. He had finished his professional basketball career there with the NBA's Milwaukee Bucks, after playing four years in the ABA with the Pittsburgh Condors and the Memphis Tams.

Three of my friends are fans of George Thompson, and I told him this. Dallas Frey grew up in Edgewood and still lives in the suburb east of Pittsburgh, and his high school team used to play in preliminary basketball games at the Civic Arena.

GEORGE THOMPSON   GUARD

"George Thompson is the godfather of Marquette's basketball legacy."
—Doc Rivers

Marquette University's basketball record for George Thompson's three varsity seasons was 68–20 with three post-season tournaments. Near the end of a close game, Coach Al McGuire would instruct the team to clear out one side and let George do his thing. "We'd break the huddle and Al would say, 'George, what do you think we need to do?'" *recalled Thompson.* "Seven was the magic number. If we got up by seven with two or three minutes left, it was a done deal."

Jim O'Brien

George Thompson with Billy Knight

"I followed him," offered Frey while I was writing this story in June of 2020, "because he seemed fearless. He took the ball inside against much bigger players. He had a great mid-range game and he usually guarded the other team's best perimeter player."

"George seemed like the kind of person I would have as a friend," said Jack Sega of Oxnard, California, another of my proof-readers, who had the same kind of personal drive to succeed in the business world.

"He was built like a fullback," said Tom McGuire, "but he could jump out of the building."

George Thompson's story was one I really didn't know, not outside the game itself. Like another George, namely George Tinsley, he was a bigger winner in the game of life. His is an exciting success story. He is richer in more ways than today's multi-millionaires and it doesn't matter how much money they might acquire. They won't acquire what George Thompson possesses and he and his family can be proud of that.

I remember once telling Bill Mazeroski, the Hall of Fame second baseman and 1960 World Series hero of the Pirates, that he was a rich man. "How can you say that?" asked Maz.

"Well," I said, "you are married to the same woman (Milene) you met while you were playing for the Pirates. You have two sons who are college graduates and, to my knowledge anyhow, have never been in trouble. You get up each day and have to decide what to do: go golfing, go hunting, go fishing, go have a few beers with your buddies, or sit around the house and do nothing. Yes, Maz, you've made it. You are, indeed, a rich man."

I told that story to George Thompson and I think he got the idea that he, too, is a rich man. But he already knew that. He never told me, until he called me one day out of the blue, that his mother died when he was 15. "I didn't need that," he said. So you were raised by your father? "Well, yes and no; he could make more money if he traveled, so my aunt and a friend of my mother looked after me."

George Thompson has been honored by the Wisconsin Athletic Hall of Fame, the New York City Basketball and the Brooklyn Hall of Fame.

He deserves to be honored somehow for having the craziest collection of roommates from his ABA days. When he was with the Condors, he claimed John Brisker as a roommate on the road as well as sharing an apartment together in Pittsburgh, and roomed on

Simmie Hill

Wendell Ladner

John Brisker

All-ABA roomies

the road with Simmie Hill, and when he was with the Memphis Tams for two seasons, he roomed on the road for one of those seasons with Wendell Ladner.

John Brisker, Simmie Hill and Wendell Ladner. Now there's a trifecta for you. If you are not that familiar with their lifestyles you have to read the prequel to this book, *Looking Up*, that has chapters on each of them. Suffice to say, they were different. If you knew them you have to be shaking your head and wondering how one man could withstand their wild ways.

In his story-telling efforts, Thompson spoke of "Brisk" and "Junior" and "Wendy." Sounds like a children's storybook and in a way that's just what it was.

Talking about Hill, he said, "Jim, he was a pretty scary piece of work. I'm from New York, I'm from Brooklyn, and I know scary people when I see them. They probably say the same thing about me. I have absolutely no fear of anybody.

"As for Ladner, Wendy was the closest thing to look like Elvis who could play ball. He was rough and tough, a rock-em, sock-em kind of guy, and another of my crazy roommates. Wendy sure liked the women.

"Brisk was a bad boy from Detroit, and his game was to intimidate people," recalled Thompson. "Rick Barry hated to play against Brisker, and Brisker knew it and always played him very physically. Brisk would bully Barry right from the tip-off. Brisk could play; he was a lot like LeBron James, though he couldn't jump as high as LeBron. His whole thing was intimidation.

"I got along fine with Brisk; no problem after we established boundaries. His intimidation act didn't work with me. I'm from Brooklyn; I know how to deal with bad dudes. I had a few skirmishes with Brisk, but it never got really bad. If you got into a fight with me, you might win but you are going to know you were in a battle. I didn't back down from nobody.

"I told him, 'John, I've had fights with guys bigger than you.' When guys got into it with me, they know they were in for a fight. I'm going to be 73 soon, and I still feel that way.

"I'm talking to somebody else now, and I hope that makes sense. I'm not looking for trouble anymore.

"Brisk and I lived together during the season. We had to re-arrange the furniture a few times in our apartment, but we were fine once we respected each other. Brisk and Wendy got into a lot of fights in ABA games."

I took advantage of Thompson's offer to call him anytime, and I did during the month of June, 2020. Each time, I got more information, more stories and more

Albert Hall

George "Tip" Thompson of Pittsburgh Condors at the foul line at Civic Arena in 1972. Thompson holds ABA record for most free throws (30) attempted in a game. He's been honored in the Brooklyn Sports and Wisconsin Sports Hall of Fame. Check out his huge thighs.

discoveries. I asked him about his nickname—"Tip"—and he told me that Dr. J dubbed him with the name, but the explanation made no sense to me so I won't pass it along. You figure it out. Something to do with him "tipping" the baseline.

It got interesting when I asked him where he and Brisker had an apartment in Pittsburgh. "In the eastern end of the city," he said. I asked him if was the Pennley Park Apartments, a complex at the corner of Penn and Negley avenues. He wasn't sure.

Finally, after a little more conversation, we came to realize it *was* the Pennley Park Apartments. He had mentioned that there were Steelers and Pirates who lived in the same complex. When I mentioned it was in East Liberty, that struck a familiar note with Thompson.

That was the first apartment for my wife Kathie and me. We were married in August of 1967 and remained there for two years. She could catch a bus to Oakland where she was employed as a social worker at Presbyterian University Hospital, now part of the UMPC conglomerate.

I mentioned that several Pirates were living there when we occupied a second floor two-bedroom apartment and one of our neighbors on the fourth floor was none other than the great Roberto Clemente.

"He was there when we first moved in," Thompson said. "I used to talk to him and use the little Spanish that I knew on him. He'd see me and he'd say, 'Buenos dias, Jorge.' And I'd say 'muy bien, Roberto, gracias.' That about exhausted my Spanish vocabulary. He was always very nice to me."

I told Thompson that there was a basketball court and a police station I could see from our apartment windows. I recalled that Connie Hawkins had conducted a summer clinic for school kids when I was living there.

It was a tough neighborhood. I recall coming home one day and seeing an acquaintance coming out of the apartment with a friend, carrying a television set. "Hey, are you guys doing a little second-story work?" I asked in jest. I later learned that was exactly what they were doing, stealing a television set from someone else's apartment. Kathie and I moved to Miami in the summer of 1969, just before Thompson and Brisker became tenants. Those were fairly new apartments at the time, but they have since been razed and replaced by another apartment complex.

I recalled that it cost $185 a month for our two-bedroom apartment, and that I had read that new high-end apartments nearby, where Google and a UPMC technology development center and other corporate giants have offices, are going for steep rentals. A two-bedroom apartment is now going for $3,000 to $4,000 a month.

"Looks like we got there at the right time," Thompson said.

Not so much, as far as the caliber of the Condors and team management and ownership. "I always played for ABA teams in Pittsburgh and Memphis that sucked," he said. "I had a coffee once with Bob Leonard of the Indiana Pacers and told him of my desire to play for the Pacers. He said he'd have to trade a guard to make room for me, but it went nowhere. He expressed interest in me but nothing came of it. I would have loved to play where basketball was more popular."

He could only dream about what life was like for Walt "Clyde" Frazier in George's hometown of New York. He had played one season with Dean "The Dream" Meminger at Marquette and Meminger got to go home and play for the Knicks. "More power to him," Thompson said. "Dean deserved it. He was a sophomore when I was a senior. Then Luke (Maurice Lucas) came along. They were my guys."

Basketball maven Peter Vecsey of *The New York Post* told me that Meminger and Thompson were "a dream backcourt combination."

When I mentioned Spencer Haywood, Thompson said, "The Woodman! We used to play against him when I was at Marquette and he was at Detroit. He was special, too. But we crushed him in Detroit."

When I asked Thompson how he got to Marquette in the first place, he said Al McGuire and his assistants Hank Raymond and Rick Majerus helped sell him on the school and its opportunities.

"Hank had a plan for me to get into a sales/marketing program at Marquette," Thompson said, "and he had everything organized for me. He told me I could always switch my major if I wasn't satisfied.

"Al came to visit me in our family apartment in Brooklyn. He came with Majerus, who was built like a wrestler, and we figured Coach McGuire felt safer in our neighborhood with Majerus with him as a bodyguard. McGuire was from East Rockaway on Long Island and he knew Brooklyn well. He knew a bad neighborhood when he saw one.

"McGuire is giving my dad a sales pitch on why Marquette would be so wonderful and the best fit for me, and, finally, my dad got bored and went into his bedroom and turned on the TV. He said to McGuire, 'It's my son's decision. I'm not the guy you should be talking to. You should be talking to my son. He's old enough to make his own determination, not based on any aspirations I might have. He's your boy now.' "

He said Lou Carnesecca of St. John's University recruited him as well, and he always liked Looie.

Marquette worked out fine for Thompson. He set scoring records that lasted 40 years until Markus Howard broke them. "McGuire used to tell us, 'Use basketball; don't let basketball use you.'"

*　*　*

Thompson ranked in the ABA's Top Ten for career scoring average with 20.15 points per game for 364 games. Ahead of him were Julius Erving, Dan Issel, George McGinnis, Artis Gilmore, George Gervin, Bob Verga and Ralph Simpson, and behind him were Darel Carrier and Mack Calvin. So he was in good company.

"I could drive on guys like Artis Gilmore any time I wanted to," said Thompson, "and guards like Bob Verga and Fatty Taylor couldn't contain me."

He set an ABA record for most free throws in a single game with 30, which points up that he drove to the basket a lot and got fouled a lot while doing so. "The referees knew I was getting beat up, so they decided to keep calling fouls."

He remembers that when he played for the Condors he often left complimentary tickets for two local high school basketball stars, Braddock's Billy Knight and Maurice Lucas from the Hill District. Both became stars later in the ABA and NBA, and the friendship followed.

I told Thompson a story about how Billy Knight told me that drugs were never a problem for him because he wouldn't want to disappoint his mother.

"My mother put the fear of God in me about drugs," Thompson said. "So I didn't dare do drugs."

Thompson was a 6-3 guard who could score outside and inside. He was quick. So were two other Condors' backcourtmen he enjoyed playing with, "Sweet" Charlie Williams and Chuck Williams. "Chuck Williams was my guy," he added. Williams went to Denver, but he and Thompson still stay in touch.

"I was as good a guard as there was in the league," Thompson said. "I could handle myself with small forwards as well as guards."

Thompson's ABA/NBA scoring average was 18.6 points per game, not too shabby as Al McGuire might have said. After his playing days, Thompson stayed in Milwaukee and became the courtside basketball analyst and color man at his alma mater for 27 years.

"Who was better at that, you or McGuire?" I asked.

"I was better," said Thompson, never shy about offering opinions. "I had played the game longer and understood it better. I had a better command of the language. But Al could make people laugh. That erases a lot of shortcomings."

I mentioned that I had just written a story about Billy Paultz, a big man for the Nets and Spurs, in which I referred to him as "an aircraft carrier," as McGuire would have called him. "We called him The Whopper," Thompson said, "as in The Big Whopper."

He enjoyed playing pro basketball, but it was never the piece of cake fans thought it was. "There was a lot of hard work involved," he said. "Practices could get rough, so could the games. We were on the road a lot. There was pain; bumping and grinding with others in practice. And when I was done with basketball, I didn't sit around praying for a pension that would never come. I went to work.

"My mother and father stressed hard work. My father was in the Merchant Marines as a career, transporting cargo and personnel to different places. He worked out of Hoboken, New Jersey, Frank Sinatra's hometown. My mother stayed home. I came from a great family.

"I still have my father's military dog tags. They're brass and I polish them now and then. That's my way of taking him with me wherever I go. I wore them when I was playing in college and in the pros. His name, of course, was George Robert Thompson and her name was Anna. They didn't want me bringing any shame to our name. I never heard my parents arguing. I had an older sister, Joyce. She was a year-and-a-half older and never let me forget that. She'd also say, 'I'm smarter than you.' But she was a sweetie pie and she would do anything for me."

I asked him what he thought he'd be making today if he were playing to his same ability. "I think I'd be making $1.5 million a year, at least," he said. I told he was shooting way too low. The average salary for an NBA player during the 2018–2019 season was $6.4 million and there was nothing average about George Thompson. "I guess it's what the market will bear," said Thompson. "You still have to go out and earn it. You can't mail it in. I took it as a personal affront if anyone thought I had it made."

I checked with Peter Vecsey, a big fan of George Thompson, and he said George would be paid $12 million a year easily in today's marketplace.

"Jack McMahon was my coach with the Condors," Thompson said. "We got along fine. He was a New York guy, from Brooklyn, and we had a lot of New York conversations. And people would say 'What the hell are those guys talking about?' When we traveled, I'd always sit at the back of the bus and McMahon would make his way back there and borrow my manicure kit. So did Brisk. I told them I thought they could afford to buy their own, but they never did."

Marquette was the perfect place for George Thompson on another level. That's where he met his wife Karen Vagner. He was looking forward to their 50th wedding anniversary on August 6, 2020. "We met when we were students at Marquette. I saw her on the campus one day when I looked across a crowded room, as they say, and I said, 'There's the girl for me. There's the girl I'm going to marry.'

"I don't think her parents were thrilled when we said we were going to get married. I think her dad saw me as a ballplayer, one of those love 'em and leave-em kind of guys. We didn't worry about that. I know some people in the travel business and I want to take Karen on a trip around the world for our 50th anniversary."

*   *   *

When he was finished playing for the Bucks, he got a job in sales and marketing with Briggs & Stratton. It was a Milwaukee-based Fortune 500 company at the time (now Fortune 1000), a manufacturer of gasoline engines and lawn care machinery that is sold in over 120 countries. "I did everything, really," he said of those days. "My boss used to say, 'George, take care of this,' and I did. I traveled all over the world, to Japan, China, Germany, you name it." In time, he became vice-president for corporate communications and community relations.

He worked for Briggs & Stratton for 31½ years, doing basketball games on the side, before retiring in 2010. He had stopped doing the Marquette basketball games in 2008. "My boss appreciated how I'd be in early the day after a night road game," he recalled.

"My boss said I didn't have to do that. He'd say, 'What are you doing here?' And I said, 'I have things to do here.' They appreciated that I respected my role and what I was to do. They let me do the Marquette games, but I didn't want that to detract from what they were paying me to do.

"I'm proudest of the wonderful wife and two kids that I have, and that I rose to be a corporate executive with a Fortune 500 company. I had three goals when I was growing up. I wanted to be good at basketball, I wanted to climb the corporate ladder, and I wanted to get into broadcasting. That last one was easy. I was just myself.

"One of my sons, George IV, is a graphics artist, and he did some work for the singer Prince in Minneapolis. Prince provided him with a large wall, and told my son to draw whatever he wanted to on it. He wanted my son to show his talent. He said, 'Just let him do what he's going to do.' My son, Chris, is a mechanical engineer.

"I don't watch much basketball anymore. I don't like the pro game. And I should, because it's the kind of free-wheeling game I played on the playground in New York. There are millions of dollars in pro ball today, and I don't blame them for going for the cheese, going to the highest bracket, more power to them.

"Three of the most important things in my life outside of my family are my lawyer, my accountant and my get-away place in the Bahamas. So, I'm doing okay. I'm not out to see what's going to happen next. I appreciate your interest and how you do things. We had a conversation. I never heard a negative thing about you. You called them as you saw them."

I knew I'd be calling Thompson from time to time. I told him I was going to send him a book on basketball that I had written. "Do I have to pay for it?" he asked. "That's what Al McGuire always said, "Do I have to pay for it?"

Basketball is the city game.

Its battlegrounds are strips of asphalt between tattered wire fences or crumbling buildings; its rhythms grow from an uneven thump of a ball against hard surfaces.

It demands no open spaces or lush backyards or elaborate equipment.

It doesn't even require specific numbers of players; a one-on-one confrontation in a playground can be as memorable as a full-scale organized game.

Basketball is the game for young athletes without cars or allowances—the game whose drama and action are intensified by its confined spaces and chaotic surroundings.

—From the introduction for *The City Game*, a book by Newsweek sports editor Pete Axthelm that was published in 1970, when Jim O'Brien was among the writers covering the New York Knicks in their first championship season, and immensely enjoyed Axthelm's book.

Howard Cosell and Pete Axthelm

Larry Brown
He was always looking for an opening

Larry Brown was the littlest guy on the basketball court all his life, from his schoolboy days in Brooklyn and Long Island to his long, long career as a coach on a college and pro level. He loved the game and the game loved him, lavishing him with so many honors, so many multi-million-dollar coaching contracts, so many moves, to the basket and the bank.

He stood 5–9 at best, but I doubt he was a half-inch taller than I am, I know from interviewing him many times when he coached 13 different college and pro teams over four decades. As a player, he was small enough and swift enough to slip through the slightest gaps in a team's defense and, as a coach, he gained a reputation for moving on, always looking for a bigger and better opportunity. He's the only basketball coach who can claim championships on a college and pro level, at the University of Kansas in 1988 and with the Detroit Pistons in 2004.

Lawrence Harvey Brown was inducted as a coach into the Basketball Hall of Fame in 2002. Alan Iverson had verbal clashes with Brown when he coached him with the Philadelphia 76ers, but Iverson said, "He was the best basketball coach in the game."

Brown was named the MVP and won a car in the ABA's first all-star game in 1968. He and Doug Moe, James Jones, Jackie Moreland, Gerald "Go Go" Govan, Austin "Red" Robbins and the immortal Marlbert Pradd of Dillard University—I'm not making this up—combined to lead the New Orleans Bucs to the seven-game championship series against the Pittsburgh Pipers at the end of that same season. The Pipers prevailed with Connie Hawkins winning MVP honors.

Larry Brown stands small between ABA Commissioner and Hall of Fame center George Mikan and Rick Barry when he received MVP honors at ABA's All-Star Game in 1968.

Larry Brown did more jumping in his career than another University of North Carolina alumnus, Billy "The Kangaroo Kid" Cunningham, and "Jumpin' Joe" Caldwell. Loyalty and long-term relationships were never his long suit, and some of the mod suits and denim overalls he wore in the '70s while strutting the sidelines quickly faded from fashion. When he was a child, he even made a brief stop to live in Pittsburgh.

The thing that stands out most when I look back at Larry Brown, or study the photos and images that surround my computer at this time, were the veins that protruded from his forehead and temples. This was an intense little guy.

He was always thinking, always looking for an edge.

He made the most of his ability, from beginning to end. Like most of us, he didn't know when to quit. For good. But he quit on a lot of teams and franchises for a bigger buck somewhere else. That, of course, is very fashionable these days in the college and pro basketball world. Brown was way ahead of his time.

Larry Brown

I always liked Larry Brown. When he and Doug Moe worked together, as they often did, they were favorites for so many sportswriters. They were always available and willing to discuss the game. Brown was the straight man to Moe's funny-man sidekick.

He coached the Carolina Cougars for two seasons (1972–74) and the Denver Nuggets for two seasons (1974–1976) in the ABA, then three more (1976–1979) with the Nuggets in the NBA. He coached two seasons (1979–1981) at UCLA, two seasons (1981–1983) with the New Jersey Nets in the NBA, five seasons (1983–1988) at the University of Kansas. This was followed by four seasons (1988–1992) with the San Antonio Spurs, one season (1992–1993) with the Los Angeles Clippers, four seasons (1993–1997) with the Indiana Pacers, six seasons (1997–2003) with the Philadelphia 76ers, three seasons (2003–2006) with the Detroit Pistons, one season

Doug Moe

(2005–2006) with the New York Knicks, two seasons (2008–2010) with the Charlotte Bobcats, four seasons (2012–2016) at Southern Methodist University. His last employer was Fiat Torino of the Italian Basketball League and he was fired, at age 78, after being booed at a home game when his team had a 5–19 record at the outset of his final season.

If you read that last paragraph aloud it will take your breath away.

He would turn 80 in September of 2020 and may still be available to the highest bidder. Makes one wonder how he kept his furniture from being lost in the shuffle.

I had a lengthy interview with him in January of 1989, the season after he had won the NCAA championship at the Kemper Arena in Kansas City.

He told me he had received a congratulatory call from John Chaney, the basketball coach at Temple University, after winning that national championship.

Chaney had a mostly successful run at Temple and before that at Cheney State, where he won an NCAA Division II title in 1978.

"One day you'll be driving down the highway with the windows down and the radio up," Chaney told Brown, "and all of a sudden you'll start grinning. That's when you'll know you've won a national championship."

Brown had been down a lot of highways and airways since his team had defeated Big Eight rival Oklahoma to claim the NCAA title on April 4, 1988.

Brown admitted he'd been too busy to start grinning.

Brown had been too busy to have had time to reflect on that fantastic accomplishment and some of the events that had transpired since then had stolen some of the fun and smiles, or grins, from that special day.

Almost immediately, he nearly returned to UCLA to coach the Bruins' basketball team once again, then switched plans and signed on to coach the San Antonio Spurs with a five-year $3.5 million contract.

I caught up to him in Oakland, California, of all places, where he was waiting to coach the Spurs against the Golden State Warriors. Gertude Stein once wrote of Oakland, "There's no there *there*." Jack London was my favorite writer from Oakland. Brown's Spurs had started the season by upsetting the defending champion Los Angeles Lakers, 122–107, before a sellout crowd of 15,861 at the HemisFair Arena in San Antonio.

That's the story, or half the story, of Larry Brown since he was born under a lucky star in Brooklyn 47 years earlier. He has been a success just about everywhere he has been, starting out at Long Beach (N.Y.) High School and then at the University of North Carolina where he was an All-ACC guard for the great Frank McGuire.

He was a member of the gold medal-winning U.S. Olympic basketball team at Tokyo in 1964. He was one of the original players in the American Basketball Association and, indeed, one of its top playmakers. He was drafted on the seventh round by the NBA's Baltimore Bullets but signed instead with the Akron Goodyear Wingfoots of the Amateur Athletic Union. He was the MVP for the AAU Basketball Tournament.

He became a coach in the ABA in 1972 with the Carolina Cougars. His team improved its record by 22 wins over the previous season. He did the same at his next two pro stops, improving the record by 28 wins at Denver, and by 20 at New Jersey, all in his first year. Only ten times in NBA or ABA history did a first-year coach improve his club's record by 20 or more wins.

In between the Denver and New Jersey jobs, he coached at UCLA for two seasons, taking the Bruins to the championship game the first year before losing to Louisville in the final, and leading them back to the NCAA Tournament the next time around.

At Jersey, he may have turned in his best coaching job ever, but he left before the season was finished to coach at Kansas. Most of the changes were on the messy side with a lot of people's noses out of joint and blemishes on Brown's little-boy face.

Looking back on 1988, Brown swallowed hard and his Adam's apple appeared more prominent than ever. Funny what sticks out in your mind, and Larry Brown's neck. "It was a crazy year," he said. "I remember that everybody's expectations were so high when we started the year. Danny Manning was in his final year. Archie Marshall was coming back after missing a year with a knee injury. But then Archie got hurt again, and things just didn't seem to fall into place. It was the kind of year in which you were really disappointed.

"Then all of a sudden I found myself in Kansas City with a chance to win the championship. Few people ever get that chance. When I was at UCLA, we played Louisville in the championship in 1980. We had beaten Louisville twice that year, but we lost the big one (59–54) in Indianapolis.

"Then at Kansas in 1986 we got to the Final Four, and we thought we had the best team in Dallas. We had played Duke close (losing 92–86 in New York) earlier in the year, and our kids thought we could beat them this time. But we lost (71-67) in the semis. I thought then, 'Hell, I might be destined to be the coach that comes close, but never wins it.' And then we win it in Kansas City. It was an unbelievable experience."

Brown often sprinkles adjectives in his comments, such as unbelievable, fantastic, monumental, phenomenal, impressive and incredible because that's the kind of life he had led to that point.

Brown said he did not rate the date he signed with the Spurs as one of the super special days he had the previous year. "I don't look at that as one of the highlights," he explained. "I was full of mixed emotions at the time. Every time I move it's a monumental thing. They say, 'There he goes again.' I had a real hard time. I thought it was the right time. I thought it was the right thing, that it was best for me and my staff.

"I still really liked Kansas and the kids that were there. My five years there were very special. But San Antonio was an incredible opportunity, an unbelievable challenge. But I also had unbelievably mixed emotions.

"The job offers at UCLA and San Antonio came right after winning the national championship. I don't think I got a chance to enjoy it.

"The six-to-ten weeks at the end of the season at Kansas was the greatest period I'd ever experienced as a coach. Then all of a sudden, we won it, and I was faced with the UCLA decision. I had always wanted to go back to UCLA.

"I told the officials at UCLA that I would come, and that I had to go back to Kansas to tell my players and our University officials. I needed some time. UCLA wanted it done right away.

"I had one day. We won the NCAA championship and 30,000 people were in the football stadium to welcome us back. I was on a plane to UCLA the next day. I was up all night for three or four straight nights. I was hoping UCLA could wait at least a week. We had a banquet set up at Kansas, and there was a reception hosted by the University president. I wanted our kids and our fans to have time to celebrate what we'd done. I didn't want to throw a damper on their good feelings."

It's easy to be critical of someone jumping from job to job as Brown did, but I was guilty of similar behavior in the newspaper business. I accepted a job at the *Detroit Free Press*, but changed my mind when offered a position a week later at *The New York Post*.

When I called my wife Kathie from New York to tell her we would not be moving from Miami to Detroit, she said, "Just let me know where to send the furniture."

Years later, in the late '80s, I talked officials at Virginia Commonwealth University into upping my salary, and returned home after two weeks on the job because I knew it was not right for me. I had taken an intern with me, Joe Onderko, a student of mine at Robert Morris, and left him in Richmond. It worked out well for him and we remain friends. Today, he is the commissioner of the Presidents Athletic Conference (PAC).

"When you left," he told me, "they started calling me Orphan Joe."

I was offered the best position ever as sports columnist at large at *The New York Daily News* in 1989, but turned down the job when they wouldn't pay for my move from Pittsburgh to New York. Two weeks later, they fired Larry Fox as sports editor. Had I gone to New York, I would have been in a lame duck situation. I've had employers disappoint me in Miami and at Pitt, so it works both ways.

In the next game that counted, Brown steered the Spurs to that season-opening victory over the vaunted Lakers. "I was shocked," said Brown during his stay in Oakland. "I admired their team so much and what they'd done. It was kind of a strange thing when I heard them introduce the players from the Lakers. I was like a fan. Magic Johnson, for instance, to me was such a good example for the kids I was coaching in college.

Larry Brown with Billy Cunningham

"There was an unbelievable atmosphere. It was a sellout, and there hadn't been many sellouts in San Antonio the last few seasons. Our team played exactly the way I would hope we could play night in and night out.

"It was a phenomenal night. When you consider the commitment Mr. (Red) McCombs has made to me and my staff, I wanted us to get off to a good start. By NBA standards what he gave me was unbelievable. People read what I am getting paid compared to some of the great coaches around the league, and it has to make them wonder. Damn, when I think about what the team has done and it bothers me. I want to see this work. I feel an unbelievable burden."

This is how bad things started off following that first regular season game for the Spurs. On December 20, 1988, the Spurs lost their eighth straight game, to the Suns in Phoenix. The Spurs were 2–12 in December, the worst month in the history of the Texas franchise.

"We haven't given our fans what they came for," Brown said at one point in our conversation. "I feel sorry for our fans. There have been some unbelievable disappointments. I was so disappointed that whole time. We had a lot of chances to win."

I felt like I was talking to an old friend from school days, and we were discussing how our lives were playing out. Brown was *unbelievably* honest.

It should be pointed out that the Spurs did come up with some *impressive* wins over some good teams, like the Atlanta Hawks and New York Knicks, in addition to the Lakers.

It wasn't enough. In a sense, Brown was being haunted by his own success, his many moves, the amount of money he was making, the expectations held for him and his team, his own high standards, and the personal demons that inhabit his body.

As if things weren't bad enough, the NCAA put the Kansas basketball team on probation for three years and banned them from that season's NCAA Tournament.

"It was a shock, first of all," recalled Brown. "That investigation went on so long. I visited with NCAA officials and didn't think it would be a major thing. I thought of some of the things we'd done. I'd given a kid a plane ticket to go see his dying grandmother. If I had to do it over again, I'd have done the same thing to help him in a difficult time. Stuff like that. And, all of a sudden, a bunch of innocent kids aren't allowed to defend their national championship."

Brown also accused the University of Pittsburgh of breaking rules in their recruitment of Curtis Aiken of Buffalo, among others. It was a real mess.

Asked if he felt the NCAA could find a hundred Division I schools guilty of some of the same things that had been unearthed at Texas A&M, Oklahoma and Kansas, just to name a few, Brown said, "Try 294 Division I schools, and that's not just sour grapes on my part. They didn't find us offering one kid a thing to come to Kansas.

"At our first game in Houston this year, I had some fans get on me. One guy hollered at me as I came out on the court, 'Hey, cheater,' and another one shouted, 'Hey, when are you gonna give my kid a car?' That hurts. I don't feel I deserve that."

Suddenly, I felt as if I were in a confessional box with Larry Brown. And Brown, being Jewish, had never been in a confessional box before. He thought he was getting a bum rap. It wasn't the first time he felt misunderstood. He didn't duck out on our interview.

In a sense, Brown has been haunted by his own success, his many moves, the amount of money he made —chump change these days—his own high standards, the price the kids at Kansas paid for indiscretions by him and the others associated with the school and the personal demons that inhabit his body, and have stretched his skin taut against his hollow cheekbones.

He always tried to have the best kind of kids on his team—in the pro and college ranks—and he liked to teach his players about basketball and life. He said he was having a tough time getting his message across to the players on the Spurs. Maybe his credibility or sincerity had been hurt. It was too early to tell.

The Spurs had some outstanding young talent in Greg "Cadillac" Anderson, Willie Anderson, Frank Brickowski, Johnny Dawkins, Vernon Maxwell and Alvin Robertson. There were some pieces to put together a good team, but at that time the pieces didn't fit that well. There was hope in San Antonio that things would turn around in a hurry once David Robinson got out of the Navy.

Some of the skeptics weren't fully convinced that Robinson was a sure thing, a franchise-saver. Robinson was great in his All-America days at Navy, but something less in international competition, especially in the Olympic Games.

"I think he'll be great," said Brown. "But I'm tired of people telling our players, 'Wait till David gets here' and stuff like that. We have to work

Albert Hall

Spurs' coach Larry Brown with David Robinson

hard and play to our potential every night so we're ready."

The Spurs beat the Warriors, 104–102, that night in a real to-the-end battle, and that snapped a seven-game road losing streak. But it was a rare victory.

The Spurs bottomed out that season, finishing with a 21–61 record, the worst in franchise history. Brown had promised better than that. Even Brown had no idea what David Robinson would mean to the Spurs. "The Admiral," as he was known, steered the Spurs' ship in the right direction.

His rookie season (1989-90) was spectacular and the Spurs had one of the greatest turnarounds in NBA history, boosting their record to 56–26, a 35-victory improvement.

That's all behind Larry Brown. Hopefully, now that he's into his 80s, he experiences that special trip down a highway with the windows down and the radio up, with a grin on his face. When he looks in the rear view mirror, he will see himself, not the Larry Brown of Long Beach and Tarheel days, but a distinguished career not many can claim. He was one of the best basketball minds of all time, and a mind still worth examining.

CAROLINA
COUGARS

SYMBOLS OF SUCCESS

Jerry Lucas
A whiz kid who could play the game

Jim O'Brien

Jerry Lucas likes to have fun with the youngsters who approach him for autographs when he appears around the country at celebrity golf outings. He likes to quiz them with math or memory games, riddles and the like. Sportswriters are also fair game. Lucas takes pride in being the first basketball player to be on championship teams in high school, college and the NBA, as well as on a gold-medal-winning Olympic basketball team. "There have only been two others do it," said Lucas. "Can you name them?"

Well, can you name them? Lucas looks like the cat that swallowed the canary when he lets you know the answer: Earvin "Magic" Johnson and Quinn Buckner.

Lucas loves stuff like that. He once wowed a national TV audience when he demonstrated how he had memorized the first 500 pages of the Manhattan telephone book. Why? He has developed and taught memory-improvement courses and has authored over 30 books on the subject, many of them aimed at children. He was always an outstanding student and athlete at Middletown (Ohio) High School and The Ohio State University. He graduated from OSU with Phi Beta Kappa honors. He appeared on the cover of *Sports Illustrated* a few times.

"I knew I wanted to go to school in Ohio," said Lucas, "and Ohio State was the only school out of all of them that talked about academics first. The rest talked about athletics." Lucas even delayed his pro career to attend graduate school at Ohio State, which tells you something about him as well.

Lucas was a big fan of Fred Taylor, who coached the Buckeyes' men's basketball team at that time.

As a senior in high school, Lucas was the leading scorer in the state of Ohio. The second-leading scorer was a 5–10 center for Warren Consolidated High School in Tiltonsville, Ohio by the name of Bill Mazeroski. Yes, Maz, the hero of the Pirates' 1960 World Series triumph over the New York Yankees.

When Maz first joined the Pirates they may have had a better basketball team than a baseball team, led by Dick Groat, an All-America in basketball and baseball at Duke, Johnny and Eddie O'Brien of Seattle University, and Nellie King, Paul Smith and Dick Hall. The Pirates also had two All-America football players during that decade, Heisman Trophy winner Vic Janowitz, a catcher from Ohio State, and Paul Giel, a pitcher from Minnesota.

Lucas was a graceful 6–8 center/forward who led the Buckeyes to their best period of basketball from 1959–60 to 1961–62. Ohio State, under coach Fred Taylor, won 78 of 84 games with Lucas leading the way. They won the NCAA championship in his sophomore season, and lost in the NCAA championship game in both his junior and senior seasons. Rival Cincinnati beat them in the finals both times. He was the Final Four MVP in 1960 and 1961.

Ohio State won the Big Ten title, of course, all three of his varsity seasons in order to qualify for the NCAA Tournament. Only the winners went back then.

The Buckeyes, who also included John Havlicek, Gary Bradds, Mel Newell and Bobby Knight, posted a 40–2 record in the Big Ten and won 27 in a row over that three-year span.

I remember that Lucas, Havlicek and Newell all wore top coats and hats when they came to Frankie Gustine's Restaurant to promote their upcoming appearance in the first main attraction at the Civic Arena when they played Pitt in the third game of a triple-header.

Duquesne defeated Carnegie Tech 78–40 in the first game, Pirates of the present and Pirates of the past played an exhibition in the second game. Former college and pro basketball standout Dick Groat played in that game. The celebrity referees were Bobby Layne and Gene "Big Daddy Lipscomb. The Press Newsboys Fund and Children's Hospital got a share of the gate. I took a picture of the Ohio State trio in front of Gustine's Restaurant. Two were wearing men's dress hats, uncommon even then. Ohio State, which had lost to Cincinnati in NCAA final the previous season, had no trouble beating Pitt that night, 99–79.

Pitt's starting lineup included sophomores Brian Generalovich, Cal Sheffield and Paul Krieger, and seniors Tom Maloney and Bob Sankey. Ben Jinks led Pitt in scoring with 28 points. Lucas led Ohio State with 23 points and 17 rebounds.

Every player from Ohio State who played for Fred Taylor thought the world of him. Bobby Knight said he never made a decision as an adult that he didn't consult with Coach Taylor. A life-size statue of Taylor was erected in his hometown of Zanesville in May of 2017. I stopped to see it while traveling from Pittsburgh to Columbus to visit our daughter Sarah and her family. Taylor's record in 18 years as head coach of the Buckeyes was 297–158. He was a class act. I had an opportunity to interview him once at the Pizza Hut Classic in Las Vegas.

Lucas led the nation in field goal percentage all three years and led the nation in rebounding his final two seasons. Assists records were not kept then, or he would have been among the national leaders in that category as well. He averaged 24.3 points per game

Jubilant Knicks after winning NBA championship in 1973, from left to right, Jerry Lucas, Walt "Clyde" Frazier, Willis Reed, Phil Jackson and Bill Bradley.

Lucas puts move on Celtics' John Havlicek, his former teammate on great Ohio State basketball team, and with Warriors he drives on Los Angeles Lakers' Harold "Happy" Hairston, former NYU standout.

for his varsity career, but he took less shots each year. He averaged only 16 field goal attempts per game as a sophomore, 15 as a junior and 14 as a senior.

"The more I played the less I cared about points," Lucas said. "Anybody can score if his teammates set him up." He seemed to take more pride in his rebounds, even as a pro, and his assists. His rebounding average went up each year he was at Ohio State. His teammates in the pros used to point out that Lucas was always eager to get rebounds when opponents were shooting free throws.

In a holiday tournament game against UCLA, Lucas scored 30 points and grabbed 30 rebounds, his points coming on 11-of-13 field goals and eight-of-eight free throws. John Wooden, the legendary coach at UCLA, told Lucas afterward, "I want you to know you are the most unselfish athlete I've ever seen."

He was determined to do whatever was needed to help his team win a contest. Lucas was a star for the Team USA that won the 1960 Olympic gold medal in Rome. Oscar Robertson and Jerry West were on that team, too, yet California's Pete Newell, said of Lucas, "He was the best player I ever coached."

I was covering the Knicks on occasion when he joined the team for the 1971–72 campaign and helped them win their second NBA title in three years in 1973. I was always struck by the contrasting figures of Lucas and another newcomer to the team, Earl "The Pearl" Monroe.

Monroe put on a show when on the floor and was so serious off the court. Lucas was so serious on the court, never smiling, and was a cut-up off the court, especially on long airplane rides with the team.

I can recall one airplane trip in which Lucas went up and down the aisle, trying to get someone's attention, asking all kinds of trivia questions. The last

Photos by Jim O'Brien

Jerry Lucas at Mario Lemieux's celebrity golf outing at The Club at Nevillewood.

Mel Newell, John Havlicek and Jerry Lucas pose in front of Frank Gustine's Restaurant in Oakland before Ohio State game with Pitt to open the Civic Arena in 1961. Lucas removed his hat for the picture.

time I saw him was in 2005 when he was playing golf in Mario Lemieux's Celebrity Invitational at The Club at Nevillewood. He seemed happy to be signing autographs. Rick Murray, a friend of mine from Upper St. Clair and co-owner of Rusmur Flooring, played with Lucas in a pro-am golf event and had a hole-in-one on No. 17, using a 7-iron for the 185-yard hole. It was his second hole-in-one of his career. Lucas, at 6–9, had the longest golf clubs and tallest golf bag in the tournament.

One fan brought a copy of the *Sports Illustrated* that had Lucas on the cover when he was a senior at Middletown (Ohio) High School. Lucas was also on the *SI* cover as the Sportsman of the Year with a watercolor portrait in January of 1962 when he was at Ohio State. Some research turned some interesting tidbits about Jerry Lucas as a pro. He wasn't a particularly big or bruising ballplayer—at 6–9, 235—but he averaged 15.3 rebounds and his career rebounding totals trailed only Wilt Chamberlain, Bill Russell and Bob Pettit. He knew how to block out and gain position inside, and had a neat 25-foot jump shot. He could play center or forward, and returned to playing center—his college position—with the Knicks when Willis Reed was sidelined by injury and the Knicks continued to win.

Jim O'Brien

Lucas signs autograph on *Sports Illustrated* cover that had his likeness.

Two little guys who made
their mark in ABA with the league's
first title team—the Pittsburgh Pipers

My association with the American Basketball Association—the ABA—began with a telephone call to our apartment in the Pennley Park Apartments at the corner of Penn and Negley Avenues in East Liberty in the summer of 1967.

Kathie Churchman and I had gotten married on August 12, 1967, and had just moved into our new digs. The voice on the other end of the telephone was a man I'd never met. His name was Gabe Rubin.

He was often referred to in the Saturday notes column of Al Abrams, the sports editor of the *Pittsburgh Post-Gazette*, as "a theater mogul." Abrams filled his "Sidelights on Sports" column with notes and observations about Billy Conn and Fritzie Zivic and their friend, Joey Diven, Steelers owner Art Rooney, and a host of his own celebrities such as Beersie Gordon, Archie "Tex" Litman, Parlay Henry, Pittsburgh Phil, Ralph Swingbelly and the Japanese Ambassador. He wrote for the *P-G* for 51 years and was a familiar man about town. He was Pittsburgh's answer, and a poor one, to New York's Damon Runyon. Abrams always looked unhappy, and he had the face of a bloodhound. He dressed well, however, rare for a sportswriter even then.

Rubin owned the Nixon Theater and brought Broadway shows and first-run movies to his theater. Rubin resided in the penthouse of the 21-story Carlton House Hotel on Bigelow Boulevard near the corner of Grant Street and Sixth Avenue. Abrams lived in the same building and

Al Abrams

hung out at the hotel bar with sports and entertainment figures.

Archie "Tex" Litman, a local entrepreneur and sports enthusiast and Lenny Litman, who contributed stories on showbiz to *Variety*, frequented the Carlton House. So it was no problem for Gabe to get Connie Hawkins, whom the Litmans had adopted, to sign a contract to play for the Pipers. I think they paid him $18,000, and Tom Kerwin, a likable backup center who had set rebounding records at Centenary (La.) University and played for the Phillips 66ers in AAU basketball, was paid a few thousand more on a two-year no-cut contract.

Rubin had a raspy voice and sounded like Edward G. Robinson, the movie actor who often played the part of a tough-talking gangster. In fact, Rubin knew Robinson and had hosted him in his penthouse apartment once upon a time.

"Hi, I'm Gabe Rubin and I'm getting into the basketball business," he said in the way of an introduction. "I hear you know a lot about basketball. I'd like to meet you and talk to you about what we're doing."

He invited me to come to the Carlton House Hotel. His penthouse apartment was large. Keep in mind I grew up in a row house in Hazelwood that was 15 feet wide at both ends, so Rubin's residence was striking and impressive. His furniture was better than ours, and none of it had cigarette burn marks. His wife Ellie was an elegant woman, quick to smile, and she offered me a drink as soon as I came through the door.

Charles "Brute" Kramer was there. He had been a scholastic sports writer for the *Post-Gazette* and then a publicist at Parsons College in Iowa and helped recruit a number of Western Pennsylvania athletes to the Midwestern school. Kramer was going to handle publicity for Rubin's team in the ABA. The team was going

George Von Benko

Rubin, Shapiro and Lenny Litman owned the Penn Theatre, now Heinz Hall. With profits from Carol Channing as "Hello, Dolly" at the Nixon Theatre, they bought the Pittsburgh Pipers' franchise in the ABA in 1967. Author is flanked by Gabe Rubin, left, and Jason Shapiro at ABA's 30th anniversary reunion in Indianapolis.

Jim O'Brien

Connie Hawkins towers over Hope and Jason Shapiro and Gabe and Ellie Rubin at ABA's 30th anniversary in Indianapolis in summer of 1998.

to be called the Pittsburgh Pipers. He would later hire Ans Dilley, a veteran sports scribe from New Jersey, to handle the same duties. Dilley liked to talk and he always looked after me.

*　*　*

Rubin wanted me to help get things organized and handle some tasks as he assembled a team. He introduced me to his partner, a gentleman named Jason Shapiro, who owned National Record Mart on Diamond Street, now called Forbes Avenue. It was the main store for a chain of 70 some NRM stores in the area, one of the largest record chains in the country. It started out as Jitterbug Records when Jason's father, Hyman, opened a shop for used records in 1937.

Rubin and Shapiro both were about 5-5 or 5-6, the same as *Post-Gazette* sports writer Myron Cope. All three were Jewish and, understandably, proud of it.

It's hard to believe that introduction to Gabe Rubin and the ABA was 53 years ago, as this book comes off the press at RR Donnelley in Pittsburgh's East End, but Kathie and I would be celebrating our 53rd wedding anniversary in the summer of 2020 so it must be so.

The Carlton House Hotel was considered a prestigious address in Pittsburgh. It had apartments, offices and businesses. It was imploded in eight seconds in 1980. The New York Mellon Bank Center now stands on the same site, across the street from the William Penn Hotel. Among those who stayed at the Carlton House Hotel were Muhammad Ali, the Rolling Stones, Carol Channing, Richard Nixon, Nikita Khrushchev and Lassie. Khrushchev came to Pittsburgh in late September of 1959 as part of a whirlwind tour of the United States. He visited Washington, D.C, a farm in Iowa, Hollywood, San Francisco and Pittsburgh. He wanted to meet some "real workers" in Pittsburgh.

Carlton House Hotel was home on the road for the likes of Russian czar Nikita Kruschev, stage performer Carol Channing of "Hello, Dolly" fame, and Lassie and his buddy Timmy. Seated to the right of Kruschev is Pitt chancellor Edward H. Litchfield.

He visited Mesta Machine Company in West Homestead on September 24, and met with the workers in the company cafeteria. My dad, Dan O'Brien, two uncles, Rich and Robbie O'Brien, and my brother Dan O'Brien were among those in attendance to hear the Russian leader.

Pittsburgh was the only city where Khrushchev was given the key to the city and the Russian leader proclaimed Pittsburgh "the friendliest city" he visited.

Channing stayed at the Carlton House while starring in her signature musical "Hello, Dolly" at the nearby Nixon Theater. Rubin used the $30,000 he cleared on that production to pay the entry fee to the ABA. Keep in mind that Art Rooney Sr. purchased a franchise in the National Football League in 1933 for $2,500. That turned out to be a better investment. The Steelers rank in the top 30 most valuable sports franchises in the world, worth $1.9 billion according to a report in *Forbes* Magazine in the summer of 2016. The Pipers never showed a profit.

Rubin grew up in Pittsburgh's East End and graduated from the University of Pittsburgh in 1932. He remained a big fan of Pitt teams and all the pro teams in Pittsburgh. He liked to bet on the games.

Rubin might have cashed in if he had the power to stay the course. The Pipers lost $250,000 their first year and Rubin and Shapiro sold most of their interest for the second year. The Silna brothers, Ozzie and Dan, both made one of the greatest deals in professional sports history when they consented to fold the Spirits of St. Louis when the NBA accepted four of the seven remaining ABA teams in 1976.

The Silnas got $2.2 million up front and a percentage of future NBA TV revenue "as long as the league existed" that would amount to over $300 million by

Carol Channing in "Hello, Dolly!" was a big hit at Nixon Theater with $30,000 profit giving Gabe Rubin the money to buy an ABA franchise for Pittsburgh.

2014. They picked up just over $500,000 the first year, but it would grow to around $20 million a year before long when the NBA signed lucrative network TV deals. The Spirits of St. Louis—to me, the best name ever in pro sports—never played a game in the NBA, but the Spirits' owners made more money than most of the NBA owners. I suggest you read this paragraph again just so the enormity of their good fortune sinks in, and why Dan Silna is the one smiling the most at ABA reunions. He did buy all the ballplayers ABA rings for the last reunion. "The guys really appreciated that," said Bob Leonard of the Indiana Pacers.

With all the different publications I was involved with in those days, I made more money on basketball than most of the owners.

* * *

I have always remembered that Rubin once remarked, "I like it when people are attending movies at theaters all over town. If I have a good movie they'll come to my theater. It's good for everyone when people are going to movies."

It's the same way in sports and other businesses. Around the same time, I heard an official with the National Bowling Proprietors Association (NBPA) tell a group of Pittsburgh bowling operators, "Some of you are hoping the bowling alley down the street goes out of business so you can get their customers. You're better off when everybody is attracting bowlers to their lanes."

It still makes sense. There is now a Carlton Restaurant in that neighborhood owned by Mike Joyce and is noted for fine dining and an impressive wine list.

Beano Cook and I had collaborated on publishing an irreverent and hard-hitting sports tabloid called

Pittsburgh Weekly Sports in 1963, my senior year at the University of Pittsburgh. I had made about $11,000 a year in 1964 with jobs as publicity director of the Pittsburgh Valley Ironmen, a minor-league football team that played its home games at Duquesne High Field, and as a copywriter and junior partner at Marc & Company, now one of the largest agencies in the country.

I wasn't doing either of those jobs when I got married. I was coming out of Army after a 21-month spell, divided between Kansas City, Missouri and Fort Greely, Alaska, and was attending grad school in literature at Pitt when Kathie and I first met. She was in the graduate School of Social Work and living in an apartment with two other coeds on Oakland Avenue, two blocks from Forbes Field. I was making about $3,500 a year. She was making $7,500 in her first year as a social worker at Presbyterian University Hospital in Oakland.

We had a pre-nuptial agreement. I would have two years to see if I could make a go of *Pittsburgh Weekly Sports*. If that didn't happen I would have to get something closer to a real job. Rubin and Shapiro paid me a few hundred dollars here and there for doing this and that. Let's just say I didn't get rich helping Rubin and Shapiro prepare the Pittsburgh Pipers for play in the newly-established ABA.

One of my first assignments was to play host to Craig Raymond, a 6-11 center from Brigham Young University who was a first round draft pick of the Philadelphia 76ers. He could have been a backup center to Wilt Chamberlain on the 1967–68 76ers team. The 76ers had won the NBA title the previous season with a 68–13 record, the best in league history to that point, and were named the league's all-time best team for its 35th anniversary.

Even though the 76ers' team was great, they still booked six of their "home games" at Pittsburgh's Civic Arena. Jason Shapiro and Gabe Rubin promoted those Pittsburgh games. Their only previous experience in basketball was betting on games. As franchise owners, Rubin and Shapiro would not be permitted to bet on basketball games. They figured they could save enough money that way to bankroll their ballclub.

Wilt Chamberlain set league records for scoring

Pittsburgh Pipers publicity photo

Craig Raymond

consecutive baskets without a miss in those games in Pittsburgh that still stand in the NBA. He hit all 18 field goal attempts for 42 points and 30 rebounds in 159–118 beating of Baltimore Bullets.

Raymond had told Rubin he was interested in going to graduate school, so Rubin instructed me to show Raymond around our respective alma mater, the University of Pittsburgh. We were quite the odd couple on campus, Raymond at 6–11, and me at 5–8½.

Raymond did not sign with the Pipers. He ended up playing pro ball in Europe for Olimpia Simmenthol Milano. A year later, he was playing for the Wilkes-Barre Barons of the Eastern Basketball League (EBL). He went on to play for the Philadelphia 76ers, the Pittsburgh Condors, Los Angeles Stars, Memphis Pros, the Floridians, San Diego Conquistadors and Indiana Pacers. As you can see, he came by the reference as a "journeyman player" honestly.

403

Connie "The Hawk" Hawkins is flanked by Pipers' principal owners Gabe Rubin, at left, and Jason Shapiro at ABA's 30th anniversary reunion in Indianapolis.

* * *

Rubin signed two players, Connie Hawkins and Charlie Williams, who had been banned from the NBA for alleged associations with gamblers. In truth, neither had committed a crime. They were starters for the Pipers along with Tom "Trooper" Washington, Charles "Chico" Vaughn and Art Heyman. Vaughn and Heyman had both played in the NBA, but were regarded as "head cases." The early ABA abounded with such talents. "Chico sure liked his wine," said one former teammate.

> *"For a young basketball junkie, the ABA Pipers and Condors were a lot of fun to watch. A lot of outstanding basketball players came through Pittsburgh. Unfortunately, not enough people in Pittsburgh were interested."*
> —Sam Sciullo, Pittsburgh sports historian

PIPERS ARE PLAYING—ABA Commissioner George Mikan, once the original big man in the NBA, towers over, from left to right, Pittsburgh Pipers' publicist Charles "Brute" Kramer, Pittsburgh Press artist Bill Winstein, coach Vince Cazzetta and owner Gabe Rubin at the Carlton House on June 9, 1968.

George Mikan, its first commissioner, began a p.a. announcement at an Oakland Oaks game, by saying he was happy to be in Oklahoma. Mikan had been the NBA's first true big man, but he wasn't much of a commissioner. He ran the league from his travel agency in Minneapolis. He is credited with coming up with the idea of having the ABA play with a red, white and blue basketball. He stole that idea from Abe Saperstein, the owner of the Harlem Globetrotters, who also introduced the three-point field goal to basketball.

That's how the Pipers ended up in Minneapolis as the Minnesota Pipers in the league's second season. The Minnesota Muskies had folded after their first season and relocated in Miami. The Pipers won the first ABA title, defeating the New Orleans Buccaneers in a seven-game series and filled the Civic Arena for the final game, but moved to Minneapolis after Rubin and Shapiro sold an 80 per cent interest in the team to Bill Erickson, a 38-year-old attorney who resided in Minneapolis.

Rubin brought the team back to Pittsburgh after a year in Minneapolis-St. Paul, but did so without star performer Connie Hawkins. Hawk had managed in the interim, thanks to the efforts of his attorneys, Roz and David Litman, to win their suit against the NBA and he was signed by the Phoenix Suns.

Rubin said he stayed up at nights wondering why his team, now called the Condors, couldn't draw fans to the Civic Arena. He said Art Rooney Sr. was his idol and, like Rooney, he tried to be patient. He tried all kinds of promotional gimmicks, but still the Condors couldn't draw crowds or enough to keep the franchise afloat. He couldn't even buy time to have the games aired on a local radio station, but Pitt's basketball games were not aired by any station at that time either.

Beano and I kept *Pittsburgh Weekly Sports* going on a shoestring budget for over five years and it was a big success because it led to Beano going to ABC Sports in New York, me going to Miami and then New York because of what I had accomplished with our newspaper, and Bob Smizik was able to leave a teaching career and become a sportswriter for *The Pittsburgh Press*.

Kathie and I moved to Miami in the summer of 1969. I was going there to cover the Miami Dolphins in their final season in the American Football League for *The Miami News*, the afternoon paper in the South Florida city. I continued to do an early-morning sports show on WEEP Radio in Pittsburgh. That wasn't easy to do then because there were no I-Pod gizmos or social media.

When the Minnesota Muskies folded after the first year, I saw an opportunity because Bob Fulton from Minneapolis was writing a column on the ABA for *The Sporting News*. The Floridians were in the ABA. So, I applied for the position of writing the ABA column for *The Sporting News* and landed it. I would move to New York early in 1970. I would cover all sports teams for *The New York Post*. I wrote a column on the ABA and then the NBA for nine years for *The Sporting News*.

I landed a lot of free-lance gigs writing about basketball while in Manhattan. That's where I first made my mark writing about basketball. The kid who grew up on Sunnyside Street pretending he was Wilt Chamberlain would meet Wilt Chamberlain and all the great basketball players of his generation.

*   *   *

That last time I saw Rubin and Shapiro was at an ABA reunion in Indianapolis on August 23, 1997. I went there at the urging of George Von Benko, a friend and sports broadcaster from South Connellsville, who had been an ABA fan. All the great ABA players were present with the exception of Rick Barry. He wanted to be paid to attend and there was no money in the budget to pay anybody to attend. Barry missed out on a great time. I sold many of my ABA media guides and programs to a collector from Japan and came home with about $3,000.

Connie Hawkins and Dr. J were there, and so were some of the best and best-natured ballplayers you'd ever want to meet. Jim Eakins, for instance, who had been a teammate of Craig Hamilton at BYU, and later starred in the ABA, was there. Eakins had a Virginia Squires uniform that belonged to Charlie Scott and, I think, sold for $300 at the reunion. Covering the

ABA was like covering boxing. You had full access. The league and its players needed publicizing so they welcomed writers into their domain, eager for any media attention. It was fun to cover the ABA. I always was intrigued with outlaw leagues and found some of my favorite subjects in their ranks. Gabe Rubin died at age 92 in Fort Lauderdale. He had given me his apartment address in case I wanted to get in touch with him. "He had a tremendous life," said Ellie, his widow. "Everything he did, he had fun doing it."

That's when I learned that, in addition to the Nixon Theater, Rubin also was the first entrepreneur to bring drive-in movie theaters to Pittsburgh. He owned the Star Lake Drive-In near Homewood and the Art Cinema in downtown Pittsburgh. Those theaters, along with the Casino Burlesque House on Diamond Street, were critical to my sex education. In 2018, Groat finished a 40-year run as analyst for Pitt basketball broadcasts with Bill Hillgrove as part of the longest-tenured radio tandem in Division I basketball history.

Pittsburgh Condors hired Dick Groat

The Condors hired Dick Groat, who had starred in baseball and basketball, to work in the front office in ticket sales and marketing. He had previously worked in sales for Jessop Steel in Washington, Pa., when he was playing for the Pirates. He also played one year with the Fort Wayne Pistons of the National Basketball Association while he was finishing school at Duke University. Groat had a great career in sports at Duke. He led the nation in scoring as a senior and was the collegiate Player of the Year (1954).

They might have drawn more fans if Groat were still able to play basketball for the Condors.

On the nose of a seal
Nine seasons on the brink

I remember the ABA. I still have a shiny never-used red, white and blue basketball that was signed by Commissioner Jack Dolph that is still in the Rawlings' box. It's stored away in a room next to one in which I am writing this reflection. It's worth something, especially with the box it came in, I'm told by collectors, and it brings back many special memories. That's why I have a security alarm system.

When I attended a reunion of ABA players in Indianapolis August 22–24, 1997, Mel Daniels, one of its most decorated players, signed a photo of himself: "To Jim, a prized member of the ABA family."

Daniels died before the 50th anniversary reunion of the ABA. I saw and spoke to another ABA original, Les "Big Game" Hunter at the 50th gathering. I learned as I was writing this story that he had died.

I felt like a member of the ABA family. I think I brought some attention and respect to the upstart league by the many stories I wrote about it in *The New York Post, The Sporting News, Basketball News, Basketball Weekly, Basketball Digest, The Complete Handbook of Pro Basketball* and *Street and Smith's* and guide books. There was some skepticism on the part of my bosses at *The Post* for awhile because they didn't think the ABA players compared with the NBA players—they were big fans of the Knicks and *The Post* was the first newspaper to cover NBA teams on the road—but I knew that the ABA had a lot of talented players. They included Connie Hawkins, Julius Erving, George McGinnis, Mel Daniels, Spencer Haywood, Jim McDaniels, Freddie Lewis, Ron Boone, Al Smith, Bob Netolicky, Charlie Williams, Byron Beck, Willie Wise, Bobby Jones, James Silas, George Gervin, Louie

Dampier, Darel Carrier, Artis Gilmore, Roger Brown, Billy Paultz, Moses Malone, Marvin Barnes, James Jones, Donnie Freeman, Steve Jones, Mack Calvin, Larry Jones, John Beasley, Larry Brown, Doug Moe, Caldwell Jones, Billy Knight, Dave Twardzik, Maurice Lucas, Dan Issel, Larry Kenon, David Thompson, Charlie Scott, John Williamson and John Brisker and some others. They were first-rate basketball players. I was not exaggerating their talent or skills.

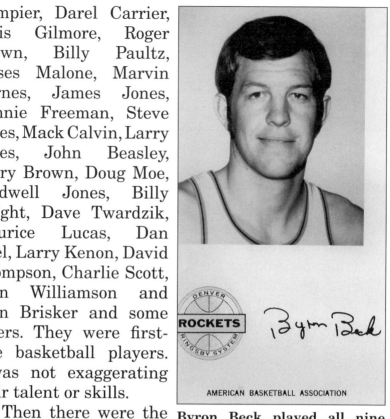

AMERICAN BASKETBALL ASSOCIATION

Byron Beck played all nine seasons of ABA with Denver entry.

Then there were the established stars who jumped from the NBA to the ABA, such as Rick Barry, Zelmo Beaty, Billy Cunningham, Joe Caldwell, Don Chaney, Mickey Davis, Billy Melchionni and Nate Archibald.

I was elected president of the ABA Writers Association at the All-Star Game in Norfolk, Virginia in 1974. I was often referred to as "Mr. ABA." It was a fun league to look after. I wrote about it during its nine-year existence (1967-1976). I also covered games in the NBA, the NFL, MLB and NHL during that time, so I had a measuring stick. What was best about covering the ABA was that the door was always open. I was welcome at all ABA outposts and owners, front office people, coaches and players were all eager to share their thoughts. You had complete access and that's a dream world for a sportswriter. I could be critical and not be barred from the locker room, as happened to New York free-lancer Phil Berger with the Knicks.

George Mikan comes to mind, for starters, when I think about the ABA.

It was Big George, all 6-10 of him, ol' No. 99 when he was a monster center and leading the Minneapolis Lakers to a string of NBA titles back in the late '40s and early '50s, before the franchise was moved to Los Angeles. And, yes, there are lakes in and around Los Angeles, if not many jazz joints in Salt Lake City.

One of my editors, George Morris pointed out that Mikan, whom he once met in Minnesota, was inducted into the Basketball Hall of Fame in 1959. Mikan, of Croatian descent, was called "Mr. Basketball" and rule changes such as widening the foul lane and goal-tending and the shot-clock because of his dominance under the basket and he led the Lakers to several NBA championships.

Bespectacled George Mikan hits the floor for loose ball.

411

ABA Publicity Archives

ABA Commissioner George Mikan, at right, presents the first Coach of the Year Award in 1968 to Vince Cazzetta of the Pittsburgh Pipers.

A friend of mine, the late Jack Curley, a truck-driver from Mount Washington, told me a story that when DePaul played Duquesne at the Dukes' campus gym, Mikan led the DePaul players up the steps to the gym floor, and tossed the ball the length of the floor into the hoop at the other end.

"That was the ballgame right there," recalled Curley. I can find nothing to confirm that story, but it's a good story.

Whoever thought of having the three-point field goal for shots from 25 feet or more deserves equal enshrinement. That was borrowed from the old ABL, the American Basketball League, which was the brain-child of Abe Saperstein, a Chicago-based businessman better known for bringing us the Harlem Globetrotters.

Globetrotters publicity photo

Abe Saperstein, seen with Wilt Chamberlain, founded the Harlem Globetrotters and the American Basketball League.

The Globetrotters drew huge crowds across the world with their wild antics and showbiz flair, entertaining fans above all else, and played many doubleheaders with NBA teams. Many of the fans came to see the Globetrotters more than the NBA teams.

It was fitting that Mikan chose to run the ABA out of his travel agency in Minneapolis.

It was important to have links with the NBA more so than the ABL or the Globetrotters, and Mikan, a member of the NBA's 50th anniversary team, certainly gave it a major-league link.

So did Alex Hannum, who had played and coached in the NBA, including the 1967–68 Philadelphia 76ers team that was later judged the best team in the league's first 50 years. That team, by the way, played six of its "home" games at the Civic Arena in Pittsburgh where Wilt Chamberlain set some shooting percentage records for field goals and consecutive field goals records that still stand. I saw those games. I had just gotten home from two years of military service and was married in 1967. As I write this, my wife Kathleen and I will be married 53 years when the book is printed.

What did Hannum have to say about the ABA's red, white and blue ball?

"It belongs on the nose of a seal," he said. If I ever wrote a book exclusively about the ABA, I thought of calling it *On the Nose of a Seal.*

Lee Meade, a sportswriter in Denver, became the first publicity director of the ABA and he added some items to the statistics-keeping. The NBA did not differentiate between offensive and defensive rebounds.

Alex Hannum
Great coach in any league

The ABA did. He introduced turnovers; the NBA didn't keep track of them. He introduced steals and blocked shots and team rebounds. The NBA soon added all those stats to their sheets. The guys who love numbers ought to hold a Lee Meade Day in his honor.

Connie "The Hawk" Hawkins was the ABA's first superstar and its first MVP. He had been barred from playing in the NBA because he had been linked to a college game-fixing scandal, unfairly and wrongly as it turned out. He had played in the ABL (1961-62) with the Pittsburgh Rens and with the Harlem Globetrotters, and the Porky Chedwick All-Stars at a gym across the street from Heinz Chapel on the Pitt campus. Chedwick was a popular Pittsburgh WAMO radio deejay. Hawkins was great to watch with his high-flying heroics. He could hold a basketball in his huge hands like most of us hold a baseball.

When I asked him once when he finally was free to play in the NBA what his thoughts were about the

ABA. "You know," he answered, playing with his mustache for a moment, "I really don't think about the ABA."

Ah, that's too bad. Because the ABA was fun while it lasted and it contributed greatly to Connie's image as one of the game's greatest talents, yet something of a mystery because he was not performing on the highest level or on its biggest stage. It's the way they once told stories about how great Josh Gibson and Satchel Paige were when they were playing in the Negro Baseball League.

The ABA began, according to whomever you believe, in New York, New York or in Oakland, California. It began operation for the 1967–68 season—the same year the NHL expanded for the first time—and it went the way of the World Football League in 1976. The Pittsburgh Penguins in my hometown also celebrated their 50th season during the 2016–2017 season.

The idea for starting such a league, even when the NBA wasn't exactly knocking 'em dead at the box office, belonged to Connie Seredin. He owned a public relations and marketing firm in Manhattan and wanted to make money providing those services for a new sports enterprise. He's not the Connie that comes to mind for most ABA fans.

One of the first thing the original owners decided was that Seredin was an expense they could ill afford to take on, so they deserted him in a hurry. They were smart enough, on the other hand, to allow another Connie—Connie Hawkins—play with their red, white and blue ball in their new league. They also called for a 30-second shot clock rather than the NBA's 24-second time limit.

It began in earnest with Dennis Murphy, a sports promoter looking for a new gig, and Gary Davidson, an attorney looking for a new way to make money fast without printing it himself, talking to some wealthy gentlemen from around the country and convincing them that pro basketball was about to become more popular than ever, and that they could profit from starting a new league the way the guys did with the American Football League.

They figured they could get their game on TV, without breaking a sweat, and force a merger with the NBA in fast-break time. But they figured wrong. Or at last their outlooks were overly optimistic. If there had been as many TV outlets as there are today, they surely would have found a suitable home on a national network.

There weren't as many media suitors in those days. ESPN started in 1979, three years after the ABA as a league no longer existed. ESPN was desperate for sports product—how about kick-boxing and roller derby?—and the ABA would have been a perfect start-up for the sports and entertainment network.

Miami Floridians photo

Dennis Murphy might have done a lot of praying from press row seat at Floridians' games in Miami.

416

ESPN could have saved the ABA if it had come along a few years earlier.

The ABA never really made it on TV. It was a decade too early in that respect. It went through a lot of owners and a lot of cities and a lot of financial problems. Some of them bounced checks as much as basketballs before they and the league were through.

It was fun for those of us who didn't have any money at stake.

The ABA was like the AFL, easy for sports writers to write about. It abounded with characters, both in the front office and on the court. Sportswriters sat at courtside in those days and now the press row has given way to the richest customers who can afford to pay a thousand dollars or so for a seat where they can bump fists with the ballplayers and be seen on television. The owners were eager to get attention and opened their doors to everybody with a notepad, tape recorder or TV camera. It was like boxing, where everybody is a promoter, a glad-hander and their time is your time.

And they said funny things.

Gabe Rubin owned several movie theatres in Pittsburgh, and thought he was the second coming of Sonny Werblin, the theatrical genius who bought the New York Jets and signed Joe Namath to a $400,000 contract and saved the AFL. Rubin often made trades without talking to his coach about it, even though he had absolutely no background in basketball, unless the fact that he was about as short as Abe Saperstein. He liked to bet on basketball games and other sports.

After he had obtained Art Heyman, a Hall of Fame character in pro basketball annals, he said, "No, I didn't trade for Art Heyman because he's Jewish. I traded for Art Heyman because I'm Jewish." He traded away another Jewish player, Barry Leibowitz, to get Heyman. Leibowitz later became captain of the Israeli national basketball team.

During the Pipers' 50th year anniversary, I learned from Leibowitz that the Israeli basketball team failed to qualify for the 1972 Summer Olympic Games in Munich, Germany. Those were the Olympics where a Palestinian terrorist group, Black September, seized 11 members of the Israeli Olympic team and held them hostage before killing all of them along with a German police officer.

Barry Leibowitz

"Who knows?" allowed Leibowitz. "I might've been one of the victims, so I am lucky to be here."

Heyman, who had been the first pick overall by the New York Knicks in 1963, died in Florida in 2012 at age 71.

Ned Doyle, one of the founders of Doyle, Dane and Bernbach Advertising, the Madison Avenue genius who gave us those great commercials for Avis, Volkswagen, Alka-Seltzer and Sara Lee, was asked why he bank-rolled the ABA's Miami Floridians.

"I'm just a sports nut," he said. "I wanted my own team since I was a kid."

Fine, but why the Floridians?

"The Brooklyn Bridge wasn't for sale."

Then there was John Y. Brown. He made his money with Kentucky Fried Chicken. He bought the recipe and the operating rights from Colonel Sanders. And he bought the Colonels' franchise from Joe and Mamie Gregory, whose show-dog Ziggy was pictured on the team's original logo chasing after a Kentucky colonel. The Colonels were the winningest team in the ABA and should have been absorbed into the NBA, but Brown took a $3.5 million payoff and later owned two different teams in the NBA, the Buffalo Braves

Colonels' publicity photo

Kentucky Colonels' charter owners, Joe and Mamie Gregory with their prize dog Ziggy, who was listed as one of the owners.

and the Boston Celtics. He wanted to be President of the United States, but had to settle for being president of pro basketball teams, and the governor of Kentucky. Brown was a sharp businessman and made out nicely on his pro basketball involvement.

He had a beautiful wife, Ellie, one of my favorites in the ABA ranks, but they were divorced and he married former Miss America Phyllis George. My wife and I were invited to a party at the palatial home of Ellie and John Y. Brown during an All-Star Game Weekend.

Brown was one of the best movers and shakers in the ABA, and pushed it to improve its posture and power. He was not one of the seven or eight commissioners (depends on how you count), but he boosted Dave DeBusschere of New York Knicks fame to be the ABA's last commissioner.

Jim O'Brien

ARTIS GILMORE

It was Brown and DeBusschere who took the ABA on a fast-break to the bargaining table with the moguls who ran the NBA, beginning with Commissioner Larry O'Brien. I attended a meeting of the powers of both leagues at Hyannis, Massachusetts—a resort community O'Brien first came to know when he was Postmaster General for President John F. Kennedy—where four of the ABA's best franchises were absorbed into the NBA. It was never officially referred to as a merger. The franchises were the Indiana Pacers, the New York Nets, the San Antonio Spurs and the Denver Nuggets.

The two other teams that remained—the Kentucky Colonels and the Spirits of St. Louis—gave up the ghost and worked out payouts. Four other franchises—the Memphis Sounds, San Diego Conquistadors and Utah Stars and Virginia Squires had already folded their teams and got nothing when the merger came.

Players from the St. Louis, Kentucky and Virginia team were taken by NBA teams in a dispersal draft.

Looking back, the seven teams that remained in business in the last year of the ABA were some darn good teams and could have been competitive if they had all come into the NBA. At the end, the ABA had a lot of talented players, fierce competition, and the fans knew the teams and players the way they once knew them in the six-team NHL.

There were 11 teams when the ABA began, seven when it went out of business. In between, there were 27 different teams altogether and a lot more groups of owners who operated those teams.

The uniforms and equipment of the aptly-named Pittsburgh Condors were sent to Attica Prison in upstate New York where they were used in the prison basketball league.

There were a lot of great players in the ABA, but a lot of fans didn't recognize or accept their ability, until they demonstrated their skills in the NBA. For sure, the real basketball junkies and the kids who bought a half-dozen basketball magazines every October, starting with *Street and Smith's Basketball*, knew about them, but the players didn't get the seal of approval until the NBA logo was affixed to their uniforms.

Consider some of the players spawned by the ABA: Start with a threesome that made the Philadelphia 76ers a contender for many seasons, certainly a cut above the current class. That's Julius Erving, Moses Malone and Bobby Jones.

Nobody was ever more entertaining than Erving, especially during the 1975–76 season when he averaged 29.3 points in the regular season and 34.7 points in 13 playoff games when he led the Nets to their second ABA championship. I was covering that team for *The New York Post.*

Erving may be my all-time favorite athlete, right up there with Jerry West and John Havlicek, because he was also such a special person. Once, while I was interviewing one of his teammates, Brian Taylor, and had my three-year-old daughter Sarah with me in the clubhouse, Erving did a small thing—yet a big thing— that I will never forget. Without a word, he walked from one end of the locker room to the other, pulled a cold orange soda out of an ice-filled cooler, uncapped it and handed it to Sarah with a smile. Then he walked back to his locker. Sarah is still a fan of Dr. J.

After he had retired as a player, Dr. J came to Pittsburgh to play in a celebrity golf outing and I caught him coming down the fairway at the Allegheny Country Club in Sewickley Heights. When he saw me, he walked over my way and embraced me. I think some other sportswriters who were present were surprised by that. I told him about his kindness to Sarah as a kid, and said that she was now in the University of Pittsburgh's medical school.

He took my writer's notebook and wrote on one blank page: "To Sarah, I hear you want to be a doctor like me. Good luck. Best wishes, Julius "Dr. J" Erving. That's been a keepsake.

Those times come to mind as much as any of his acrobatic assaults on the basket. To me, he has always been a class act, but some, understandably so, don't hold him in such high regard. According to his Wikipedia sketch, he fathered a total of nine children with three women out of wedlock.

I once asked him to identify this middle-aged woman who was always cheering for him in the end zone at Island Garden in Hempstead and Nassau Coliseum, and he said, "That's my Mom. I've got to introduce you to her. You'll like her."

Years later, whenever I'd come upon him during the All-Star Weekends, he'd say, "Stay here a moment. I want you to see my son."

And he'd bring one of his boys to meet me. That's so rare.

The day the ABA's Virginia Squires signed him— April 6, 1971—may have been the young league's brightest moment. He left the University of Massachusetts after his junior season. I have read elsewhere that it was after his sophomore season, but that is not right.

The day—October 20, 1976—the Nets sold Erving to the 76ers may have been its darkest day. At least for a sports writer who was going to cover Dr. J and the Nets in their first season in the NBA. It's one of the reasons the Nets were no longer in Nassau County where Dr. J grew up and fashioned his game. They are scheduled to play many of their games there in future years.

I recall that I was with the Nets, including Nate "Tiny" Archibald and Rich Jones when we were picking up our bags at the airport in San Francisco when we learned that Dr. J had, indeed, been sold to the Sixers. The players were still hopeful he'd be playing for them that year.

There were other bona fide stars in the ABA. In the first All-Star Game played after the NBA absorbed four of the ABA's teams that half the starting lineup was from the ABA. Five of the ten starters were former ABA players and ten of the 24 All-Star players were from the ABA and Dr. J was named the game's Most Valuable Player at The Mecca in Milwaukee.

How about Maurice Lucas and Dave Twardzik, who joined Bill Walton and the Portland Trail Blazers back in 1977 and promptly pushed that team to its first and only NBA title?

The ABA gave us George "The Iceman" Gervin, a three-time NBA scoring champion.

It was a league that signed such collegiate standouts as Artis Gilmore, George McGinnis, David Thompson, Ron Boone, Willie Wise, Dan Issel, Rick Mount, John Roche, John Williamson, Johnny Neumann, Larry Kenon, Marvin Barnes and many others.

But not even some of the smart guys in the NBA knew just how good they were.

Consider that Artis Gilmore, Maurice Lucas, Ron Boone and Marvin Barnes were all picked ahead of Moses Malone in the 1976 ABA dispersal draft. Two months later, Malone was traded twice (by Portland and Buffalo) in a span of six days. Malone died at age 60.

> **"Why is anybody not the best possible person he might be?"**
> **—William Saroyan**

The ABA had some great players and great all-star games. It put on a bigger mid-season extravaganza than the NBA for quite a while. The NBA has borrowed a lot of aspects of the ABA spectacular for their own all-star game these days. Some of those ideas, such as the slam-dunk and shooting competitions, were developed by my late friend Jim Bukata, when he was the league's public relations director. I had turned down an offer for that position and recommended Bukata, a Penn Stater from Munhall, Pennsylvania, who did a great job.

The All-Star Game was more important to the ABA, for one thing, because quite often it was the only appearance on national TV. So, the owners and the players took it seriously and strutted their stuff in all-star fashion and then some. To think of all the exciting contests that were never shown on TV.

It was a league where the average price of a ticket was $4, and students could get in for $1, or less if the owner wanted to paper the house.

It was a league with lots of 5 a.m. wake-up calls, especially in Salt Lake City, and it seemed like there were more four and five stop airplane trips than in any other major league. It always seemed like you were waiting around airports in Atlanta and Chicago and Philadelphia and New York. Life on the road in the ABA had its moments. I remember our plane, with the Nets on board, scraping the tops of trees approaching an airport in Norfolk, Virginia.

It was a league that put pretty girls on the sidelines before anybody else, and had them strut their stuff, and take the fans' mind off some of the madness that was offered as pro basketball. I was fortunate to be in Miami when the Floridians featured young women in the briefest of bikinis running back and forth in front of the press row.

Photos by Jay Singer of Jaybo Enterprises

ABA FLORIDIAN BALLGIRLS were a distraction for writers along press row who were trying to focus on the basketball action. Here the author is shown above kissing the forearm of Michelle Stephans, and below, getting vanilla ice cream wiped off his kisser after some kind of courtside promotion, by ballgirls Jeanne Jarvis, left, and Carol Flipse. "Why do you hold onto these photos?" my wife Kathie complains. "You're an old man! You should be ashamed of yourself!" Yes, Dear, I am.

It was a league that had a sense of humor. There were lots of dropouts and rejects from the NBA, players who had plenty of talent but were considered head cases, flakes or incorrigibles, or some who had gotten into trouble with the bottle, drugs or gamblers.

Simmie Hill was one of those who had great talent but had a hard time behaving himself. The LA Stars offered him twice as much money as the Chicago Bulls in 1969, but he couldn't get along with coach Bill Sharman. Hill never had anything good to say about Sharman, one of my dearest and life-long friends from my days on the pro basketball beat. Hill escaped Marty Blake, the GM of Pittsburgh Condors, by leaving the team in favor of the Eastern League.

"That was composed of a bunch of mad maniacs," said Hill. "It was like getting a bunch of guys out of a bar and throwing the ball up and letting them play. They went through coaches so fast that one time the trainer became the head coach and his wife the assistant coach." The ABA also had a special charm and warmth about it. Everybody was in the same boat. Everybody was an under-dog. Most everybody stuck together. The owners and the coaches and the players, and sometimes the sportswriters as well, pulled together to gain proper acceptance.

It's difficult to accept that so many of the individuals have died. The list includes Jack Dolph, Jackie Moreland, Jim "Goose" Ligon, "Super John" Williamson, Wendell Ladner, Art Heyman, Vince Cazzetta, John Brisker, Babe McCarthy, Lloyd "Sonny" Dove, Gary Bradds, Bill Sharman, Max Zaslofsky, Chico Vaughn, Zelmo Beaty, Moses Malone, Barney Kremenko, Les Hunter, Ron Thomas, Mike Storen, Jim Bukata and Dave DeBusschere.

I remember Malone making his pro debut against the Nets. Kevin Loughery, the coach of the Nets, had his players get physical with Malone, but Malone, just 19 but solidly built, was more than they could handle. He showed right away that it was OK for him to skip college in favor of the ABA.

Lou Carnesecca is 95, Ira "The Large" Harge is 78, George Lehmann is 78 and Al Cueto—billed as the world's tallest Cuban at 6–7— is 74. Cueto, ABA fans may recall, played for the Floridians. He had gotten out of Cuba after Fidel Castro took over the government.

Brisker and Ladner liked to fight, and even squared off a few times in some monumental battles. Brisker, it has been reported, was killed while fighting as a mercenary in Angola. Ladner died in a plane crash near Kennedy Airport.

There was Steve Chubin, who played for six different teams, in the first three years of the ABA. What a character.

There was Harley "Skeeter" Swift, who once pleaded, "Give me some ink. I don't care what you write. Can't I be on some all-star team. I don't care if it's the all-ugly team. Anything!" You can't make up stuff like this.

Worth Watching

All I ever heard about Stephon Marbury, a talented and troubled NBA performer from 1996 to 2009, was that he was difficult to deal with. He became a star and a most popular figure with the Beijing Royal Fighters in the Chinese Basketball Association (CBA). Marbury comes off better in this documentary called "A Kid From Coney Island" than he did in his NBA days. "The Last Dance," a reflection on the life of Michael Jordan in ten episodes, is also available on Netflix. Best of all, check your local library to see if you can find a copy of "Finding Forrester," starring Sean Connery as a reclusive book author who takes a liking and interest in a high school student and gifted writer who plays basketball on a court below his apartment window. They're all worth watching.

Most fans were far from madding
crowd at Civic Arena
for Pipers' playoff game

Roberta Sarraf, a member of The Writers of Westminster, told me she stayed at the Lorraine Motel once. "It's part of the Civil Rights Museum in Memphis. There is a wreath on the balcony railing where Dr. King was shot, and a vintage car (presumably his) parked outside the room. The whole museum experience was so impactful since I lived through it all. There was the bus that Rosa Parks rode and a burned-out bus from an attack on protestors. For me, it was déjà vu all over again! It traced history from slavery to current times. It's a living laboratory. Should be a required destination for all."

The preacher who practiced non-violent protest in promoting civil rights in this country had been shot dead.*

There were 1,500 National Guardsmen encamped in Pitt Stadium in Oakland, others in the Civic Arena in The Lower Hill and the parking lot outside of the Arena looked like a military post. It was filled with olive-green military vehicles. "I feel like I'm in an Army camp," said Vince Cazzetta coach of the Pipers, whose team was practicing on a Monday afternoon at the Arena. My friend, Frank Gustine Jr., son of the famed Oakland restaurateur and Pirates infielder from the '40s, was one of several Pitt football players who were dispatched to stand guard at Pitt Stadium until the National Guard got there.

---

*This was the week that wasn't for sports in Pittsburgh. This was mid-April, 1968, and this is what happened in the aftermath of the slaying on April 4 of Dr. Martin Luther King Jr. on the balcony of his room at the Lorraine Motel in downtown Memphis, Tennessee.

There was a lot going on in the world at the time. The U.S. was in a race to the moon, we were in a war in Vietnam, President Lyndon B. Johnson had created the Great Society—a war against poverty in our country—and, just ahead, on June 6, 1968, U.S. Senator Robert Kennedy, a kid brother of the late President John F. Kennedy, would be shot in a kitchen at the Ambassador Hotel and would die at Good Samaritan Hospital in Los Angeles.

There were riots and fires in American cities, including Pittsburgh.

That's not easy to digest in one paragraph...

OCCUPIED PITTSBURGH—Gabriel G. Rubin, owner of the Pittsburgh Pipers pro basketball team, pushed open the door at the Civic Arena on a Saturday evening, April 6, 1968, and looked outside.

It's something he had done before that maiden season of 1967–68, looking hopefully for a late-coming line-up of fans at the ticket windows. He had been disappointed many times. Too many times.

When he looked out and saw no one was there on Saturday night, except those in the uniforms of the Pittsburgh police force and a local National Guard unit, he was happy. He didn't know what to expect, but if he had believed all the alarms sounded by Arena security guards and one executive in the house, there would have been thousands of enraged citizens of the Black community raising hell outside. Talk about extreme weather reports...

Charlie Williams, the only surviving starter from the Pipers 1968 championship team, remembers seeing his Pipers' teammate Steve Vacendak in a National Guard uniform in the parking lot. Vacendak has been called to active duty that same day. "There was no problem with our players," continued Charlie. "The Black players showed no scorn or vindictiveness toward the white players; we were a team."

"They've broken through the police lines," cried one Civic Arena guard. "They've stopped them once, but they're liable to do it again."

I stood close to Rubin, a tough customer even though he was two or three inches shorter than me, and I'm just 5-8½. I was the editor of *Pittsburgh Weekly Sports*, a tabloid that Beano Cook, the former Pitt publicist then with ABC-TV Sports in New York, and I were publishing in our fifth year of operation. I was also a friend and confidant of Rubin, who had enlisted me to help him establish his operation because of my basketball connections and knowledge. So, I was a witness to what was going on. There was no madding crowd, not this Saturday night.

My wife Kathie came to the game with me that night, as she often did. She remembers we were escorted to our car after the game by National Guardsmen. I don't recall that aspect of the evening, but I will take her word for it.

All season long, Rubin wished that people would storm the gates when his Pipers were playing, but not with Molotov cocktails in hand, and screaming all sorts of threats.

Jimmy Jarvis, a Pipers' guard, rented an apartment in The Hill and thought his place might get torched.

The news of King's assassination was not out when I left our apartment in East Liberty to go the Arena a few nights earlier to pick up my press credentials at the Will Call window. I often drove through The Hill to get there because it was a direct route and there was hardly ever traffic on Wylie Avenue or Centre Avenue. I felt safe there—I had played in basketball and baseball games there in my teens. Nothing was going on when I was driving through the Hill. I was lucky. As an Irishman, I am whiter than most white people and would have been an inviting target.

Later that night, Pittsburgh was one of many major American cities to have crime in its streets. Businesses, most of them owned by Jewish merchants from Squirrel Hill, were the first to have bricks tossed through their storefronts and Molotov cocktails pitched into the stores.

"The way they told it," Rubin recalled in the peacefulness of his office at the Carlton House on the following Monday, "you would have thought they had crossed the moat, and were storming the walls of the Civic Arena. The cops told me they had broken through and were marching on the Arena."

Rubin had been sitting in his box at the Arena, next to his wife, Ellie, when he was told there was a disturbance outside. Rubin had been rooting for his Pipers to rally and overtake the Minnesota Muskies in the final five minutes of play.

Jack Roberts, a front office executive at the Arena, first asked if they would simply stop the game, but neither team wanted to do that. Then Roberts requested that neither coach call a timeout the remainder of the game.

Jim Pollard of Minnesota moved toward Coach Vince Cazzetta of Pittsburgh and said, "Vince, I want to win this game!"

"I don't blame you, Jim," Cazzetta replied. "If you want to call time out, you call it."

Cazzetta admitted at practice the following Monday that he expected "to see a horde charging at me when I opened the door."

This incident points up an aspect of the ABA and NBA in those days that is often glossed over. This was during yet another struggle for civil rights, and there

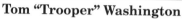

Tom "Trooper" Washington

Art Heyman

was still a lot of unrest in this country, families divided over the race issue. There were sit-ins, protests of all kinds, Martin Luther King Jr. urging for non-violent behavior to win such rights. There was tension, yet pro basketball teams made up of Black and White men, about half and half on most teams at the time, were able to work together as a team.

Tom "Trooper" Washington wanted to kill Art Heyman every day, but that wasn't because Heyman was white, just an intolerable jerk too much of the time. "A lot of guys wanted to hit Heyman," recalls Charlie Williams with a smile. "It wasn't a race thing."

Alex Medich, the team trainer from Duquesne, Pa., got tired of Heyman calling him "a stupid hunky," and charged at Heyman in the locker room one day. "Go ahead and hit me in my one-million-dollar chin," Heyman was heard to holler at Medich, letting everyone know his high opinion of his value. That's a story that became the headline in a profile I wrote of Heyman for *SPORT* magazine.

When Rubin traded Barry Leibowitz to get Heyman in an all-Jewish trade, he was asked if he got Heyman because Heyman was Jewish. "No," replied Rubin, "I got him because I'm Jewish."

Rubin, a theater man for over 30 years who had thrived on road shows with casts of hundreds, knew a crowd when he saw one, but he hadn't seen one in quite a while. His last big show had Carol Channing starring in "Hello, Dolly," which gained him the money to splurge on the ABA franchise.

His Nixon Theater had been empty for three months in the winter of 1967–68 because "Far From the Madding Crowd" has lived up to its name, and flopped in a few weeks. Then the Pipers played under the same marquee. "It's been the worst winter I've ever experienced," Rubin said glumly. "Then this. I was ready to take the pipe."

Rubin was talking about sucking on a gas pipe because he was understandably beside himself with disappointment over his team's failure to succeed at the box office even if it was a big success on the court, indeed, one of the ABA's best teams.

KDKA-TV's Dick Stockton said on the air that night that many fans who had purchased tickets stayed home for fear of their safety. Rubin said he would refund money for anyone who requested it. He said he had a good track record in that respect.

Looking back on that scary night at the Arena, Rubin remarked, "There was no commotion whatsoever when I left the building. They had no right scaring people like they did. It was needless, and just awful."

Rubin and his wife and some friends walked down Centre Avenue, where buildings were burning a few blocks away in The Hill, to get to their Carlton House suite at the bottom of Centre Avenue, where it reaches Grant Street.

Rubin has been criticized for allowing the game to be played, and this smarts as well.

"There was no decision for me to make," said Rubin. "At noon Saturday, Commissioner (George) Mikan called off the Sunday and Monday games like all the other sports were doing. At two o'clock, the Director of Public Safety here (David Craig) made a statement that there was no emergency and that the game should be played.

"I can't see what's going to happen. The criticism is hindsight. Why didn't the mayor have the foresight to impose a curfew Saturday night, instead of Sunday after the bad outbreak of violence? There were two NBA games played Friday night and they had a wrestling show with 11,000 people at the Civic Arena Friday Night. The Pirates played a meaningless exhibition game in Richmond (where there was a racial disturbance), and no one says anything about them. Why are they picking on me?"

There were seven black players on the Pipers team, and none of them said they didn't want to play, according to Rubin and Cazzetta, "Maybe we shouldn't have played," the Pipers' coach conceded. "I don't know."

Rubin had waited for a Saturday night playing date at the Arena for a long time. He had only one previous to this particular night. "The winter's not over, but it's already been a long winter," he said.

Jim O'Brien

Ira "The Large" Harge with Pipers' owner Gabe Rubin at 30th anniversary reunion in Indianapolis.

To Jim
Best Wishes
Steve Vacendak

Steve Vacendak was a guard
for Pittsburgh Pipers, but
was in the uniform of the
Pa. National Guard on a
memorable night at the Civic
Arena in the wake of the
assassination of Dr. Martin
Luther King Jr.

Somehow it seemed wrong to play a game that night

The April 19, 1968 edition of *Pittsburgh Weekly Sports* carried four stories on its front page that related to what happened in Pittsburgh with the Pipers-Muskies game, and one about what went down in Philadelphia the day after Rev. Martin Luther King Jr. was killed in Memphis.

It was written by George Kiseda, a Pitt grad who grew up in Monessen, and had previously been a sportswriter for *The Pittsburgh Sun-Telegraph.* Kiseda was one of the best sportswriters ever to come out of Pittsburgh, and he was always an advocate for fairness and sportsmanship and understanding the difficulties faced by Black athletes in America.

He had called Chet Walker of the 76ers at his apartment the afternoon of a scheduled game with the rival Boston Celtics that night in Philly.

"He was sitting alone in his apartment and staring at the walls," wrote Kiseda. "He couldn't sleep. He didn't really want to sleep. He just wanted to sit there and think about what happened in Memphis, Tenn., last night."

Walker told him, "It's a sickening thing to me," he said. "Because he's one of my favorite people. I think he's one of the greatest men of all time.

"Usually, before a Boston game, I get myself up for the game, but when I heard that Dr. King had been shot, I forgot about the game. It just doesn't seem important to me anymore. The game will probably go on, but this whole thing is really affecting me.

"I'm really shocked about it because Dr. King was the greatest civil rights leader of them all. You have all the Black militants who spoke against his non-violence, but they respected him. I think now that he's been killed a lot of people who straddled the fence, who couldn't decide whether they should go violent or non-violent, will go the violent route.

"I think the nation is in pretty serious condition. I don't know if we realize it or not."

They say history repeats itself, and I am writing this story in the wake of a week-that-went-wrong all over the world after the senseless slaying of a black man in Minneapolis by a white cop. And what followed in the streets of Minneapolis, Pittsburgh, Columbus, Paris and London, and the list goes on. So does the insanity; it never stops.

NBA Archives

Chet Walker, when he was with Chicago Bulls, splits Jo Jo White (10) and Satch Sanders (16) of Boston Celtics.

Jimmy Jarvis 'jumpy' after
his 'life or death' dash

Jimmy Jarvis was a reserve guard for the Pittsburgh Pipers basketball team, and he didn't get to play much because the starters played most of the games.

He'd replace Charlie Williams from time to time. He and Williams, along with Ira "The Large" Harge were probably the best known of the Pipers who showed up for the 50th anniversary of its championship season in the early summer of 2018.

He still reminded me of Johnny Unitas, the great quarterback of the Baltimore Colts who'd come off the sandlots of Bloomfield and Lawrenceville to launch a Hall of Fame career. Jarvis said he had been asked for his autograph and disappointed the person when he didn't sign the name "Johnny Unitas."

Even though he didn't play much against the Minnesota Muskies on this Saturday night, April 6 of 1968, he was "pretty well fatigued" at midnight after the game.

Jarvis was dressing when an Arena guard burst into the Pipers' locker room and excitedly declared that everyone had to get out, and fast. There was much alarm about a riot outside the Civic Arena and, to hear the guards tell it, the Black hoodlums, as they put it, were rushing the building.

Jarvis hurriedly dressed and went to his wife, who was holding their three-year-old son, Jeff. With his wife were her parents, a neighbor, a brother-in-law and the mother of Craig Dill, another player for the Pipers. I think Dill and Jarvis roomed together on the road.

Another guard or policeman, Jarvis didn't remember which it was, rushed them out of the door. One declared, "It's a matter of life and death. You might get shot out there!" That makes a lot of sense, but in truth, the guards wanted to get home, so they had to evacuate the building

Jarvis had parked his car in the upper parking lot at the Civic Arena. It was about a hundred yards away. Suddenly, it seemed like a mile to Jarvis.

Everyone started running for the car. Jarvis made his best moves of the season, zig-zagging across the lot, carrying his little boy in his arms.

"He sensed the panic," Jarvis recalled, "and he started screaming, and fighting for me to put him down."

Jarvis nearly ran out of his pants, or he was nearly scared out of them. Both pants legs split open, and one of his shoelaces busted.

Finally, they reached the car and eight of them jumped inside, lowered their heads for fear of being shot. Jarvis pressed the accelerator as if they were going to fly out of the parking lot.

"My father-in-law didn't know the area, and he kept hollering, 'Go up the hill, go up the hill!' But I shot out of the side exit and down the ramp to the Liberty Bridge. I must have run five red lights."

His in-laws were shocked by the episode, and most anxious to return home to Oregon. He sent his family back home. "I can't wait to get home myself," he told me.

He would have to wait until the Pipers were finished with the playoffs. Who knew that night that the Pipers would go on to win the first ABA championship?

I was preparing to write a story for a Minneapolis newspaper at my press box seat, when I was told by a guard to get out of there. "O'Brien, what good is that story going to do you if you're dead tomorrow? You're going to be writing your own obituary!"

Kathie and I went outside and there were about 20 steel-helmeted policemen holding rifles. This was at Gate 1 of the Civic Arena. We got home to our apartment in East Liberty without incident.

JIMMY JARVIS
Johnny Unitas look alike

Bowtie Bill
and the Globetrotters

Bill "Bowtie" Torrey was best known for his Hockey Hall of Fame efforts as general manager of the New York Islanders in forming the team that won four Stanley Cups in the early '80s.

But he had previously worked in Pittsburgh as the right-hand man for owner John H. Harris with the Pittsburgh Hornets of the American Hockey League. Torrey booked the Harlem Globetrotters to play in Pittsburgh the day after Christmas each year, and continued to make that booking when he worked in Oakland, California (with the expansion Seals) and Long Island.

To this day, the Globetrotters continue to be a Christmas tradition in Pittsburgh, playing the day after when kids are still out of school, because of a holiday vacation and not because of the coronavirus.

Harris, by the way, had a deal with the NBA to get a franchise, and Bill Sharman was going to be the coach. Art Rooney Sr. was lined up as one of the investors in the franchise. When Harris was unable to sign Sharman, he backed out of the proposal.

"Bowtie Bill" Torrey

Charlie Williams
They called him "Sweet Charlie"

Big men and even bigger women were struggling to climb the steep stairway to the second-floor ballroom at the Savoy Restaurant & Wine Bar on Penn Avenue in Pittsburgh's Strip District. This was in mid-May of 2018.

The Pittsburgh Pipers, who won the first ABA championship in 1968, were reuniting on the 50th anniversary of that improbable title run. The weekend celebration attracted an intriguing assortment of Pipers and Piper wannabes.

I got stuck behind a logjam on the stairway, but two sleek figures managed to snake past the big people and reached the top with relative ease. That was Charlie Williams and his wife, Madge Potts-Williams, two of the most attractive people at the gathering. Both were well-dressed for the occasion. Charlie had a pocket handkerchief that went well with his light gray suit.

Charlie Williams was the lone survivor of the starting five from the Pipers championship unit. Connie "The Hawk" Hawkins had died eight months earlier at age 74 in Phoenix, and Tom "Trooper" Washington, Charlie "Chico" Vaughn and Art Heyman had also passed away. Vince Cazzetta, the coach; Alex Medich, the trainer, and Gabe Rubin, the owner, had all died.

Williams could relate to how Joe Greene of the Steelers must have been feeling as the lone survivor of "The Steel Curtain" front four from the Steelers glory days since L.C. Greenwood, Dwight White and Ernie Holmes had died.

Williams was not only a starter on the Pipers' championship team of 1967–68, he was also one of the five players on the ABA All-League team in 1968, so

The 1971–72 Pittsburgh Condors included, first row left to right, trainer Ray Melchiorre, Jimmy O'Brien, Harlan "Skeeter" Swift, Coach Jack McMahon, George Thompson, Arvesta Kelly and John Brisker. Back row, left to right, Walt Szczerbiak, Dave "Big Daddy" Lattin, Mike Lewis, Paul Ruffner, Stew Johnson, Mickey Davis and George Carter.

honored along with Hawkins, Doug Moe, Larry Jones and Mel Daniels.

"Sweet Charlie was one of my favorite opponents," offered Freddie Lewis of McKeesport, Pa. who was the point guard for the Indiana Pacers team that won three ABA titles in the '70s. "He could play. He was so quick and you had to be extra careful with handling the ball around him, or he'd take it away in a heartbeat."

Lewis also recalled when he was a junior and senior at Arizona State University that they twice lost to Williams and a 5–10 guard named Peller Phillips of Seattle U. "They crushed us," said Lewis.

"Oh, Sweet Charlie," said George Thompson, who played with Williams when the team became the Pittsburgh Condors. "He was a great teammate and a great guy. He was cool and he was swift and, man, he could shoot with the best of them."

I hadn't seen or spoken to Charlie Williams in 50 years, but I was instantly comfortable in his company near the bar where a buxom barmaid in a low-cut black top was attracting a lot of attention, some who wanted to refresh their drink, some who just wanted to ogle one more time.

Among those in attendance were former Pipers Ira "The Large" Harge, Barry Leibowitz, Jimmy Jarvis, Arvesta Kelly, Tom Kerwin, Craig Dill and a former Condor Walt Sczerzbiak, and former local basketball stars Garry Nelson and Billy Knight, who'd gone from Duquesne University and the University of Pittsburgh to pro stints. Harge was accompanied by Cece Daniels, the widow of the late Mel Daniels, who had been a teammate of Harge at the University of New Mexico.

Harge had a history similar to Spencer Haywood. Both were born in Mississippi, but played high school basketball in Detroit.

I had seen Kerwin, whom I had shared drinks with at Atria's Restaurant & Tavern in Mt. Lebanon on more than one occasion, and had visited him twice in Pine Knoll Shores, home to the North Carolina Aquarium, where he continued to live on the Crystal Coast. I had seen Kerwin recently at a 50th anniversary reunion of the ABA in Indianapolis. Kerwin, who was a backup to Connie Hawkins, has always been good company. He remained a good friend and drinking buddy of Bill Raftery, the long-time basketball analyst and color man for network college basketball coverage. They were both Jersey Boys. Kerwin likes to tell stories.

Bill Neal of Champions, Inc., former founder and director of the Connie Hawkins Basketball League, who organized the reunion, and Mark Whited, who was writing a book about the Pipers—*Pittsburgh's Forgotten Championship Team*—were also in attendance. I learned that Charlie Williams' wife, Madge, is a dentist. That's better than any ABA pension.

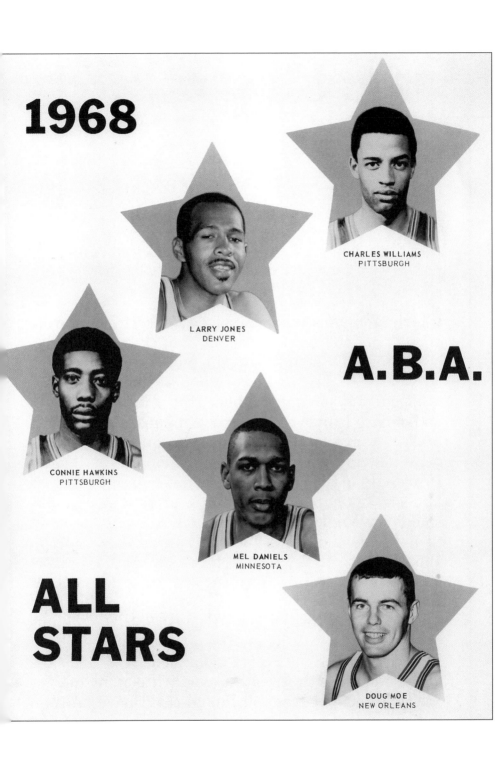

1968

CHARLES WILLIAMS
PITTSBURGH

LARRY JONES
DENVER

A.B.A.

CONNIE HAWKINS
PITTSBURGH

MEL DANIELS
MINNESOTA

ALL
STARS

DOUG MOE
NEW ORLEANS

Mack Calvin of Floridians is guarded by Charlie Williams of Pipers.

Charlie Williams was more of a quiet sort. There were enough out-there characters on that club, and he was something of a silent assassin, who could shoot from outside, go to the hoop, pass and play tough defense.

Like for so many others, the ABA was a second-chance league for Charlie Williams. He had been barred from the NBA because he failed to report a point-shaving bribe offer to a teammate at Seattle University in the mid-60s. No money had ever changed hands, no game was fixed, but it was felt that Williams should have reported it to school officials. He was about to make the final roster for the Seattle SuperSonics in 1965 when the NBA league office rejected the contract because of his failure to report that bribe attempt. Al Bianchi was the coach of the Seattle team then and he said later, when he joined the ABA, that Williams was good enough to make the team. Arvesta Kelly, a reserve guard on the Pipers' championship squad said, "That night was the greatest experience of my life."

Williams believes the Pipers could have built on that championship season. There were over 11,000 fans filling the Civic Arena for that seventh-game victory for the Pipers over the New Orleans Buccaneers.

"We had a real good following that could have carried in to the next year," said Williams at the reunion. "If we would have stayed, there might be an NBA team here now. Who knows? I think the city was ready for professional basketball."

Williams played for the Pipers in Pittsburgh and then in Minneapolis, and with the Condors back in Pittsburgh, then with the Memphis Tams, Memphis Pros and Utah Stars in a six-year ABA career. He played in the 1969 and 1970 ABA All-Star Games and averaged 16.3 points per game while scoring 6,020 career points.

Then he went to work. He started out with Armco, a steel company based in Middletown, Ohio—the hometown of the great Jerry Lucas—with mills in Butler and Cincinnati and a sales office in Cleveland. He was in corporate sales for over 30 years, based in Cleveland. His story in that respect is much like that of George Thompson. He got a job and created his own destiny.

Williams was born in Colorado Springs, Colorado and, at the time of the Pipers' reunion, was retired in south Florida, in Bradenton, where the Pirates hold spring training.

* * *

All Charlie Williams wanted was a chance.

So, Williams wrote a letter on a yellow legal-pad to Vince Cazzetta, who had been hired to be the head coach of the Pittsburgh Pipers, asking for a tryout for the new ABA team. Cazzetta had been the coach when Williams played at Seattle University.

This was in 1967 and I was sitting in the offices of the Pipers at the Carlton House in downtown Pittsburgh. Team owner Gabe Rubin pulled a letter from a file, and handed it to me.

447

Williams explained to Cazzetta that we was cut by the Seattle SuperSonics because of his failure to report a bribe offer to a teammate on the Chieftains, now called the Red Hawks.

Williams wasn't a familiar name to Rubin. "Is he any good?" he asked me.

I told Rubin that Williams had played a terrific game against Duquesne University and outscored Willie Somerset in a head-to-head duel. That was something Rubin could relate to. Williams had averaged 17.8 and 20.3 points per game during his final two seasons at Seattle.

Cazzetta called Williams who wanted to know some of the players who would be playing for the Pipers. "Well, we have Connie Hawkins," said Cazzetta.

"Connie Hawkins...that's all I need to know," Williams was reported to have said. "I'm coming." That's how championship teams were put together back then.

Williams would average 20.8 points that first season with the Pipers, almost identical to his scoring average as a senior at Seattle, in fact, .5 better.

He was a quiet operator who did his best to stay out of the mayhem that was the Pipers' and Condors' clubhouse. He was as flamboyant as a spy. He was as unobtrusive off the basketball court as he was on it. He seldom smiled, never shouted or cried. He was the son of a Methodist minister, and acted like he was always in church.

While the fans were watching his partner-in-crime, the flashy Connie Hawkins, Williams was busy frisking everyone's pockets. He was the mover and shaker of the Pipers' offense, and a stalwart on defense. The Pipers posted a 54–24 regular season record, the best in the ABA.

Jim O'Brien interviews sports author Mark Whited who has written a book about the Forgotten Champions—the Pittsburgh Pipers.

Ira "The Large" Harge, Cal Graham and Charlie Williams at The Savoy in The Strip for Pittsburgh Pipers' 50th anniversary celebration organized by Pittsburgh sports promoter Bill Neal of Champions, Inc.

Championship Pipers, from left to right, are Chico Vaughn, Art Heyman, Connie Hawkins and Charlie Williams. Missing from photo is Tom "Trooper" Washington who didn't want to be pictured with Heyman.

"He's inconspicuous out there," said Jim Pollard, the coach of the Minnesota Muskies and the Miami Floridians, "but he's always trying to pick the lock. You've got to keep an eye on him. He's extremely quick."

Williams, at his best, could hit jumpers from anywhere, drive by bigger bodies—the same way he shot by them on the steep stairway at the Pipers' reunion —and contort his body to get to the basket and drop in remarkable shots. He picked off poor passes and swiped the ball from careless opponents.

"I don't want to put the ball on the floor when I'm near him," said Donnie Freeman of the Dallas Chaparrals. "It's just not smart to handle the ball around Williams. I think he's one of the best defensive guards in the league."

At an even six feet, Williams was one of the ABA's smallest guards. In some respects, he thought it was an advantage.

"I would prefer to have a taller man guarding me," he said. "I'm faster and quicker than they are."

One of his favorite plays was the old give-and-go. He hits a teammate in the hole with a pass and darts to the basket for a return pass and an easy lay-up. He leaves the defender a three-point shot behind him.

"On defense, taller guards sometimes try to take me under the basket where they can use their height advantage for an easy shot. But they're not too successful, because I play defense before the man gets the ball" said Williams.

"A little guy can play this game, but he's got to have desire. He's also got to have speed and quickness. If you're small and slow, you're in trouble."

Williams followed Fagin's advice to "Oliver" in the Broadway show: "You've got to pick a pocket or two, boys, you've got to pick a pocket or two."

Old Guard:
Williams rates some of his all-time opponents

When Charlie Williams was asked to name his toughest opponents in the ABA, he offered two names that are not often mentioned these days, notably Levern "Jelly" Tart and Les Selvage.

Jelly Tart has to be the captain of the ABA's All-Nickname team and Selvage should have been named "More" Selvage because no one in the league shot long-distance jumpers *more* than the Anaheim Amigos "unconscious" guard.

"Tart was tough physically," said Williams.

"He was a beast; he was rough. And Les could shoot. When he was on, it was lights out! And if he was hitting, he never stopped shooting."

Tart started out with the short-lived Oakland Oaks and played in the ABA's first All-Star Game, scoring 12 points on a four-for-12 shooting effort. He was a starter for the West team that lost by 126-120 to the East in Indianapolis.

He played his college ball at Bradley and later played for the New Jersey Americans and New York Nets, and represented the Nets in the 1970 All-Star Game where he went 1-for-8 from the floor, including a three-pointer as the East lost 128–98 in Indianapolis. He died at age 68 in 2010.

During the ABA's first season, Selvage attempted and made more three-pointers than anyone in the league, hitting 147 of 401 shots beyond the 25-foot arc. He attempted more three-pointers than any other team in the ABA with the exception of the Pittsburgh Pipers.

Jim O'Brien

Chuck Williams
In May of 2018

"He acted like if he stepped on the (25-foot) line he was going to get killed or something," said former Denver Rockets coach Bob Bass. "He didn't just take 25-footers. He took 30-footers. All he could do was shoot, and he shot too much. But when he was on it was unlike anything I'd ever seen."

Before he played in the ABA, he starred for Douglas Aircraft in the Industrial Basketball League. He played briefly for the LA Stars in the 1969–70 season. He died at age 48 after a brief illness.

Williams said the Kentucky Colonels had the best backcourt combination with Louie Dampier and Darel Carrier.

Williams also said he had great respect for big guards such as James Jones and Steve "Snapper" Jones, Warren Jabali, Mack Calvin, Ron Boone, Glen Combs, Donnie Freeman, James T. Silas, Billy Melchionni, Freddie Lewis, Charlie Scott and Chuck Williams. He also had a high regard for teammates George Thompson and Chico Vaughn.

Charlie Williams and Chuck Williams were teammates, along with Thompson, on the Pittsburgh

New York Nets publicity

Condors in the ABA's third season (1969–1970) and were often confused with one another.

I saw Chuck Williams at the 50th anniversary reunion of the Kentucky Colonels and he may have looked the best and handsomest of all the ABA alumni.

There was a positive glow or aura about him, I swear. And it was easy to see how popular he was with the ABA players. "I was surprised to see how some of the players looked," said string-bean Jim Eakins. "I thought I wasn't looking so bad after all."

Levern "Jelly" Tart

Tequila and rookie didn't mix well

One night in Indianapolis, I recall staying out late with several members of the New York Nets, all white guys. They were Billy Melchionni, Billy Paultz, John Roche and Kevin Joyce. We were drinking shots of tequila, some with white worms in the shot glasses. We'd shake some salt onto the top of our left hand, squeeze some lemon on it, lick it and then toss down the tequila. Kevin Joyce was a rookie and this was his first go-round with this drinking game. We were in a grand room, nicely furnished and carpeted. Then Joyce vomited onto the rich burgundy carpet and we called for the check so we could get out of there without any problems. I hope we left some nice tips.

Wes Unseld
Wes's world was different
from yours and mine

Funny things happen when I am writing stories for one of my books. It's hard to explain. Call it serendipity or find a new word to explain what is going on in my writing world. People appear that I hadn't thought about, but fit into a story, and I wonder what brought them to me. I read a book that's not about sports and find something that stirs my mind and initiates another story. I've been told that to write well you have to read well. It's true.

Books that belong to me have scribbled notes in the margins. I have more files, all labeled as to subject, more than my wife Kathie is comfortable with having in this half of our home. She worries about what's to be done with them when I am gone. I tell her there are people you can pay to take them away. One man's treasure is another woman's junk. But they are mine, my life's work for safekeeping, and they are a gold mine of newspaper and magazine clippings, yellow ledgers with hand-written words from so many interviews, scraps with a note or two on them, personal correspondence, photos, so many photos, artwork, images. Material that is requisite and still so much alive when I hear Billy Joel in *Piano Man* singing "Play me a memory."

I have no tape recordings of interviews. I never used a tape recorder. I wanted to be a writer, not a stenographer. People felt freer to talk when there was no tape recorder. If I missed a word, I figured I wasn't dealing with Lincoln's Gettysburg Address. I still remember what they said, even today, because I was listening, and what they said prompted a follow-up question. If I misplaced my notebook, I could still write my story.

"Don't start out with a tough question," advised Jimmy Cannon, the great New York newspaper man, "or you'll end up with an empty notebook. Save the tough question for last."

In his book *Requiem for a Nun*, John Steinbeck wrote this memorable line: "The past is not dead; it's not even past." It comes alive when I cull stories from my files, stored in 38 gray metal file drawers. When I am reworking an old story, I am often able to anticipate the next word or two, or wonder why I didn't use a different word. Maybe I was typing the story on a small portable typewriter in a dimly-lit airplane heading somewhere after a night game. It could have been a night when I am on a fierce deadline and trying my best not to annoy anyone sitting near my clickety-clack writing effort.

Former President Barack Obama borrowed from that Steinbeck observation to make a point in a powerful speech about racial relations in America, and he did so long before riots broke out in over 150 cities in America following the unforgivable murder in late May and early June of 2020 of a black man in Minneapolis by a white policeman, pressing his knee down hard on the neck of George Floyd for nearly nine minutes, ignoring the man's plea that "I can't breathe."

It became a rallying call to protest injustice in the world, to protest police brutality, to repeat the phrase that "black lives matter," and it started a storm that is still going on as I write these words. It's been a difficult year, a challenge to people across the globe with, first, the plague of the coronavirus that killed and sickened and sorrowed so many people, just as unfairly as Floyd's death, cost one out of four their jobs in America, and then the perfect storm of the awful images of Floyd's final moments of life, and the cries and crimes that followed.

George Floyd's face with large pronounced features became an instant mural, like so many that can be found in downtown Louisville, a billboard crying out in pain, echoing a voice of protest for most of us. George Floyd, like President Obama, had the kind of face that caricaturists love to draw. Obama had big stick-out ears, just like Lyndon B. Johnson, another former President.

*   *   *

Westley Sissel Unseld didn't stick around long enough to see how this scenario played out. He died, at age 74, after a long illness, on June 2, 2020; the final blow was a bout with pneumonia. That, too, makes it difficult to breathe. I remember my father suffered from pneumonia whenever he went to the hospital, and too much smoking and drinking led to my dad's death from emphysema at age 62. His lungs gave out; he couldn't breathe. My father's mouth was wide open by the time I got to his bedside that morning, like he was gasping for one more breath. That disquieting image has stayed with me for over 50 years.

I recall that Wes Unseld was thin-lipped, a quiet man, not given to story-telling. He was the captain of the Bullets and, by sports columnist Peter Vecsey's viewpoint, captain of the "All Worst Interview Team" in the NBA. I saw a lot of Louisville's favorite sons and daughters memorialized on murals on buildings in the downtown sector, such as Muhammad Ali, Diane Sawyer, Victor Mature and Jennifer Lawrence, but I didn't see one for Wes Unseld. The oversight should be corrected, unless I missed something.

Wes would have been disturbed by what went down in Minneapolis, and in Baltimore and Washington, D.C. where he starred for the Bullets from 1968 until

1981, bringing the Bullets an NBA championship in 1978. He was a stand-up guy all his life. A great locker room presence. He and Paul Silas were supposedly the best in the business with keeping order in the locker room, kind of like Joe Greene's role with the Pittsburgh Steelers.

When I saw the video of George Floyd being apprehended by the police officers outside the store where he has just purchased some cigarettes. I thought he looked tall, and might have been a basketball player in his day. All tall black men are constantly asked if they were or are basketball players. I checked Floyd's background, and learned that he played basketball and football at Yates High School and for two years he played basketball at Florida Community College. His family described Floyd as "a gentle giant,"—he was thought to be between 6–4 and 6–6. Unseld's family offered a statement when his death was announced and he, too, was referred to as "a gentle giant with a big heart."

It's also been pointed out to me that George Floyd was imprisoned at least seven times in his life. That gives one pause for thought. So, he was no saint, but he still didn't deserve to be choked to death.

I remember traveling with my wife to Syracuse one summer, and stopping at a rest room along the highway. When I came out, I told my wife that a man in the rest room asked me if I had been a boxer, someone he recalled seeing in a boxing show in Syracuse. I felt good about that. "How come no one ever asks you if you were an architect or a sculptor?" Kathie came back.

I can still picture this proud man when he played ball for the Bullets. He was big and strong, but not as tall as most of the centers he contended with, at 6–6½ and 240 to 250 pounds, maybe more. He set the widest pick in the NBA, freeing the likes of Earl Monroe,

Kevin Loughery, Phil Chenier, Elvin Hayes, Gus Johnson and Jack Marin for their pure jump-shots. I can see them all at the Baltimore Civic Center. It always seemed to be dark in the upper seats of the old building. Wes walked above the crowd, a warrior with the kind of presence one found in Wilt Chamberlain, Walter Bellamy, Earl Lloyd, Willis Reed, Moses Malone, Kareem Abdul-Jabbar, Jerry West, Julius Erving, Lenny Wilkens, George Mikan, Shaquille O'Neal, Hakeem Olajuwon, so many noble men.

Kevin Loughery

I remember running into a player at a bar across the street from the Civic Center one night after a game with the Knicks. His name was Dorie Murray, and this was after his first game with the Bullets after he was traded to the team from the Portland Trailblazers. He was a slim 6-8 forward from Detroit. A woman at the bar asked him if he was a good ballplayer. "I must not be," I overhead Murray saying, "or I wouldn't be in Baltimore tonight."

Whenever I'd go to Baltimore, I'd visit the grave of Edgar Allen Poe, the boyhood reform school setting for Babe Ruth, and I remember how good the crab cakes were that they served in the press box at Memorial Stadium when I was covering the New York Yankees against the Orioles. I was at that stadium in the northeastern end of the city when the Orioles beat the Cincinnati Reds in five games to win the World Series in 1970. That World Series was the first to be played on artificial turf, the first to have an African-American umpire, Emmet Ashford, and the last World Series to have all the games played in the afternoon. Those same Orioles, managed by Earl Weaver, would lose out to the Pittsburgh Pirates in the World Series of 1971 and again in 1979. Those were the Orioles of Frank Robinson, Boog Powell, Brooks Robinson, Jim Palmer and Dave McNally, such a star-studded team. Wes Unseld knew them all.

*   *   *

In 1969, Unseld was named the NBA's Rookie of the Year and the league's MVP. Wilt Chamberlain was the only other player in history who could make such a claim. Unseld was something special until his knees went bad, always scoring and rebounding in double figures. He was the heart and soul of the Bullets and led the gifted team to the NBA championship in 1978. He was the Finals MVP.

The 1967–68 season was the ABA's first year of existence and, naturally, the Kentucky Colonels always coveted Unseld who'd have been a big draw, it was thought, in his hometown of Louisville.

He played all 13 years with the Bullets, first in Baltimore and then in Washington, D.C., and was picked to play in five all-star games. During a four-year peak, he averaged 15 points, 17 rebounds and three assists a game. He later coached and held front-office positions with the Bullets. He was inducted into the Basketball Hall of Fame in 1988, his first year of eligibility.

When he died, Unseld was cited for the class, integrity and professionalism he brought to all his roles with the Bullets' organization, a model for the rest of the NBA family, and "for his dedication for expanding educational opportunities for children."

As a player, he was renowned for his rebounding and great outlet pass. It started so many fast-breaks and lay-ins by Loughery and Monroe and Chenier.

"I was a wide-receiver like Paul Warfield," allowed Loughery whose scoring average zoomed from 14 to 20 points in Unseld's first season with the Bullets.

"He'd get a rebound and release a pass down-court," recalled Earl Monroe in his memoir *Earl the Pearl*, "that triggered our potent fast-break game. He set picks that allowed the rest of us to hit our deadly jumpers. He was very efficient in the way he played. He could shoot, rebound and pass. He contributed mightily to our cohesion factor as well. Plus, he was a great teammate and leader and a friend."

Mitch Kupchak, the general manager of the Charlotte Hornets after a similar stint with the Lakers, played for five seasons with the Washington Bullets, said that Unseld was "the consummate team player. He was very aggressive and he just wanted to win. Statistics were never important to him. You can't imagine what he did to make his teammates better."

Unseld was the second player picked in the 1968 NBA draft, behind Elvin Hayes of Houston, who would later be a Bullets' teammate. No one ever confused "The Big E" with Wes. One of his coaches, Jack McMahon once labeled Hayes "the world's worst human being." Let's just say that Hayes had a tendency to view the world through his personal periscope.

Most statisticians are fussy about when to give credit for an "assist" to a player, insisting that the pass must lead directly to a field goal, that the recipient doesn't dribble before releasing the shot. Otherwise, Wes Unseld would have been credited with more assists, and might have led the league, as Wilt Chamberlain did one year when he focused on that facet of the game, doing it mainly because he could. Nate "Tiny" Archibald led the NBA in scoring and assists in the 1972–73 season—the only player ever to do so—but he was a point guard who could shoot and make the pass.

Wes worked hard on defense though he wasn't tall enough to protect the rim, and he set those impactful picks. He was what analyst Al McGuire would call "an aircraft carrier."

Willis Reed, an equally proud warrior under the boards with the New York Knicks, once said of going up against Unseld, "when I'd turn to the hoop, there was this impenetrable wall, like a handball wall."

*　*　*

I was at my writing desk on June 2, 2020 when I received a brief, succinct note from my friend Tom McGuire, no relation to Al McGuire, but just as funny and to the point. It read: Wes Unseld. He died today."

I hated to read that, of course, but here's where it gets weird. I was sitting at my computer, as I am right this minute, and I was wearing a golf jersey with the University of Louisville emblem—a bright red cardinal, my favorite bird—over my heart. Wes Unseld once starred at the University of Louisville in the city where he was born in 1948.

Today, I am sitting in my summer pajamas, a plain gray top, and dark blue bottoms. I like to get started writing as soon as I rise from bed, sometimes as early as 5:30 a.m. At my age, you can take a nap later in the day if you care to. I'll brush my teeth and take my pills later. I don't have to check my blood today; I'll prick one of my fingers tomorrow, hoping for a good reading. I learned in January that I have Type II diabetes and I am dealing with that in real earnest. I have dropped down from 240 pounds—that's what Wes weighed in his prime—to 205, as of yesterday. But I'm only 5–8½ and that ½ is just as important to me as it was to Wes.

But why did I choose to wear that University of Louisville jersey on the day that Wes Unseld would die? It was the first time I've worn it since last summer. I received that jersey as a gift from Kenny Klein, the sports publicity director for 37 years at the University of Louisville when I visited the school's impressive athletic complex in the summer of 2018. I was given a similar jersey, only a size larger, to give to "Big John" Varoscak when I got home. Varsoscak had been a teammate of Charlie Tyra at Louisville in the late '50s. I saw Varoscak's name in the listing of former players in the UL basketball press guide. I got him a copy of that as well, which he cherishes.

Everything looks so new at the University of Louisville campus. They were renovating the KFC/Yum Football Stadium while I was there. I saw the statue in tribute to Johnny Unitas, my boyhood hero, a scrawny kid who came out of Pittsburgh to put Louisville on the national football map, and then—after being cut by his hometown Steelers without a fair trial—became a legendary quarterback for the Baltimore Colts.

I saw a student center named for another Louisville alumnus with Pittsburgh ties, namely Dwayne Woodruff, a generous donor to his school.

Johnny Unitas and his statue at University of Louisville's Yum Stadium.

Wes Unseld had done the same for Louisville's basketball program, following Charley Tyra (pronounced Tye-ray) as the Cardinals' nationally-known basketball stars. There were only two issues of *Street and Smith's Basketball Yearbook* published before I came on board as the editor in 1969, and Charley Tyra, perhaps the hairiest chest in all of college basketball, was on one cover and Tommy Kearns, a shooting guard at North Carolina was on the other cover.

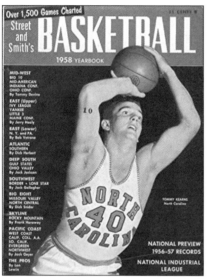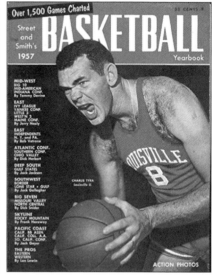

These are early Street and Smith's Basketball Yearbook covers featuring Tommy Kearns of North Carolina and Charlie Tyra of Louisville.

There is a framed copy of that *Street and Smith's* cover in the office of Kenny Klein, who has served in the sports information office at UL for 37 years, as of this writing. He was great to work with, I recalled, and there was a period when Louisville might have the best college-pro sports publicists in one city in the U.S.A., in Kenny Klein at Louisville and Dave Vance with the Kentucky Colonels.

Vince Tyra, the current athletic director at Louisville, was not present the day that Alex Pociask and I paid our visit. He is the son of Charlie Tyra. There are four former players at UL who have been honored by having their jerseys retired and they are Tyra, Wes Unseld, Darrell Griffith and Pervis Ellison. Unseld would never have been considered for a cover in the South because the powers that be in the Graybar Building didn't believe a cover with a black player featured would sell well or be accepted in the South. I convinced an old codger named Doc that the players I featured deserved to be so honored.

We had three regional covers that first year of 1970 and I had Austin Carr of Notre Dame on the Midwest cover, Jerry West and Oscar Robertson on the Western cover, Kareem Abdul-Jabbar and Willis Reed on the Eastern cover. One year, I had Michael Jordan on all the covers. He played well in every American town.

* * *

I went on a sports odyssey and boys-only vacation tour with my buddy Alex Pociask in the summer of 2018, traveling through Ohio, Indiana and Kentucky, all hot-beds for football, baseball, boxing and thoroughbred horse racing and auto racing.

We stopped at the Indianapolis Speedway, the Indy 500 Museum, baseball parks in Indianapolis and Louisville, Churchill Downs and the Kentucky Derby Museum. The Muhammad Ali Museum and Louisville Slugger museums in Louisville, horse country in Lexington, Fort Knox (where I went for basic military training in 1964) and even the Stephen Foster Museum and Camp Grounds in Bardstown, Kentucky.

Stephen Foster never stepped foot in Kentucky or any state in the South. He had a cousin who lived in Bardstown on a 265-acre farm. U.S. Senator John Rowan once lived in a stately mansion on the ground. I bought some post cards showing Stephen Foster's likeness as personal keepsakes. It would be a reminder that his statue was a campus landmark during my student days at Pitt in the early '60s.

Stephen Foster

I was planning on writing a chapter on Wes Unseld before learning of his death. I had a file marked WES UNSELD. It was at the bottom of a stack of similar player files because they were in alphabetical order. But he has been the foundation for a lot of great teams on a high school, college and pro level.

He was a star at Seneca High School in Louisville. He led his team to state championships as a junior and senior in 1963 and 1964. Adolph Rupp recruited him to be the first black basketball player at the University of Kentucky but he turned down "the Baron of the Bluegrass" in favor of his hometown school.

It was Louisville's good fortune. When I toured the basketball arena at the school in the summer of 2018, I saw likenesses and tributes to Wes Unseld.

* * *

I had a "Working Press" column for *The New York Post* with the headline "The Phone Call" that called attention to the way Wes Unseld treated people, an away-from-the-court look at the man.

"He's a brute of a center at 6–6½, 245 who's made an admirable recovery from a third surgical operation

Wes with UL coach John Dromo.

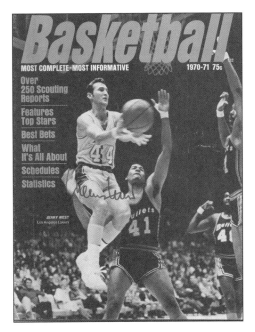

Jerry West of Los Angeles Lakers drives to the hoop against Wes Unseld of Baltimore Bullets on western region cover of 1970–71 edition of Street and Smith's Basketball Yearbook, Jim O'Brien's first effort as editor.

on his left knee and remains one of the best rebounders, play-making pivotmen and sure shots under the boards in the NBA.

"His basketball ability is just one side of Unseld's story. There's much, much more to this man, a human side we seldom hear about. Unseld is as unselfish off the court as he is on it. He cares about people and his concern is genuine. His name should be Wes Unselfish."

I had heard about what Wes did for a basketball player at Farleigh Dickinson University in Rutherford, New Jersey, a 21-year-old junior named George Lightly.

Lightly was from Washington, D.C., where he first became a fan of Unseld. A high-jumping 6–4 forward, he had been averaging nearly 18 points a game at FDU earlier that season.

He was getting great, even ranking second in the nation as a foul shooter, until he suffered a severe leg injury in an auto accident after a game on January 8. Lightly was lucky. He nearly lost his leg. His good friend and teammate Ben Johnson, who was driving the car, lost his life in the same crash. Another teammate, Redonia Duck, was badly injured when the car crashed into a utility pole on New Jersey Route 17 in Carlstadt.

Lightly, confined to his dormitory room and struggling to walk again, had been depressed quite often since the accident. He used to dream about being a pro basketball player. Now, too often, he dreamed about the auto accident.

"I see the car skidding toward the pole," said Lightly "and I see my leg after we hit. It was all busted up, bloody, and just hanging there. Then I was unconscious. It's really freaky.

"The doctors weren't optimistic about being able to save it," he told me. "But they did. I'm just so glad to be alive. I wish my friend could be."

Lightly wasn't optimistic about his chances of playing basketball again. But he was considerably cheered by a half-hour telephone call he received from Unseld when the Bullets were in New York to play the Knicks.

Unseld had just heard about what happened to Lightly, who'd worked for a week as a counselor at Unseld's basketball camp the previous summer.

"He took the time," said Lightly, "to talk to me, and boost my morale, when most professional athletes don't have the time to come back to the level where they once were.

"He's a great human being as well as a great basketball player. At camp, he treated everyone so nice. He's a gentle giant. When I received the phone call, it gave me a tremendous boost. I was really down.

"He told me he had three operations on his left knee, and that some people felt he was finished as a professional basketball player, but he came back – and look at him now.

"You know, I'm still pessimistic about the whole thing. My leg's still in real bad shape. But I talked to Wes, and I'm taking his advice above everyone else. He told me that when I was ready that I can call the Bullets' trainer (Bill Ford) so I can get a rehabilitation program under way. But it's up to me to get going again. I haven't been trying to walk as much as I'm supposed to. Wes gave me a real boost. I'll try harder."

It was reassuring to hear that sort of thing about a professional basketball player. Too often we only hear about basketball players popping off, about how abused they are, how exploited, how they want this and that. They frequently come off as self-centered, money-grubbing thankless goons.

Hey, and I was writing this in the early '70s. Nothing much has changed in that respect. If you check on the Internet, you can find the homes of the most celebrated pro basketball players, and most of them live in mansions and estates that rival the Taj Mahal in India. Is it any wonder they lose track of themselves? Then, too, he never made the kind of money even pedestrian players make today. Unseld, on the other hand, was unselfish, satisfied with the good life pro basketball had brought him and his family, soft-spoken and long active in civic affairs.

Maybe George Lightly's dream of being a professional basketball player was unrealistic to begin with. In his room at the Wilshire Apartments in Teaneck, New Jersey, Lightly's bed was surrounded by sports publications, and he said he occasionally "browses" through his schoolbooks. Maybe he would have been wise to change the emphasis and heed something Wes Unseld had also said two years earlier.

"I'm going to play as long as this thing lets me," Unseld said in reference to his bum knee, "but I'm not going to cripple myself. I feel as long as I can walk around, I can make a living."

Writing this makes me wonder how things turned out for George Lightly.

WES UNSELD

Book Review
This one's a knockout

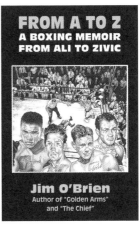

FROM A TO Z
A BOXING MEMOIR
FROM ALI TO ZIVIC

Jim O'Brien
Author of "Golden Arms"
and "The Chief"

By Abby Mendelson

It was the Pittsburgh Kid versus the Brown Bomber. On a steamy June night, 1941, in Manhattan's Polo Grounds, boxer Billy Conn came ready to take the heavyweight title from Joe Louis.

This was a tough, feisty Billy Conn, who had battled his way up from high school dropout to light heavyweight champion, then did something no one had ever done—resigned his two-year title just for a shot at Louis. Bigger, stronger, harder-hitting, Louis came into the ring outweighing underdog Conn by 30 pounds, 199 to 169.

But for 12 rounds, Conn bested the champ. In a fight many consider the greatest of the century, Conn used his famous left, his jabs and hooks, keeping away from Louis' devastating right—the one that made him champ for a dozen years. For 12 rounds, Billy Conn was the best boxer in the world.

But it was a 15-round fight, and virtually every one of the 54,487 in the house wanted Sweet William to hang on for three more rounds. Nine minutes. The champ was tired, weary—everyone could see that; everyone who had come to see East Liberty's Billy Conn, the Flower of the Monongahela, apply lessons in the sweet science.

But Conn wouldn't let himself take the title on points. Back home, his mother was dying of cancer and Conn had promised her a knock-out. So in the 13th round he went for the killer blow. A step here, a feint there—but it was Louis who saw an opening. A paralyzing right to the jaw left Conn dazed. Then another, and a third. Counted out at 2:58, Conn was two seconds shy of the bell, six minutes away from the heavyweight crown. It's the greatest "never-was" moment in Pittsburgh's rich boxing lore.

From this world-class pinnacle to Golden Gloves moments in back-alley gyms, Pittsburgh sportswriting legend Jim O'Brien's wholly wonderful *From A to Z: A Boxing Memoir from Ali to Zivic* takes us virtually everywhere with anyone who ever had anything to do with Pittsburgh and the Sweet Science. Anyone, that is, who worked out, hit the speed bag, promoted fights, wrote the stories. And it's a marvel!

A full 400 illustrated pages, with 16 more of priceless, full-color plates, O'Brien's history-cum-memoir is peppered with tasty stories, priceless photos, and precious memories. As a worthy addition to his legendary Pittsburgh Proud series, an entire shelf's worth of first-rate accounts of Western Pennsylvania sports teams and figures, Jack Lambert to Chuck Noll, Art Rooney to Roberto Clemente, *From A to Z* gives us the kind of inside information only a seasoned sports journalist can provide.

Indeed, to call Jim O'Brien a veteran chronicler massively understates the case. From his fledgling days at *The Pitt News* to stints at the *Pittsburgh Press*, *New York Post*, *Miami News*, and others, to his own 40-year career heading his own publishing empire, O'Brien's been virtually everywhere, knows everyone, seen it all.

And writes about it all with the strength and verve of a sharp uppercut. Possessing an unerring nose for a story, this hall-of- fame scrivener and world-class elbow-rubber— here he's talking with Muhammad Ali, there with Frank Deford, Roy McHugh, Jimmy Cannon, Art Rooney, Billy Conn, Howard Cosell, Bruno Sammartino, and so many others—has undreamt-of access, access where others find only closed doors, hears stories that never reach other, less ingratiating ears.

Indeed, O'Brien's obvious and enviable intelligence, vast experience, and amiable manner enable him to garner all manner of tales easily overlooked by lesser lights—writers less sophisticated, less traveled. Meaning that *From A to Z* also deserves to be an endlessly fascinating memoir about a man who's seen them all, pugs and pugilists, trainers and ticket takers, owners and promoters and newsies galore, all the characters that's made the boxing world so rich, and are sorely missed from today's corporate, antiseptic sports world. Put another way, O'Brien's been there, done that, and deservedly bought the T-shirt!

Above all the larger-than-life personalities, this latest edition aptly describes Pittsburgh. An area—a state of mind, really—that's produced such great boxers as Billy Conn, Fritzie Zivic, Harry Greb, and many, many more. Around them, O'Brien weaves a tale of triumph and tragedy, of nobility and knowledge. And, sadly, of one-way tickets to Palookaville.

Then there are the thrilling palaces of yesteryear, venerable boxing venues without which any Pittsburgh historical Baedeker* would be incomplete: Motor Square Garden, Duquesne Garden, Forbes Field, the Civic Arena, and others. Now-vanished temples, home to many sporting events, including grand boxing matches, it's worth the cover price alone just to be transported back, to hear the crowds roar, to smell the sweat seeping from the walls.

In the ring, on the street, in the locker room, at the gym, O'Brien takes us everywhere, introduces us to everyone. As idiosyncratic as it is irresistible, *From A to Z* adds up to a grand, richly-illustrated history, a ringside seat to some of the finest, and most furtive, boxing stories in Pittsburgh history.

Humor and hard work, championship fights and crushing defeats, broken noses and broken dreams, this indeed is Pittsburgh Proud!

*Karl Baedeker was a German publisher of popular guide books.

Award-winning writer Abby Mendelson is the author of three novels, two collections of stories, the number-one best-selling The Pittsburgh Steelers: The Official History, The Pittsburgh Steelers: Yesterday and Today, The Steelers Experience, Arena: Remembering the Igloo, *and numerous other books and articles about Pittsburgh. Check out Jim O'Brien's book* From A to Z: A Boxing Memoir from Ali to Zivic. *Visit his website at www.jimobriensportsauthor.com for more information.*

Book Review
"The Chief" is worth reading

By Edwin Pope
Sports Editor Emeritus,
The Miami Herald
September 2011

It's a lot more than coincidental that most of my all-time favorite sports people—Art Rooney and Dan Rooney, Dan Marino, Stan Musial and Billy Conn—are all Western Pennsylvanians.

It's more than coincidental because I've liked everybody I've ever met from there, from the late Froggy's proprietor Steve Morris, to all the guys who used to clean me out in midnight poker games at the old *Pittsburgh Press*.

And right now I'm reveling in the best book ever written about any sports figure from there—Jim O'Brien's "The Chief." People have written lovingly about the late Art Rooney practically forever. No one has done it better than O'Brien in "The Chief." I first became aware of O'Brien when I judged a college writing contest back in the early '60s. I recall telling Beano Cook, the Pitt sports publicist and Jim's friend and co-conspirator with a lively establishment-tormenting tabloid called *Pittsburgh Weekly Sports* that it was no contest—O'Brien's work for the Pitt student newspaper was clearly the best in the competition.

Then O'Brien came to Miami in 1969 to cover the Dolphins for our rival newspaper, *The Miami News*.

He started frequenting my favorite after-hours watering hole, Julie's Pad, where he and Bill Braucher, our beat

Edwin Pope died of cancer at age 88 in late January of 2017. In response to a condolence card from author Jim O'Brien, Pope's wife Eileen wrote a card that said, "Your boxing book was the last book he read. He told me more than a few times that he was enjoying it. He loved to cover boxing." It was good to know because Edwin Pope was a legendary sportswriter, author and friend.

writer on the Dolphins, and Jack Mann, a noted newspaperman, talked shop long into the night and early morning. Even Larry King came by now and then when he was doing a popular radio talk show in Miami. O'Brien told me it was like going to grad school.

Before his first year was up, I had recommended him to our sister Knight-Ridder newspaper in Detroit. Frankly, I wanted to get him out of town because he beat us on a few good stories. He accepted a job there at the *Detroit Free Press*, where Joe Falls held forth, then changed his mind, and went to *The New York Post* instead. I'd run into Jim at Super Bowls and championship boxing events, Muhammad Ali and others of that time, and he once saved my butt when I took a bad fall at the media headquarters hotel in New Orleans. He was always keeping the company of older out-of-town writers and always asking questions. I believe he looked up to us. I know he felt that way about Art Rooney. It's obvious by the way he wrote this book. I learned a lot of things I didn't know about Art Rooney and it only increased my regard for this great sportsman.

As a for-instance, I'd always understood The Chief bought the Steelers with the proceeds from a betting coup at Saratoga, New York. Wrong.

He made plenty before that running juke boxes and slot machines in bars and restaurants all over Allegheny County. He was street smart and knew how to make a buck.

Besides, The Chief paid only $2,500 to the National Football League for the Steelers' franchise in 1933. And he called them the Pirates the first seven years because he was such a big baseball fan. He changed the name in 1940 to avoid confusion with the city's Major League Baseball team. I'm sure the sports editors and headline writers at the local newspapers appreciated that change. He won up to a hundred times that NFL entry fee in a two-day gambling spree in New York City and Saratoga.

As O'Brien tells the true story, Rooney ran a $300 stake up to $21,000 gambling in Manhattan. Then he set out for Saratoga and extended the spree by betting $2,000 at 8–1 odds on a horse named Quel Jeu. He didn't stop there. As an old Pittsburgh friend of mine would say about a real plunger, "He bet what he weighed." And Art Rooney kept winning until he had upwards of a quarter-million in his pockets.

The Steelers cost him many times that much before real football money started coming in after the NFL-AFL merger in 1970. Then, too, Art Rooney gave away what he won that day, many times over before he died in 1988.

You couldn't begin to list all the things that were right with Art Rooney and wrong with the Steelers in this relatively brief space. I used to kid the great Ed Kiely, Art's right-hand man for so long, about their judgments on both coaches and quarterbacks. But when they brought in Chuck Noll and then Terry Bradshaw, they hit a double gusher.

It isn't always the nicest people who get the big payoffs in football. Hey, even Al Davis has won Super Bowls. But it was the right thing happening to the right man when Art Rooney's Steelers finally zoomed into that wild and wonderful Super Bowl championship streak.

If you had to pick one attribute that made Art Rooney the most loved figure in the history of football, and I mean ALL football, it was the common touch.

In "The Chief," Dan Marino talks about working on a summer construction job at Three Rivers Stadium when he was at Pitt, and hearing "how well Mr. Rooney treated those guys on the ground crew." Marino also heard Rooney used to take two members of the ground crew on the plane to every Steelers' road game, and even to Super Bowls. "He treated people like they were important," Marino said. "He touched people."

He sure touched me, and so did this book.

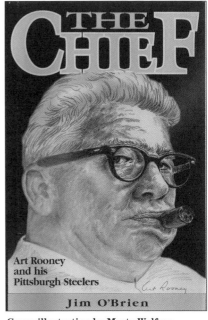

THE CHIEF

Art Rooney and his Pittsburgh Steelers

Jim O'Brien

Cover illustration by Marty Wolfson

A writer's memoir
about loving basketball

By Craig Meyer
Pittsburgh Post-Gazette
October 7, 2018

There's a certain point in Jim O'Brien's *"Looking Up: From the ABA to the NBA, the WNBA to the NCAA: A Basketball Memoir"* that the reader realizes there's a fundamental truth spread across the book's 480 pages—that in most of the basketball tales being told there's almost always a connection to Pittsburgh, however large or small that may be.

In a sports-obsessed region, one whose teams and colors are as central to the civic identity as anything else, basketball can exist as something of a forgotten stepchild. With no professional team and a deteriorated pool of local talent, basketball in Pittsburgh can, at best, seem overlooked and, at worst, exist as an object of derision.

But through Mr. O'Brien's experiences and anecdotes, collected over decades covering the sport in depth, a different world is illuminated.

The book isn't specifically about basketball in Pittsburgh. Hundreds of pages and dozens of chapters are devoted to some of the most decorated figures in the sport's history who had no connection to Western Pennsylvania.

It's a book that's personal to some extent—it's a memoir after all—Mr. O'Brien, who became the first Pittsburgh native inducted into the U.S. Basketball Writers Hall of Fame, deftly connects the sport he loves with the city he loves.

What results from it is an enjoyable and insightful read. For a basketball fan, particularly one who appreciates the nuances of the sport and its history, it's an immersive experience, even if it may not be that way for those who don't have a passion for the game.

A vast majority of the 53 chapters focus on a particular figure, helping tell the story of not only that person (usually a player or coach) and the author's experience with them, but also the era in which they lived and often helped define. In each of the stories, Mr. O'Brien illustrates that person's eccentricities and flaws, the kind only acquired by decades spent wandering arenas, traversing locker rooms and sitting in cars, with Mr. O'Brien riding shotgun and his subject at the wheel.

There's Julius Erving, with whom Mr. O'Brien developed a close relationship, a man whose afro, acrobatic game and nickname (Dr. J) embodied all that was cool and cutting edge about the upstart league in which he played, the American Basketball Association (ABA) before he took his talents to the NBA.

There's Michael Jordan, widely regarded as the best to ever play, an athlete Mr. O'Brien got to know early in his career, before a warm personality ("If you ever met Michael Jordan, you would like him," Mr. O'Brien writes) gave way to the unapproachability that has long been his public persona.

For Mr. O'Brien—a McMurray resident who was the founding editor of *Street and Smith's Basketball* and a writer for several publications, such as *The Sporting News, New York Post* and *The Pittsburgh Press*—this reconstruction of basketball history wouldn't be complete without his hometown.

The book begins with Simmie Hill, a star of Midland High School's legendary 1965 state championship team and a former ABA player. He was the kind of character who counted Jimi Hendrix and Marvin Gaye among his acquaintances and once robbed a local liquor store, as the author notes, not because he was in need of money, but "just for the helluva it."

It ends with a chapter on Suzie McConnell, a member of what's arguably the royal family of basketball in Pittsburgh today, although the book was printed before she was fired as the University of Pittsburgh's head women's basketball coach in April (2018).

In between are tales of some of the quintessential figures in Western Pennsylvania basketball history, a sampling of names that spans generations—John Calipari, the University of Kentucky coach and Moon Township native; Chuck Cooper, a Westinghouse graduate and former Duquesne University star who was the first African-American player to be drafted by an

Jim O'Brien

University of Kentucky head basketball coach John Calipari, at right, comes home to Moon Township High School to conduct clinic, joining old friends and influences, left to right, John Miller, Ron Galbreath and Joe DeGregorio. Someone asked Miller how he was doing. "I have two sons (Sean and Archie) who are millionaires, so I'm doing fine."

NBA team; Connie Hawkins, a star in the ABA with the Pittsburgh Pipers who has long been hailed as "Dr. J before Dr. J"; and Pete Maravich, a human highlight reel of a player whose extraordinary skill set was molded in Aliquippa.

With the information and insight Mr. O'Brien provides, he's not merely a sports writer, but a sports historian, a key and important distinction that adds to the richness of what he recounts.

The book is not without its flaws. It is at its best when it sticks to basketball, although some of its tales of figures around the game, particularly longtime Pittsburgh press box denizen Radio Rich, are entertaining.

There's a repetition of full names and explanations of people who are mentioned a few chapters earlier, but it does little to take away from the reader's experience.

It's a collection of stories that serves as a time capsule, one that's informative without being dense. As a memoir, it is meant in some way to be about himself, but through his career and the exploits it brought, one learns about so much more.

Craig Meyer is a *Pittsburgh Post-Gazette* sports writer: cmeyer@post-gazette.com

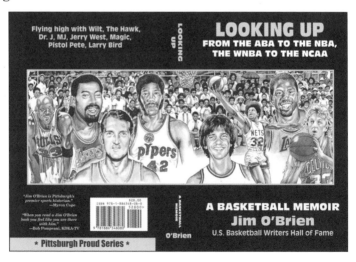